The Attachment Therapy Companion

The Attachment Therapy Companion

Key Practices for Treating Children & Families

ARTHUR BECKER-WEIDMAN

LOIS EHRMANN

DENISE H. LEBOW

W. W. NORTON & COMPANY

New York • London

Previous edition published under the title
ATTACHMENT-FOCUSED THERAPY: A Professional Practice Guide

For information about permission to reproduce selections from this book, write to
Permissions, W. W. Norton & Company, Inc., 500 Fifth Avenue, New York, NY 10110

For information about special discounts for bulk purchases, please contact
W. W. Norton Special Sales at specialsales@wwnorton.com or 800-233-4830

Manufacturing by Hamilton Printing
Book design by Gilda Hannah
Production manager: Leeann Graham

Library of Congress Cataloging-in-Publication Data

Becker-Weidman, Arthur, 1953-
The attachment therapy companion : key practices for treating children & families /
Arthur Becker-Weidman, Lois Ehrmann, Denise H. LeBow.
     p. cm.
  "A Norton professional book."
  "Previous edition published under the title Attachment-focused therapy:
    a professional practice guide"—T.p. verso.
  Includes bibliographical references and index.
  ISBN 978-0-393-70748-9 (pbk.)
1. Attachment disorder--Treatment. 2. Family psychotherapy. I. Ehrmann, Lois
Pessolano. II. LeBow, Denise. III. Title.
  RC455.4.A84B43 2012
  616.85'88—dc23

                                   2011049616

ISBN: 978-0-393-70748-9 (pbk.)

W. W. Norton & Company, Inc., 500 Fifth Avenue, New York, N.Y. 10110
www.wwnorton.com
W. W. Norton & Company Ltd., Castle House, 75/76 Wells Street, London W1T 3QT

1 2 3 4 5 6 7 8 9 0

This book is dedicated to the many families with whom we have had the privilege of working.

They have taught us much and we hope this book reflects what we have learned.

CONTENTS

ACKNOWLEDGMENTS

We would like to acknowledge the members of the Association for Treatment and Training in the Attachment of Children's Professional Practice Manual Committee who prepared the original draft of this book, under the leadership of chairperson Victoria Kelly, PhD, past president of the association. This committee worked for over a year reviewing best practices, current research, and trends to prepare the early version of this book. Under the leadership of Dr. Kelly, that document became a nationally recognized standard. It is with deep appreciation that we would like to thank the committee for its groundbreaking work.

I would also like to thank the board of directors of ATTACh for allowing me, along with my colleagues Denise and Lois, the opportunity to offer readers a revised edition. This dedicated group of individuals has been a source of support and inspiration to me and I value their friendship. For over ten years I have been associated with ATTACh and am pleased to have had this opportunity to help the organization.

On a personal note, I must acknowledge my family. Without the support of my spouse, Susan, and my children, Emily, David, and Samantha, I could not have completed this work. Their understanding of my many hours attending to this manuscript gave me the peace necessary to complete the work.

Finally, I thank Lois and Denise for their hard work on this project. Each of them took responsibility for particular chapters, and their work resulted in a substantially new and improved professional resource. I am grateful for their efforts and their friendship.

—Arthur Becker-Weidman, PhD, November 1, 2011

ORIGINAL COMMITTEE MEMBERS

Arthur Becker-Weidman, PhD

Chris Diani, LCSW

Lois P. Ehrmann, PhD, NCC, LPC, CAC

Victoria Kelly, PhD

Keith Kuboyama, LCSW

Todd Nichols, MA, MPAff

Sally Popper, PhD

PREFACE

This book began as a project of the Association for Treatment and Training in the Attachment of Children (ATTACh), the first edition of which the organization published over 3 years ago. Since then, a number of advances in the treatment of complex trauma and disorders of attachment have occurred. My colleagues, Denise LeBow and Lois Ehrmann, and I have worked hard to update and improve that document.

I would like to highlight several points for readers with regard to this new, re-titled edition, which has been substantially edited and updated. We have added many new, more current references and citations to support the latest emerging research on attachment and trauma. We have worked hard to include a good deal of new, up-to-date material and case examples that reflect cutting-edge knowledge of the nature of attachment disorders and complex trauma. We have included more recent research and materials about complex trauma, the neurodevelopmental treatment implications of trauma, and new treatment information that describes, in attachment theory terms, the phases of treatment within a relational model. This new material greatly expands the range of options for clinicians. For example, a better understanding of the phases of treatment and the importance of creating an alliance and safe base enables clinicians to use various interventions differentially, depending on the phase of treatment and the child's neurodevelopmental functioning.

The order of chapters has also been changed—and some chapters combined—to create a more user-friendly flow to the material. The reader will find that the reference section is much expanded, as is the study guide (Appendix D).

This book is an important contribution to the field of trauma treatment and attachment-focused therapy. It provides clinicians with a framework to assess, develop, and evaluate treatment plans, and to provide treatment in a comprehensive and integrated manner. Judges, attorneys, and child welfare professionals will find this book quite helpful in their work. It provides a comprehensive description of the standards of care for evaluations and treatment within an ethical framework. The material in this book can be used to evaluate the adequacy of evaluation and treatment, and act as a guide when service decisions are being made. College professors will also find this book a useful adjunct for family therapy, treatment, and ethics classes, and the study guide will assist in classroom instruction. Consumers and clients are provided the necessary tools and information to make better-informed decisions regarding the adequacy of care they are getting. It is my hope that this book will mark a new stage in the development of attachment-focused therapy by delineating the standards of care for the treatment of attachment and trauma disorders.

—Arthur Becker-Weidman, PhD, November 1, 2011

The Attachment
Therapy Companion

Introduction

Attachment-Focused Therapy Today

Attachment-focused therapy is based on improving the relationship between child and caregiver, so that the caregiver can be a resource and a source of safety, comfort, and security to the child. For the purposes of this book, the term caregiver applies to whomever is caring for the child: parent (birth, foster, or adoptive), primary youth worker in residential settings, or other custodial guardians, depending on the circumstances of the case.

Our purpose in writing this book is to provide the reader with a comprehensive text describing the principles, components, and framework of attachment-focused therapy. While much of the book is focused on providing attachment-focused therapy for families of children with trauma and attachment disorders, the general framework described in this book can be used with a variety of other populations and problems. This book provides the practitioner of attachment-focused therapy with the necessary guidelines for the ethical and professional practice of this very complex and rewarding treatment approach.

> This book is not intended and should not be used as the basis for practicing attachment-focused therapy by clinicians who have not had specialized training and supervision in this area.

Purpose and Scope

The primary intended audience for this book is mental health professionals (e.g., social workers, psychologists, mental health counselors) who work with children who have experienced significant relational trauma and their families, social service and protective service professionals, and members of the legal system such as judges, attorneys, and guardians ad litem. Professionals who work with children in the child welfare system, or who have been in the child welfare system, will find this book of value. It is our opinion that psychotherapy in general, and specialized attachment-focused therapy in particular, requires a combination of graduate training in theories of human development and treatment approaches, coupled with postgraduate supervised practice under the direction of an experienced and skilled clinician.

This book may also be of benefit to others who are interested in emerging practice guidelines for attachment- and trauma-informed care. A related goal of this book is that we want to articulate current principles and rationales for attachment-focused interventions based on current research and theory. In so doing, we hope to promote important criteria for well-reasoned treatment interventions with this challenging population of psychologically wounded and behaviorally disordered children and their caregivers. As such, this book may be informative to other clinicians working with children for whom attachment issues are part of the foci of treatment, insurance companies attempting to evaluate whether treatment plans include important components of care, and professional licensing boards and judicial courts attempting to evaluate whether appropriate standards of care were implemented.

Use by Clinicians

This book is intended to be a guide for clinicians in the delivery of attachment-focused interventions to children who have experienced relational trauma (Briere & Lanktree, 2011; Cook, Blaustein, Spinazolla, & van der Kolk, 2003; Schore, 1994). Attachment-focused therapy is a complex set of interventions dictated by the individual needs of the children and families who seek these services. There cannot be a cookbook approach to interventions and treatment. Attachment-focused therapy, while having distinct phases, is also not a linear, step-by-step treatment process. Instead, trauma processing and developmental remediation in the areas of social and emotional skills are often an iterative process. By this we mean that each step toward resolving attachment-related trauma may provide an experience of empathy that creates scaffolding for another step in emotional awareness and connection. Evolving emotional awareness and connection then provide scaffolding for deeper exploration, communication, and greater emotional support, which in turn can support greater exploration and processing of traumatic material, which leads to further integration and healing. In attachment terms, phases of treatment include creating an alliance, maintaining the alliance, exploration, integration, and healing. These phases occur in a cyclical and iterative manner. The alliance allows for exploration, which leads to integration and healing, which allows for deeper exploration (Becker-Weidman, 2010b, 2012).

We are attempting through this book to provide a framework for the development of a guiding treatment rationale and ongoing decision making, rather than a step-by-step guide for this treatment approach. Further, it is our hope that as clinicians become well grounded in related areas of research, theory, and treatment guidelines, they will more effectively integrate these into their own clinical training, skills, and judgment. By doing so, clinicians will be less dependent upon techniques and, instead, will have a broader, more sophisticated understanding of this complex phenomenon. As this relatively new field continues to evolve, well-informed clinicians can then better evaluate and select evidence-based models that are congruent with this approach. Clinicians may also be better prepared to express their own style of treatment in a way that adds innovation to this approach, while remaining guided by the core principles we discuss in this text.

This book should be used in conjunction with the clinician's professional code of ethics and clinical judgment. No text can ever substitute for the clinician's assessment of a client, or the clinician's clinical judgment.

Use by Parents, Caregivers, and Others

Parents, other caregivers, child welfare professionals, advocates, members of the legal profession, courts of law, and others may use this book as a resource for a variety of purposes. This book provides information on what is currently considered best practice in the field of attachment-focused therapy and the treatment of children with trauma-related difficulties. This information may be used to educate consumers, advocates, and the general public. There has been much misinformation and distortion in the media in recent years, so it has often been difficult for consumers to make informed decisions about attachment-focused treatments. This book provides information to support informed decision making.

Consumers may use this book when interviewing clinicians regarding treatment for a specific child to determine if the clinician's philosophy and approach are congruent with these standards. In this way, this book will help consumers of attachment-focused therapy become better informed and able to distinguish between various approaches that may or may not be congruent with these best practice standards. Similarly, this book may help consumers identify components of treatment that might be missing in other treatment approaches, especially if a child is not making adequate progress and has a history of attachment-related trauma.

Limitations

No text can identify and address every situation a clinician may face, or prescribe a strategy or intervention for a specific client. Nor can any text replace the depth of information gathered by a thorough assessment of an individual client and family. Therefore, this book is intended as a general guideline for practice only. The clinician's judgment, based on the assessment of the family, must always take precedence.

The nature and dynamics of attachment can inform rather than define interventions and clinical thinking:

Attachment theory offers a broad and far-reaching view of human functioning that has the potential to change the way clinicians think about and respond to their patients, and the way they understand the dynamics of the therapeutic relationship. At the same time, an understanding of attachment organization does not define all aspects of the human experience. Nor does it substitute for other, equally important, and equally valid kinds of clinical understanding. (Slade, 1999, p. 577)

This book represents the current understanding of research in academic attachment, trauma, child psychopathology, developmental psychology, and neuroscience as it relates to this population of children and youth. These are dynamic areas of research and it is expected that this book may change as new information emerges that should inform clinical care.

Providing Attachment Therapy

This book does not endorse or recommend specific models of attachment-focused therapy. Rather, it sets out the framework that should guide attachment-focused therapy and its related interventions. Clinicians are encouraged to be familiar with published works on the various approaches, including such models as the following:

- Attachment and bonding therapy (Keck & Kupecky, 1998)
- Corrective Attachment Therapy (Levy & Orlans, 1998)
- Dyadic Developmental Psychotherapy (Becker-Weidman, 2010b, 2011, 2012; Becker-Weidman & Hughes, 2008; Becker-Weidman & Shell, 2011; Hughes, 2007)
- Family Attachment Narrative Therapy (Lacher, Nichols, & May, 2005)
- Theraplay (Jernbeg & Booth, 1998)

Clinicians should also be familiar with specific techniques that can support attachment therapy, including:

- EMDR (Tinker & Wilson, 1999)
- Neurofeedback (Budzynski, Budzynski, Evans, & Abarbanel, 2008)
- Sensorimotor therapy (Ogden, Minton, & Pain, 2006)
- Sensory integration (Ottenbacher, 1991)

These models and approaches share many common features, but also differ in theoretical and research foundations, clinical conceptualizations and priorities, processes of therapy, and respective roles of the therapist and the caregiver.

This book is offered as a guide to current best practice for the treatment of trauma and attachment disorders. We expect that the field of attachment-focused therapies will continue to develop as it is informed by research in neuroscience, attachment, and trauma, as well as the further development of evidence-based practices for children and adolescents in order to more effectively address the unique needs and challenges of this population.

We seek to provide guidance on the core concepts and elements that should be part of any best-practice approach for attachment-focused therapy. Therefore, the primary purpose of this book is to provide a framework for the principles that guide such models. Different models may prioritize these principles in several ways. For instance, they may incorporate diverse techniques and approaches in the service of these core elements. We believe that the diversity of these approaches is critical for two reasons. First, this is a developing field, where innovation and creativity support the ongoing refinement of effective strategies. Second, the complexity inherent in the children and youth who present with attachment-disordered behaviors clearly argues for a comprehensive continuum of approaches, interventions, and adjunctive therapies.

The framework for the overarching principles we recommend is grounded in several important core guidelines of treatment:

- Attachment-focused interventions are based on a relational model of change. If children have been wounded physically and/or psychologically through relational trauma, then a safe, supportive, and well-attuned relationship with a primary caregiver provides a critical foundation for safety. Providing the child and the caregiver with emotional, physical, and psychological safety are critical foundations for trauma resolution work and healthy development.
- Parents and primary caregivers are central to helping children heal. It is imperative that caregivers feel supported, accepted, and understood, and experience the empathy of the therapist. "Whatever you want the parents to do with the child you must be able to do with the parents" (Becker-Weidman, 2010b, p. 52).
- Increased security in the caregiver-child relationship is essential for positive therapeutic outcomes and, to a large degree, is a function of the caregiver's capacity to be sensitive, reflective, committed, and insightful. As psychologically wounded children experience greater security, they can more effectively recognize, challenge, and resolve negative and distorted thoughts and beliefs. As these thoughts and beliefs change, their behavioral problems will resolve or will be more amenable to other interventions. While serious behavioral problems typically accompany trauma and attachment-related difficulties, the focus, at least initially, is more often on understanding and resolving the cause of the behavior than on behavior management strategies alone. Generally, it is causes, not symptoms, that are the focus of treatment in most psychological and medical approaches.
- Treatment focuses on building reflective capacity, a process that helps

reduce the parent's and child's reactivity to traumatic triggers, dysregulation due to overwhelming emotional states, and rigid defensive coping strategies, by being able to stay emotionally engaged in, and cognitively aware of, how the present is different from the past. This enables the child to be increasingly able to distinguish between the past and present, hurtful and helpful beliefs, and the feelings, emotions, and intentions of self or others. Treatment supports the caregiver's increased reflective capacity, since this is essential for good therapeutic outcomes, so that the caregiver can better understand and respond to the child with empathy and active support—even in the face of serious behavioral problems.

- Corrective emotional experiences in treatment are grounded in intersubjectivity, a process of mutual interaction and engagement that promotes the child's "feeling felt by" (Siegel, 1999) the primary caregiver (Trevarthen, 2001). As the primary caregiver both feels what it has been like for the child and begins to help the child put words to this experience, this process creates critical scaffolding for shared understanding in the moment. As the caregiver is better able to provide empathic supports to the child so that both can jointly make sense of the experience, then the child can better access, rely upon, and learn to trust in the caregiver as a secure base and source of safety. This process of intersubjectivity then also promotes an increased likelihood of greater sensitivity to and receptivity toward attunement in subsequent encounters.

- Enhanced reflective capacity, grounded in experiences of emotional support, promotes the building of a coherent narrative, which is usually defined as:
  1. The ability to make sense of one's life experiences
  2. Integrating both positive and negative experiences into a more holistic understanding
  3. Resolving negative and distorted conclusions to allow for more constructive and helpful beliefs about oneself, others, and the world

- Relational trauma can take a toll on children's development. Developmental effects can be seen across multiple domains of development (Becker-Weidman, 2009). Therefore, specific attention must also focus on skill building, especially in the social and emotional areas of functioning.

It is our hope that our colleagues in the child welfare system will continue to partner with us to address the very real needs of children who have experienced significant maltreatment and who do not respond predictably to other forms of treatment. Increasingly, state child welfare departments, adoption agencies, Medicaid departments, and other important stakeholders are reaching out to us for consultation, recognizing our experience and expertise with a group of children whose needs are overwhelming the system. We believe that healing and permanency are possible for these children, and we see proof of it every day.

Attachment-Focused Therapy Today

Attachment therapy, as a new and developing field in the late 1970s and early 1980s, relied heavily on "holding therapy," a methodology that had been used with some success with very troubled youth in residential facilities. It was an outgrowth of an approach called rage reduction therapy (Zaslow, 1975). Like many other therapeutic interventions of that time (e.g., cathartic emotional releases, highly intrusive systematic desensitization), the approach was very confrontational. By current standards of psychotherapy, the techniques were coercive, and they are no longer accepted. The guiding theory of that time was that only through confrontation could hardened defenses be challenged and "broken through." This theory assumed that rage was the predominant underlying and driving emotion of an "attachment disorder." Rage was believed to lead in turn to a profound need to control others and resist emotional closeness. Thus, the theory condoned confrontation as a method to evoke rage, for the purpose of facilitating a breakdown of the defenses so that the individual could access underlying emotional needs and vulnerability.

Later advances in neuroscience, and attachment theory as defined by Sir John Bowlby, have instead begun to clarify that the underlying process in trauma is profound, dysregulated fear and insecurity instead of rage. These findings, coupled with the advent of other attachment-focused interventions that do not utilize coercive techniques, have guided the evolution of attachment-focused therapy away from coercion and toward methods that support greater affective and behavioral regulation in affected children through a focus on relationship and the creation of an alliance and a secure positive relationship. This paradigm shift is exemplified in the ethical guidelines outlined in Appendix A.

Over the last 30 years, the field of attachment-focused therapy has seen a variety of models and interventions that are more congruent with emerging findings from the fields of academic research on attachment, trauma, neuroscience, and developmental psychopathology. It is important to also recognize that this evolution continues to parallel the evolution of other forms of therapy. For example, current forms of cognitive-behavioral therapy to address phobias are a much gentler approach that allows the client to gradually face exposure to fearful stimuli, but always with the chance to integrate the thoughts, feelings, and reactions such exposure generates. Indeed, even therapeutic approaches to work with sexual offenders, arguably some of the most treatment-resistant clients today, increasingly recognize that empathy and resolution of trauma are much more effective than the intense confrontations of the past.

Attachment-focused therapy covers a broad continuum of interventions that seek to more sensitively help caregivers help children resolve the developmental effects of early maltreatment and provide attachment-facilitating parenting. Today, the focus is much more on helping children learn to regulate the intense fear and avoidance that are the hallmarks of their traumatic reactions—especially fear of caregivers and adults in authority positions. To accomplish this, the attachment-focused clinician works to identify and challenge the negative, distorted, and limited beliefs that developed during the maltreatment (e.g., "others are hurtful," "the world is unsafe"). Similarly, the clinician works to help the child develop increased trust in the caregiver so that the caregiver can become more of a secure base for the child (i.e., providing soothing, security, guidance, and protection—the things the child missed when the maltreatment occurred at the hands of an earlier caregiver). There is substantial recognition that the primary caregivers are the cornerstone of treatment success. As such, there is increasing recognition that treatment of the child occurs through the caregiver-child relationship and that therapists increasingly help caregivers act in an attachment-facilitating manner.

Current forms of attachment-focused therapy focus on helping children make sense of their early experiences in ways that counter the sense of shame that is so profound in children who are abused and/or rejected by their birth parents and others. Progress toward these goals is carefully and sensitively titrated in a way that recognizes and honors a child's level of coping, capacity to tolerate affect, and age. Resources for coping include both internal resources (e.g., distress tolerance, internal beliefs, and current coping ability) and external resources (e.g., availability and acceptance of significant supportive relationships and ability to utilize these relationships for actual support).

The hallmark of current best practice in attachment-focused therapy is the primary focus on sensitively responding to the child in the moment (the intersubjective sharing of experience). Failure to ensure this can be retraumatizing for the child and must be avoided. Attachment-focused therapy does not have a cookbook approach, since it is necessarily finely attuned to the individual child's needs, in terms of both trauma resolution and developmental remediation.

Consequently, the use of coercive holding is not synonymous with attachment-focused therapy. And coercion is never an aspect of treatment. Many current approaches to attachment-focused therapy do not use any holding or touch at all. Attachment-focused therapies and approaches utilize a range of modalities such as family, dyadic, and group therapy, as well as different models and techniques. If holding (a better description would be cradling) is used, it is now more likely to be a position in which the therapy may be conducted and is better described as cradling. For example, to help children feel safe while exploring early traumatic memories, the caregiver may hold a younger child on the caregiver's lap or may hold an older child's hand.

Since many of these children missed out on early experiences of nurturing, physical closeness, cuddling, and playful dyadic games, these experiences may be provided within a therapeutic context that is playful, accepting, and empathic. The purpose of this is to provide reparative experiences of positive sharing of emotions between the child and caregiver. The "amplification of positive affect" is considered to be a critically important component of facilitating secure attachment (Schore, 1994). Some critics have complained that these interventions are inherently "infantilizing" for children. These critics argue that there should be no touching or nurturing. We disagree. We know, and there is extensive research to support this, that nurturing experiences are critical to healthy development. Current brain research continues to point out how neglected children have significant deficits in the brain chemistry that reinforces social connectedness (Fox, Hane, & Pines, 2007). Appropriate, sensitive use of touch and nurturing helps foster healthy brain development that in turn helps foster healthy social connectedness. In addition, many of these children are significantly younger developmentally than their chronological age (Becker-Weidman, 2009). It is therapeutic to treat the individual where that individual is developmentally rather than chronologically. It is important to stress that we must be very cognizant of the needs of the individual child. All interventions must be done in a way that is respectful of the child's chronological age, developmental age, comfort with closeness, and immediate needs. The sensitive use of touch and nurturing will only be corrective experiences if the child is able to accept and tolerate them at the given moment. The chronological needs of the child (e.g., an adolescent's strivings for autonomy and independence) must be sensitively balanced against the unmet developmental needs (e.g., the maltreated child's needs for comfort and protection) and developmental delays (Becker-Weidman, 2009). Our intention is always to help facilitate the child's greater sense of security, connection, regulation, and healthy development while mitigating the risk of any retraumatizing.

We expect that this brief summary of the current state of attachment-focused therapy will provide a context of understanding how this field has changed and continues to change as new research informs practice, as is the case in all fields. Attachment-focused therapy continues to develop, as do other fields of therapy such as psychodynamic and cognitive-behavioral treatments. Professional peer-reviewed journals have published empirical outcome research, using experimental and control groups, regarding the evidence base for some new approaches to attachment therapy, such as Dyadic Developmental Psychotherapy (Becker-Weidman, 2006a, 2006b; Becker-Weidman & Hughes, 2008). Other small studies are also underway. In light of emerging neuroscience findings that inform our understanding of how attachment patterns develop in the brain, the field is increasingly evolving and growing in importance.

Problems With Research

We recognize that the field of attachment-focused therapy is still relatively young and there is need for additional research. Significant attention in the field of mental health in recent years has focused on the need to ensure that treatment interventions are grounded in a sound, scientific basis. The goal of this movement has been to support effective treatment and enhance public health (American Psychological Association, 2005).

For many disorders and treatment interventions, double-blind, randomized, multisite outcome research has not been performed. However, it is important not to assume that interventions that have not been studied in such controlled and rigorous trials are ineffective; they are simply untested (American Psychological Association, 2005) or are evidence based at a different level (Craven & Lee, 2006; Saunders, Berliner, & Hanson, 2004). There is not one evidence-based standard, but several levels, each with differing criteria of increasing rigor. Many of the approaches described in this book meet the criteria of being evidence-based and effective treatments, just not at the level of having double-blind, randomized, multisite outcome studies.

As treatment models continue to evolve, the techniques and interventions become better operationalized. This provides a greater opportunity for clinicians to study outcomes of their work, either through single-case experimental designs (individual client change over the course of therapy), or more systematic case studies to compare client variables and outcomes across multiple clinicians. We expect that these important first steps will eventually support more thorough studies of the effectiveness of attachment-focused models.

Continued progress in the evolution of evidence-based approaches faces several important challenges. Applications of existing approaches must consider the unique needs of the population served. Clinical research has predominantly been conducted on the application of well-defined treatment delivered to a set of children with clearly defined problems as the focus of treatment (Shirk, 2001).

The children and youth with typical trauma and attachment disorders have historically been excluded from empirical studies of other treatment approaches because they present with multiple, serious behavioral and psychological difficulties, complex histories of multiple traumas, and often significant developmental delays, especially in the areas of social and emotional functioning. In addition, they often meet Diagnostic and Statistical Manual of Mental Disorders (DSM-IV-TR; American Psychiatric Association, 2004) criteria for multiple disorders and so are often not included in studies exploring the particular efficacy of a treatment approach with a specific diagnosis. Additionally, most treatment approaches assume some degree of capacity for trust so that a therapeutic alliance can be developed. This can be a significant barrier for children and youth with disorders of attachment and likely needs to be addressed to some degree before other treatment techniques can be successfully implemented.

We hope that the continued evolution of evidence-based models will eventually include more of an attachment-focused approach when indicated. Until that time, we believe that many of the children and their families treated using evidence-based approaches (albeit not randomized, multisite, double-blind studies) have benefited from an approach that incorporates attachment security, trauma resolution, emotional regulation, and enhanced social and emotional functioning. Moreover, the often serious behavioral difficulties of these children and youth pose very real risks to the stability of their placements, present significant challenges to their development, and may simultaneously be exclusionary criteria for their participation in other community treatment programs.

The issue brief "Systems of Care: A Framework for System Reform in Children's Mental Health," published by the National Technical Assistance Center for Children's Mental Health in partnership with the federal Substance Abuse and Mental Health Administration (Stroul, 2002) makes several important recommendations in the search for establishing a scientific evidence base for mental health interventions for children. Several with particular relevance to this book are as follows:

- Existing evidence-based interventions have been developed within specific contexts and for specific client groups. Little is known about whether these interventions are as effective when utilized in more highly diverse groups of youth with multiple needs, problems, and often co-occurring problems in community settings.
- All services do not have a strong evidence base at this time, and where such a base is lacking, common sense and experience take over.
- It is important to identify unique and creative practices within systems of care that are candidates for development of an evidence base.
- It is important not to allow innovation to be limited by the desire to use only proven interventions.
- We need to expand the definition of evidence and research methods considered acceptable for providing evidence, so that these are relevant to community clinicians and services.

The Relationship Between Attachment-Focused Therapy and Trauma Therapy

One area in child mental health that has received focus is the treatment of trauma (see Chapter 4). The Substance Abuse and Mental Health Administration has been actively addressing issues of childhood trauma through its National Child Traumatic Stress Network (www.nctsn.org), which defines complex trauma as follows:

the dual problem of exposure to traumatic events and the impact of this exposure on immediate and long-term outcomes.

Complex trauma exposure refers to children's experience of multiple traumatic events that occur within the care-giving system—the social environment that is supposed to be the source of safety and stability in a child's life. . . . [This] exposure to simultaneous or sequential [maltreatment can result in] emotional dysregulation, loss of a safe base, loss of direction, inability to detect or respond to danger, and often leads to subsequent trauma exposure. . . .

Complex trauma can have effects across the following domains:

attachment, biology, affect regulation, dissociation, behavioral regulation, cognitive function, and self concept. (Blaustein, Cooke, Spinazzola, & van der Kolk, 2003, pp. 5–6)

As stated above, neither complex trauma nor attachment disorder are diagnoses in the DSM-IV-TR (American Psychiatric Association, 2000). As such research is conducted, the degree of similarity versus distinction should become more clear. Due to the differences in basic conceptualizations of these clinical phenomena, there are differences in the assumptions that underlie the current models of intervention.

We have been encouraged to see that this broadened conceptualization of trauma now more closely relates to the clinical phenomena we understand as disorders or disturbances of attachment in older children. We think that the term relational trauma (Main & Hesse, 1990; Schore, 1994) is another useful construct since it focuses on the specific nature of the trauma addressed by attachment-focused interventions. Relational trauma and complex trauma are very similar and overlapping terms. Relational trauma has been described as the convergence of:

- Maltreatment by a caregiver
- Resulting loss of the caregiver as a secure base
- The resulting overwhelming dysregulation that children experience without access to safety or comfort

Many of the children treated for complex or relational trauma have experienced simultaneous and/or sequential forms of maltreatment, as well as exposure to other traumas (e.g., domestic violence, parental mental illness or substance abuse, multiple placements). However, the emphasis of treatment, at least initially, is not so much on resolution of the traumatic memories per se as on the loss and building (or rebuilding) of a secure base in the caregiver relationship. With the achievement of a secure base, these children experience a greater sense of safety, so that they are then better able to explore, address, and resolve their traumatic memories and reactions.

Research has demonstrated that the availability of one secure attachment bond can offer significant protection against psychopathology induced by trauma (Finkelhor & Browne, 1984; McFarlane, 1987). This protection derives from the critical role the attachment plays in both buffering the stress and facilitating the development of psychological and biological capacities to manage distress (van der Kolk, 2005). Moreover, Luthar and Zigler (1991) found that access to the presence of a supportive caregiver can mitigate the effects of trauma on children, even if the caregiver is unable to alter the outcome of the events. The absence of a secure attachment, on the other hand, leaves the child defenseless and vulnerable in the face of trauma and its impact.

One example of an evidence-based model used for the treatment of trauma in children and youth is trauma-focused cognitive-behavioral therapy (TF-CBT;

Cohen, Mannarino, & Deblinger, 2006). TF-CBT is an empirically supported treatment model of components addressing psychoeducation on trauma and post-traumatic reactions, cognitive-behavioral principles, attachment security, and skill development. Similarly, integrative treatment of complex trauma (ITCT; Briere & Lanktree, 2011; Lanktree & Briere, 2008) is a model being developed to address the range of disturbances evident in complex trauma. One of the important commonalities between these models and attachment-focused interventions described in this book is the use of exposure to reminders of trauma.

TF-CBT and ITCT utilize, in different approaches, the technique of a trauma narrative in which the clinician sensitively guides the child over time in describing traumatic experiences in greater detail so that accompanying thoughts and feelings can be identified. This process helps reduce the child's defensive avoidance of reminders and allows dysfunctional thoughts to be challenged so that more helpful beliefs can be developed. The purpose of this is to reduce the symptoms of post-traumatic stress disorder (PTSD). ITCT is a more flexible model that attempts to address symptoms beyond PTSD, such as attachment difficulties and emotional dysregulation, more directly through supportive and skill-building approaches.

In attachment-focused interventions, the initial focus is the loss of the secure base and the child's resulting feelings of being alone and overwhelmed by the dysregulation resulting from maltreatment by, or loss of, the caregiver. In other words, it is a recognition that the child has been hurt in the past by caregivers and the child understandably felt alone in coping with the overwhelming feelings. Further, it is a recognition that the very things the child learned to do to survive the trauma, alone without help or comfort, are things that now interfere with the child's ability to access or accept support and help in the present.

In this model, processing of traumatic memories is secondary to the development of a secure base. Exposure is utilized, but the traumatic reminders are more commonly a complex and confused paradox of unmet longing for emotional connection with, and protection by, a caregiver, coupled with fears of maltreatment by that same caregiver. There may also be specific traumatic reminders of maltreatment, abandonment, or loss, but in children with attachment-related traumas, the offer of help or comfort is itself a trigger.

Children with histories of relational or complex trauma typically avoid or actively resist connection with others; usually out of fear. Moreover, their severe behavioral and emotional dysregulation persists because they actively resist guidance, assistance, or support from adults; based on their severely negative prior experiences with caregivers. The new caregiver's sensitive and gradual intentions and efforts to understand the child's feelings and provide support and assistance in managing the feelings are the initial focus of attachment-focused interventions. This focus seeks to promote and strengthen a sense of a secure base so that processing of other traumatic reminders can then be done safely.

Identification and processing of specific traumatic memories about maltreatment, abandonment, or loss are not the focus until a child can experience a greater sense of safety and security with a protective and helpful caregiver. Specific traumatic memories that might emerge in this initial phase may be recognized and used as an opportunity to clarify the current caregiver's intentions as distinctly different from the past (e.g., to offer comfort instead of hurting; to offer help in coping instead of leaving the child alone; to help the child make sense of what has happened instead of blaming the child).

Another important distinction between the two approaches is the relative role of the caregiver in the treatment process. TF-CBT and ITCT consider one of their core components to be the therapeutic relationship between the child and the clinician. While this model encourages caregiver involvement as important to overall outcomes, TF-CBT could be conducted without the participation of the caregiver. The essential treatment components are led by the clinician and the primary client is the child. In attachment-focused therapies, the caregiver is recognized as central to therapy and the clinician takes more of a coaching or consultant role. The primary client is the caregiver-child relationship. These differences likely emerged out of how these models evolved.

TF-CBT had its origins in structured work with children who had been sexually abused. ITCT evolved as a treatment approach for children who had experienced multiple traumas, both maltreatment and exposure to violence. Both of these models often included the birth parents or caregivers, who may or may not have been involved in the abuse of the child. In other cases, the caregivers were often foster parents who had a temporary commitment to the child. These caregivers had varying degrees of readiness, willingness, and/or ability to deal with the abuse that occurred.

By contrast, attachment-focused therapies have evolved primarily out of efforts to help adoptive and foster parents connect with and support their adopted or foster children. These children come into their new families with histories of trauma from others, and often reenact the conditioned patterns of fear from the earlier relationships in the new families. These caregivers then struggle to help the children heal from past hurts and accept nurturing and guidance in the present. Yet when the chronic patterns of resistance, defiance, and aggression continue in spite of the absence of maltreatment, caregivers can become overwhelmed by their perceived inability to connect with and support these children. When this occurs, the placements can often be at risk, especially if the children's often serious behavioral disturbances continue to escalate. Therefore, in the attachment-focused approach to treatment, the caregiver's involvement with therapy is deemed a critical component and essential initial focus. An example of an evidence-based and empirically validated attachment-focused therapy is Dyadic Developmental Psychotherapy (Becker-Weidman, 2010b, 2011; Becker-Weidman & Hughes, 2008).

Another important distinction between the two approaches is the underlying assumption about the neurobiology of trauma. The TF-CBT approach to trauma focuses more on explicit memories that can be verbally reported so that distorted thoughts associated with the trauma can be identified and resolved (Clark, Beck, & Alford, 1999). This approach is grounded in the "top-down" psychological resolution of explicit memories of trauma through very conscious reworking of distorted thoughts and beliefs. It recognizes the critical role of the hippocampus and language centers of the left hemisphere.

While increased affect regulation is included in this model, it is more of a means to support improved cognitive processing than a goal of treatment per se. Conversely, attachment-focused therapies, such as ITCT, initially work to enhance the capacity for affect regulation and security of attachment. This approach is more of a "bottom-up" resolution of implicit memories acquired through the experiences of both maltreatment and the lack of a secure base. It recognizes the important role of subcortical structures such as the amygdala and other limbic system components, as well as the prefrontal cortex and orbital frontal cortex, in trauma resolution.

Attachment-focused therapies draw from the work of Alan Schore (1994, 2003) in recognizing that early child maltreatment by caregivers can result in significant dysregulation of the right hemisphere, interfering with the development of capacities for affect regulation, self-awareness, social functioning, and ability to learn from experience. While cognitive processing and resolution of distorted beliefs are essential components of this approach, they are believed to be more effective (and indeed only possible) once a foundation for security, affect regulation, and intersubjectivity (e.g., the child "feeling felt by" the caregiver [Siegel, 1999] or the understanding of mental states in self and other [Fonagy, Gergely, Jurist, & Target, 2002]) is experientially established.

Another difference between ITCT and the attachment-focused interventions described in this book is that ITCT is driven by ongoing objective assessments. Attachment-focused interventions also use objective assessments to help guide the treatment planning process, but then may rely on subjective assessments of how the caregiver-child relationship is evolving and improving. As the caregiver-child relationship provides greater security for the child, evidence of increased reflective capacity, emotional sharing, and accessing the caregiver as a source of support in skill building becomes apparent.

The reader should now have a clear understanding of the purpose of this book and the material we will be discussing. We intend to provide a comprehensive and detailed description of the practice of attachment-focused therapy as a general approach to treatment. In the process we describe the principles and elements of this approach, its relationship to trauma-focused therapies, and what are best practices in this developing field.

CHAPTER ONE

Terminology & Diagnosis

One of the challenges facing us in writing this book is the lack of consensus and clarity about terms and diagnoses. A major contribution to the field was the "Report of the Taskforce on Attachment Disorders and Attachment Therapy," by the American Professional Society on the Abuse of Children (Chaffin et al., 2006). The report avoided definitions, but acknowledged lack of consistency in terms currently utilized in the field. The terms *attachment disorder*, *attachment problems*, and *attachment therapy*, although increasingly used, have no clear, specific, or consensus definitions. Unfortunately, this lack of clarity is a major contributing factor to the confusion regarding approaches and methods of treatment and what they do and do not include.

For many years, clinicians recognized that significant impairments in development could result from deprivations and/or disruptions in the caregiver-child relationship. The field of developmental psychology has recognized the complexity of the effects of such experiences:

> It is critical to distinguish among deprivation that results from not developing a close attachment relationship during the infancy and toddler period; distortions in care that are the result of insensitivity, unresponsiveness, and often physical neglect and abuse within an attachment relationship; and finally the loss of a relationship that has been established. (Greenberg, 1999, p. 470)

Clinical diagnostic approaches have been slow to recognize and address these impairments.

Children who have experienced loss of an attachment figure or trauma within the context of the caregiving relationship in the first few years of life (complex trauma) are seriously damaged by that experience. One of the problems we as clinicians struggle with is how best to assess the range of emotional, psychological, and behavioral problems that can present as a result of attachment-related trauma. The approach to diagnosis embodied in the *DSM-IV-TR* (American Psychiatric Association, 2000) is largely symptom driven, without a formal way to conceptualize the diagnosis from a developmental perspective and without any connection to the cause of the symptoms, which is what, ultimately, is treated. As such, children who present with a complex array of disturbances have frequently been given a myriad of diagnoses by other clinicians (e.g., ADHD, ODD, PTSD, conduct disorder, bipolar disorder). We then become frustrated because, although the child may nominally meet the criteria for the diagnoses, we find that too often the diagnoses reflect disturbances that are better understood as symptoms of a more comprehensive developmental disturbance, which is itself the product of the attachment-related trauma experienced by the child.

The current symptom-focused diagnosis approach of the *DSM* system fails to capture the reasons behind the symptom presentation. The significance of this is that the purpose of a diagnosis is to develop a working hypothesis to direct treatment. In our experience, the typical treatments for the various disorders listed in the previous paragraph do not adequately address the underlying dynamics of a child who has lost, or never had, a secure base and who has experienced chronic early maltreatment within a caregiving relationship. As such, these diagnoses fail to incorporate the reality that many of these areas of disturbance are essentially symptoms of disturbances in attachment. The typical interventions for these other disorders, such as psychopharmacology, behavior management, and cognitive approaches to treatment, are not sufficient to address the underlying core issues for children with attachment-related traumas. Children who have experienced complex trauma often show impairments in such domains as attachment, behavioral and emotional regulation, cognition, defensive functions, biology, and self-concept, as well as difficulties in forming and maintaining emotionally meaningful and supportive relationships.

A central issue for a child with attachment-related trauma is its pervasive negative effects on the capacity to build and use relationships in a constructive way. These children have, to differing degrees, turned away from and resist human contact, remaining profoundly stuck in what Bowlby termed "compulsive self-reliance" (1980, p. 365). Such a child must find a way to trust another human being enough to begin to use that relationship to access the supports necessary to learn, develop, and grow. Most therapies assume this ability and do not explicitly address how to facilitate it. Until a child has developed some capacity for this ability, it is unlikely that the child will respond well to any treatment approach. As a result, we suggest that helping the child build trust, perceived safety, and comfort within a caregiving relationship must be the foundation of any good attachment-focused treatment.

The *DSM-IV-TR* (American Psychiatric Association, 2000) and *ICD-10* (World Health Organization, 1992) identify reactive attachment disorder (RAD) as the only formally accepted diagnosis that recognizes the effects of disturbed or absent attachment relationships. This diagnosis is characterized by two subtypes, both of which are believed to be the result of pathogenic care. The inhibited type is characterized by hypervigilance and fear expressed more often as avoidance and withdrawal in social relationships. Conversely, the disinhibited type is characterized by indiscriminate sociability, even with strangers, coupled with failure to discriminate an attachment figure. While the clinical manifestations of these subtypes are different, the commonality is that neither type of child had trusting relationships with adults who provided a secure base.

RAD was first introduced into the *DSM-III* in 1980, at a time when biological psychiatry was at its height. RAD was clearly not biologically based, but rather reflected an awareness that something unusual happened when children were maltreated early in life. This meant it could not be captured well enough by other diagnoses. Unlike the process by which diagnoses are typically included in the *DSM*, RAD was included without the kind of rigorous research usually required to establish and define a diagnosis. The RAD diagnosis was essentially based on "pathogenic care."

As is clear from this description, the diagnosis of RAD is remarkably opaque in its description. It is also clear that many children have no selective attachments, or are seriously damaged in ways other than early neglect or maltreatment, but do not meet criteria for RAD. In this regard, clinical constructs such as complex trauma, relational trauma, and developmental trauma disorder better reflect the pervasive negative impacts of chronic early maltreatment within a caregiving relationship. There was general consensus from the start that the diagnosis was useful as a first step, but not adequate to describe the symptom patterns that were found in children who had experienced institutional deprivation, or serious neglect and maltreatment within their birth families (Zeanah, 1993).

Researchers involved in the development of the RAD diagnosis for the *DSM* have argued that although this disorder does not fit attachment as explained by the developmental research, it does provide "clinical evidence for a constellation of symptoms and atypical development not captured by other diagnostic categories" (Richters & Vollkmar, 1994, p. 331). These researchers further argue that a truly reliable and valid diagnosis will require longitudinal, prospective studies that will help characterize the disorder, validate the criteria, and document developmental trajectories (p. 332).

Among the first researchers to focus on the difficulties with the *DSM* diagnosis of RAD were Neil Boris and colleagues, who in 2004 proposed several diagnostic subcategories that they had been able to reliably describe in toddlers, including nonattachment with emotional withdrawal or with indiscriminate sociability; disordered attachment with inhibition, with self-endangerment, or with role reversal; disrupted attachment disorder; and RAD with either inhibited or indiscriminate sociability. Since that time, these authors and a number of others (Rutter et al., 2007) have been working to provide more detailed and comprehensive descriptions, especially of children who have experienced early institutional deprivation.

Around the same time an organization called Zero to Three (2005) published a new diagnostic manual, *Diagnostic Classification of Mental Health and Developmental Disorders of Infancy and Early Childhood, Revised* (*DC:0-3R*), specifically focused on children aged three or under. They suggested the diagnostic category of reactive attachment deprivation/maltreatment disorder of infancy. Its definition described a child who failed to initiate social interactions or showed ambivalent or contradictory social responses, including social indiscriminateness after a history of maltreatment. These classifications have not been extended to older children.

Therefore, the diagnosis of RAD offered a meaningful, if imperfect, label for the profound difficulties some children demonstrate in social relatedness and, in particular, the ability to discriminate caregivers as a source of comfort and safety. For many caregivers and clinicians, the RAD became widely used within the burgeoning field of attachment-focused therapy. For some caregivers and clinicians the term RAD became reified and used to explain a broad range of emotional and behavioral problems that were not included in the *DSM-IV-TR*.

Several checklists evolved that purported to help identify children with RAD. Typically, these lists included a number of behaviors that can generally be described as antisocial: for example, lying, stealing, preoccupation with fire, blood, and gore, or cruelty to animals. Frequently the children were described as manipulative and controlling or good at conning others. These lists were typically based on the experience of working with or parenting children who do not trust because of early experience, so they reflected a range of behavioral disturbances that other diagnoses failed to capture. However, in focusing on the behavioral manifestation alone, without understanding the effects of attachment-related trauma on development, they also attributed a level of intentionality to the child that we question. These checklists have been appropriately challenged for their lack of validity and reliability (Chaffin et al., 2006). In addition, such checklists ignored the fact that RAD, complex trauma, relational trauma, and developmental trauma disorder are all evidenced primarily within relationships.

The resulting reality is that the field continues to lack a fully meaningful and coherent term to adequately describe the clinical phenomenon that we attempt to address in attachment-focused therapy. This has created much confusion, but we are not alone in this confusion.

> many clinical reports and virtually all of the research on "attachment disorders" do not use *DSM-IV* or *ICD-10* criteria; therefore, we need a more generic term that does not necessarily invoke a diagnosis but

instead refers to a parallel set of behaviors implied by the diagnosis and is consistent with the broader class of disturbances considered in previous reports. *No very adequate term exists, so we use the term "attachment disorder behavior."* Finally, the terms "Secure," "Insecure," and "Disorganization/Disorganized" are used strictly in relation to the research on individual differences that have been the focus of attachment research with children who have had a history of selective attachment relationships. (O'Connor & Zeanah, 2003, pg. 225, emphasis added)

In this book, we use the term *attachment disorder behavior* to represent the common clinical presentation of children and youth who either have not had selective attachment relationships or have had significantly disorganized attachment relationships marked by serious and persistent behavioral difficulties deriving from interpersonal difficulties, emotional dysregulation, negative internal working models and deficits, and/or delays in social-emotional development. Other useful constructs and terms we use are complex trauma, relational trauma, and developmental trauma disorder.

Another distinction we would like to make clear is the importance of understanding the underlying emotions driving attachment-disordered behaviors within relationships and the impact of caregiver caring on these behaviors. Historically, the core underlying emotions of "attachment disorders" were more typically understood as rage and the need for control. When behavioral disturbances were conceptualized in that way, too often the approach to treatment was control based and coercive. We do not support coercive approaches, nor do we conceptualize the difficulties these children present as issues of control. Often the underlying affects are fear and shame. Instead, we believe that research on trauma, neurobiology, child maltreatment, and attachment makes a more compelling case for the underlying emotions being fear (even terror) and shame. Furthermore, the difficulties are primarily relational in nature, and, therefore, effective treatments must also be relational. Understanding the complex presentation of symptoms from this perspective leads to very different treatment approaches based on safety, regulation, and support. We strongly advocate that attachment-focused therapists should continue to keep current with the evolution of research in these areas so that treatment approaches to working with children damaged by attachment-related traumas remain informed by cutting-edge research.

Differential Diagnosis

The same symptom can come from many different sources and can have many different causes; this is true for mental health, medical, and other issues. Therefore, it is important that all clinicians providing attachment-focused therapy approach the process of diagnosis with good preparation in normal child development, developmental psychopathology, the assessment of trauma, and the ability to screen for various related issues such as sensory integration, cognitive and neuropsychological issues, and mental health issues, as well as an open mind capable of scientifically weighing evidence both for and against specific diagnoses.

It is important to recognize that the question of differential diagnosis with respect to attachment disorders is extremely complicated. A high rate of comorbidity appears intrinsic to child and adolescent developmental psychopathology (Sonuga-Barke, 1998, p. 119). This is due to the fact that many disorders include poor self-regulation among their criteria, yet its etiology can be very different (e.g., neurological, developmental, pathogenic care, prenatal exposure to alcohol or drugs, and other causative factors). Moreover, increased self-regulation can be observed in children as they make developmental progress, which argues that the behavioral symptoms should be understood as developmental deficits rather than a mental disorder. This is especially important when working with younger children. It is for this reason that complex trauma may be the most clinically useful construct for understanding the pervasive effects of relational trauma and for guiding the domains to be considered in assessing a child and family.

Sonuga-Barke's (1998) review of the literature on diagnostic schemas for children and adolescents addresses the special challenges of comorbidity by arguing that in the face of complex and ambiguous presentations, clinicians may rush to impose order through diagnosis. Clinicians with the greatest need for structure may be most likely to interpret behavior as trait based and quickest to impose a diagnosis. This can lead to a premature foreclosure of other considerations. It can also lead to an insistence on one diagnosis to the exclusion of others. We strongly encourage all clinicians involved in attachment-focused therapy to utilize a broad-based and developmentally sensitive approach to assessment and diagnosis. This is discussed further in Chapter 6.

While understanding the impact of relational trauma under the rubric of attachment-disordered behaviors may be helpful in integrating treatment approaches, this approach must not exclude the consideration and inclusion of other relevant diagnoses as additional foci of treatment. For example, sensory integration issues, medical complications, neurological concerns, and other issues may need to be considered.

A more sophisticated understanding of the impact of early trauma and loss on children's development means that no one diagnosis properly sums up the issues with which such children present. Instead, we must consider a number of diagnoses and related issues to fully describe these children. In addition to the diagnosis of RAD, which, as explained above, is a limited and problematic diagnosis, clinicians must look at symptoms more broadly from both trauma and developmental perspectives. Trauma can include situational forms, including maltreatment and exposure to violence, as well as biological forms including in utero exposure to toxins. The developmental effects of trauma must also be understood from the dual perspective of symptoms that are related to:

- a primary failure to develop appropriate regulation of physiological, neurological, affective, and behavioral systems; and
- secondary failure to develop those expected skills at appropriate ages.

PTSD and Situational Trauma Exposure

Many children who were taken from their birth families or were victims of maltreatment (e.g., neglect, abuse, exposure to domestic violence, parental substance abuse, and mental illness) exhibit some symptoms of PTSD but may not meet all the *DSM-IV* criteria for this diagnosis (most notably the criteria regarding experiencing a life-threatening event). Frequently, their symptoms of anxiety, such as hypervigilance or difficulty concentrating, are mistaken for attention-deficit/hyperactivity disorder (ADHD) or other disorders of attention. Unfortunately, mental health clinicians may fail to consider PTSD as a potential diagnosis and as a result may miss what may be the more correct diagnosis. On the other hand, it is also true that many children have experienced trauma but do not meet criteria for PTSD. This is especially true of young children. It is for this reason that the clinical construct of complex trauma may be much more useful from an assessment and treatment point of view.

Scheeringa, Zeanah, Myers, and Putnam (2005) have followed preschool children who met only some of the symptom criteria for PTSD over a period of 2 years and found that even those who were not able to report a full complement of symptoms for the diagnosis showed impairment equal to those who did. However, the *DSM-IV* does not permit the diagnosis of PTSD unless a child meets full criteria for the disorder. It is also important to recognize that PTSD is a diagnosis for acute trauma and may not capture the range of symptoms associated with complex trauma (see next section).

Further, some may question whether a child who has not been abused but has "only" lost his or her parent(s) has actually experienced trauma. This perspective fails to appreciate the needs of the young child and the significance of the attachment relationship (Bowlby, 1982, 1988). As vulnerable and dependent beings, young children are only too aware that access to responsive parents means survival, so life itself is in danger when parents are lost, either through actual physical separation or unresponsiveness.

Complex and Developmental Trauma

In recent years, the National Child Traumatic Stress Network (NCTSN) and some researchers, including Dr. Bessel van der Kolk, have proposed that when children are chronically maltreated within a caregiving relationship during the first few years of life, the impact is far more serious than when trauma occurs in an older person. This may be because the child is exposed to trauma at a very vulnerable age and development in many areas is skewed as a result. Very important developmental, neurological, and psychological processes are occurring within the first few years of life. The NCTSN has suggested that complex trauma disrupts development in the following seven areas: attachment, biology, affect regulation, dissociation (defensive functions), behavioral control, cognition, and self-concept. The following list of symptoms related to these areas makes it clear that this clinical construct would be appropriate for many children who come to clinics focused on attachment disturbances (Blaustein et al., 2003):

Attachment
- Uncertainty about the reliability and predictability of the world
- Problems with boundaries
- Distrust and suspiciousness
- Social isolation
- Interpersonal difficulties
- Difficulty attuning to other people's emotional states
- Difficulty with perspective taking
- Difficulty enlisting other people as allies

Biology
- Sensorimotor developmental problems
- Hypersensitivity to physical contact
- Analgesia
- Problems with coordination, balance, body tone
- Difficulties localizing skin contact
- Somatization
- Increased medical problems across a wide span, such as pelvic pain, asthma, skin problems, autoimmune disorders, pseudoseizures

Affect Regulation
- Difficulty with emotional self-regulation
- Difficulty describing feelings and internal experience
- Problems knowing and describing internal states
- Difficulty communicating wishes and desires

Dissociation
- Distinct alterations in states of consciousness
- Amnesia
- Depersonalization and derealization
- Two or more distinct states of consciousness, with impaired memory for state-based events

Behavioral Control
- Poor modulation of impulses

- Self-destructive behavior
- Aggression against others
- Pathological self-soothing behaviors
- Sleep disturbances
- Eating disorders
- Substance abuse
- Excessive compliance
- Oppositional behavior
- Difficulty understanding and complying with rules
- Communication of traumatic past by reenactment in day-to-day behavior or play (e.g., sexual, aggressive)

Cognition
- Difficulties in attention regulation and executive functioning
- Lack of sustained curiosity
- Problems with processing novel information
- Problems focusing on and completing tasks
- Problems with object constancy
- Difficulty planning and anticipating
- Problems understanding their contribution to what happens to them
- Learning difficulties
- Problems with language development
- Problems with orientation in time and space
- Acoustic and visual perceptual problems
- Impaired comprehension of complex visual-spatial patterns

Self-Concept
- Lack of a continuous, predictable sense of self
- Poor sense of separateness
- Disturbances of body image
- Low self-esteem
- Shame and guilt

We are hopeful that clinical constructs such as complex trauma or developmental trauma disorder will be accepted as diagnoses because these constructs better capture the range of symptoms typically associated with chronic early maltreatment within a caregiving relationship, attachment-disordered behaviors, and may eliminate the problems inherent in the diagnosis of RAD. However, attachment disturbance is but one of the domains of impairment caused by complex trauma. Consequently, it may be possible for an individual with complex trauma or developmental trauma disorder to have impairments in the other areas and less in the area of attachment.

Symptoms Related to Neglect and Institutional Deprivation

In recent years, there has been a flurry of research on children who have experienced institutional deprivation as a result of orphanage placements. This work adds to a limited body of work from the 1940s through the 1960s, including the seminal work of Rene Spitz (1945) and that of Michael Rutter (1981). In general, children who have histories of institutional deprivation have been found to have more serious delays and aberrations in development than children who are moved to foster care in the same country, or children adopted domestically in the UK (Kreppner et al., 2007; Nelson et al., 2007; Rutter et al., 2007; Smyke et al., 2007).

Gunnar, van Dulmen, and the International Adoption Project Team (2007) found that children with institutional histories were more likely than other internationally adopted children to have social problems and difficulty managing attention. In particular, disinhibited attachment, and what has been termed "institutional autism," appear to be more common in children who have lived in institutions (Rutter et al., 2007). Yet the factor of institutional care does not always predict poor outcomes for children. Several studies (Rutter et al., 2007) have found that many children adopted later (after 6 months and after 2 years of age, respectively), following institutional care, do not consistently exhibit persistent marked delays or disturbances in development. This is an important reminder that resilience is possible for many children in the face of very challenging life experiences. Anecdotally, many international adoption workers suggest that some children are able to establish important relationships with orphanage workers and become favored children, which may be a mitigating factor and foster resilience.

Unfortunately, the high quality of research carried out on children from foreign orphanages, particularly those in Romania, has not been duplicated on other groups. There is ample and compelling evidence from the Adverse Childhood Events study by the U.S. Centers for Disease Control that maltreatment of all types contributes significantly to negative outcomes in all areas of functioning, even into adulthood (Anda et al., 2006).

Bipolar Disorder and Difficulties With Affect Regulation

Many children with histories of trauma and loss present with both extreme emotional reactivity and deficits in regulating affective states. Schore (2001) has posited that teaching an infant to regulate affect is one of the primary jobs of the caregiver in the first years of life, so it is easy to understand why a child without that experience would likely have significant difficulties regulating affect later in life. However, this does not mean that all children with difficulties regulating affect, especially those who move easily into rage states, should be diagnosed as having bipolar disorder, a practice that is currently far too common (Carlson, 2007). We would suggest that in order to be fairly confident that a bipolar diagnosis is correct, one should look for clear evidence of cycling, with periods of hypomania or mania (which may be dysphoria or irritability in children) and periods of depression. It is also wise to check for the neurovegetative symptoms of bipolar disorder, since it is unlikely to be present without at least some of these symptoms. A careful review of the *DSM-IV* criteria for bipolar disorder is essential before giving this diagnosis, as should be the clinician's practice before giving any *DSM*-based diagnosis.

Fetal Exposure to Cocaine, Alcohol, and Other Substances

Concerns persist about prenatal exposure to cocaine, although research has indicated that cocaine is a less teratogenic substance than either alcohol or nicotine (Chiriboga, 2003; Slotkin, 1998). It has been difficult to tease out specific effects of fetal exposure to cocaine since cocaine use is typically associated with multiple substance exposures as well as poverty and its associated risks (Tronick & Beeghly, 1999). The general thrust of the research is that prenatal exposure to cocaine can lead to significant neurodevelopmental impairments. Fetal alcohol exposure has been well researched and has been found to cause serious long-term effects including mental and developmental retardation, microcephaly, and many associated deficits in memory, executive functioning, social skills, and communication skills (Niccols, 2007), as well as marked physical deformities, primarily of midline development (Chasnoff, 2010).

Few are aware of the teratogenic effects of nicotine, which has been associated with higher rates of low birth weight and sudden infant death syndrome, as well as a host of neurodevelopmental abnormalities including hyperactivity and cognitive impairment (Ernst, Moolchan, & Robinson, 2001). Marijuana has been researched fairly thoroughly, and has been found to have a number of subtle effects on later functioning. These include some cognitive deficits, impulsivity, inattention and hyperactivity, and increased levels of some psychological disorders and substance abuse (Sundram, 2006). There are also indications that a number of environmental contaminants cause fetal damage, although research in this area is far from comprehensive (Wigle et al., 2008). Davies and Bledsoe (2005) reviewed the impact of a variety of substance use effects in adoption and, when available, provided country-specific information on exposure.

In brief, the research on substance and environmental exposure risk to children indicates that it can be serious, and, especially when interacting with other risk factors, such as histories of loss and trauma or maltreatment, can cause significant deficits in a number of areas of neurological, developmental, and cognitive functioning. It is remarkable to note how much the spectrum of substance exposure–related symptoms coincides with those of complex trauma. It can be important to assess the impact of each since the effects of alcohol and other substances on brain functioning may not be reversible, while the psychological and emotional effects of trauma and attachment disorders are often reversible with treatment. It is important, however, to recognize that most of these symptoms are not consciously used by the child to manipulate or con adults, as has been suggested in the past in writing about children with attachment disturbances. Rather, they more likely represent effects on brain development and psychological and emotional functioning.

Issues With Terminology Regarding Therapy

Just as there are significant issues with terminology over diagnostic labels, there is also confusion about what to call the therapy or treatment itself. Many terms have been used: attachment therapy, attachment-focused therapy, attachment-trauma therapy, and holding therapy. It is important to clarify that attachment-related therapies are not synonymous with holding therapy; many forms of attachment-related therapy do not rely on any form of touch or holding (see Introduction). Moreover, holding therapy is more commonly associated with coercive and confrontational practices, which are not endorsed by us or any professional association such as the Association for Treatment and Training in the Attachment of Children, the National Association of Social Workers, or the American Psychological Association, to name just three.

We think that *attachment-focused therapy* is the most accurate name for the approach described in this book. This form of therapy includes joint attention to the concepts of attachment and trauma. Since the specific form of trauma addressed is relational trauma, which negatively impacts the security of attachment, it follows that the therapy itself focuses first and foremost on the creation (or re-creation) of a secure base for the child and is focused on relationships. Attachment-focused therapy seeks first to facilitate greater security between the child and caregiver. Other forms of trauma-focused therapy may be utilized as an adjunct to resolve specific issues related to the maltreatment itself, as needed.

CHAPTER TWO

Overview of Attachment Theory: Synopsis of Key Concepts

Note: It is beyond the scope of this book to provide a comprehensive review of attachment theory and research. The purpose of this chapter is to briefly highlight the most salient elements of attachment theory that guide the practice of attachment-focused psychotherapy.

Attachment theory has become the predominant theory in the field of infant mental health and in our understanding of the impact of chronic early maltreatment on a child's development, mental health, and capacity to form emotionally meaningful relationships. Most trauma therapies either explicitly or implicitly rely on attachment theory as part of the basis for conceptualizing treatment. The purpose of this chapter is to provide a primer on attachment theory. Attachment theory is the primary theoretical framework for attachment-focused treatment and provides the framework of assessment treatment methods and approaches.

Bowlby and the Origins of the Theory

John Bowlby's (1944, 1969, 1973, 1979, 1982) development of the theory of attachment grew out of his observations that children separated from their primary caregivers were more vulnerable to develop psychopathology. He concluded that attachment, or the significant, discriminated tie to a primary caregiver, grew out of a biologically based need to maintain proximity to the caregiver so that the young child would survive. Bowlby then asserted that this "attachment behavioral system" is an inherent motivation in the child and is not dependent upon merely being fed or feeling pleasure with the primary caregiver. Indeed, children were observed to form attachments even to abusive caregivers. This attachment behavioral system was understood as including an organization of a variety of attachment behaviors developed to respond to both internal and external cues and directed toward ensuring proximity to a preferred caregiver. Internal cues relate to the child's perceived sense of distress, while external cues relate to the child's perceived sense of threat.

Sroufe and Waters (1977) helped clarify how attachment proceeds through development. The child may maintain a relatively stable internal organization of attachment over time, while specific behaviors may change as the context changes and the child develops. For example, the infant may only be able to cry in response to a caregiver's departure; an older toddler might actively pursue the caregiver; and an older child might be able to hold an internalized representation of the caregiver, so as to be able to self-soothe in the caregiver's absence; while a teenager or young adult might use the telephone or electronic media to maintain contact over extended absences.

It is important to clarify that the child's seeking proximity is not just about physical closeness to a specific caregiver. Rather, it is the emotional state the child experiences when optimally close to the caregiver in specific contexts and circumstances. This is important since the child's optimal degree of closeness to the caregiver will fluctuate over time and across different experiences, depending on the child's level of development and degree of perceived vulnerability and distress.

While Bowlby's theory was rooted more in biological and physiological processes, he also recognized that emotions are strongly associated with attachment. The positive emotions that are inherent in the formation of an attachment include love and joy. Anxiety is associated with threats to attachment. Sorrow and despair are associated with loss of attachment. These feelings can give way to anger and detachment.

Attachment Styles

Attachment theory, developed by Bowlby, focused on the attachment existing not in the child, but rather in the caregiver-child relationship. Mary Ainsworth and her colleagues (Ainsworth, Blehar, Waters, & Wall, 1978) identified four patterns of attachment: secure, two insecure patterns (ambivalent and avoidant), and the disorganized pattern.

Note that the four patterns of attachment represent different degrees of perceived security in the child with regard to the relationship with the caregiver. They are organized patterns of expectations (about the self and the caregiver) the child has learned and developed through experience with a specific caregiver. These expectations serve as "road maps" for how to negotiate the relationship with the caregiver so as to maximize care from the caregiver. These are not diagnoses and were never intended to be used as indicators of pathology. Instead, they merely represent differences in the human experience of development.

Secure

The secure pattern of attachment is evidenced by a child's ability to effectively use the caregiver as a secure base, that is, seeking comfort when needed, being able to be comforted when distressed, and then being emotionally refueled and able to resume age-appropriate exploration. The relationship then becomes marked by comfort with physical and emotional closeness, coupled with an easy exchange of emotional expression between the partners. This pattern of attachment develops when the care by the caregiver is empathic and provides a "good enough" level of support relative to the child's needs, especially within the emotional and social areas of development. In an adult, this pattern is called the secure or resolved pattern of attachment.

Insecure-Avoidant

The insecure-avoidant pattern of attachment is evidenced by the child's apparent independence; an example is more exploration than comfort seeking or reliance on the caregiver. The child with this pattern of attachment does not easily seek comfort from or share emotions with the caregiver. This child's inability to expect and rely on the caregiver to meet the child's needs derives from a lack of sensitivity in the caregiver and/or discomfort with emotional and/or physical closeness with the child. This child then learns to minimize expression of need and emotions, while learning to function more autonomously. This child may learn to focus on activities or objects in an effort to occupy and distract the self from discomfort in the interpersonal relationship. This pattern often develops with a caregiver who is unavailable and whose responses to the child's demands are rejecting. In this manner the child learns that the best way to secure comfort and safety is to not place many demands on the caregiver. In an adult, this pattern is called the dismissing pattern of attachment.

Insecure-Ambivalent

The insecure-ambivalent pattern of attachment is evidenced by a combination of clinging behavior coupled with a difficulty in being soothed and a limited relative willingness to explore independently. The child appears to fail to find comfort in the caregiver and then appears stuck in a bid for affection and attention, coupled with frustration that the needs of the self are not adequately addressed. This child's reactions are the result of the caregiver's inconsistent and unreliable responses and availability to the child. This pattern often develops when the caregiver is preoccupied and the child learns that the best way to secure comfort and attention is to be loud and demanding of attention. In an adult, this pattern is called the preoccupied pattern of attachment.

Disorganized

The disorganized pattern of attachment is marked by confusion, fear, and often contradictory behaviors of approach and avoidance toward the caregiver (Main & Solomon, 1990). The behavioral stilling or freezing that is often observed appears to be a direct response to the child's fear of the caregiver and uncertainty about how to organize intentions and behavior toward a consistent way of interacting with the caregiver so as to maximize the chance of having one's needs met. This pattern is most often learned in relationships with caregivers who themselves act in frightening and inconsistent ways, typically due to serious child maltreatment, untreated mental illness or substance abuse, or the caregiver's own unresolved history of trauma. In an adult this pattern is called the disorganized pattern.

Frequency Distribution of Attachment Styles

When Ainsworth and colleagues (1978) began identifying attachment patterns in nonclinical samples, the following pattern of frequency distributions emerged:

60–65% exhibit secure attachment
20–25% exhibit avoidant attachment
10–15% exhibit ambivalent attachment
5–10% exhibit disorganized attachment

When Mary Main and Judith Solomon (1986) began replicating this research in clinical populations, including settings providing child welfare, mental health, or social services, the pattern of disorganized attachment (Solomon & George, 1999) was identified. In clinical samples it was more common for anywhere from 50% to 90% to exhibit this style (Carlson, Cicchetti, Barnett, & Braunwald, 1989; Cicchetti, Rogosch, & Toth, 2006).

Impact of Attachment Disruptions

In the 1940s and 1950s, Bowlby observed children who were exposed to prolonged separations from their parents. Observations of children who were placed in institutional care, separated from their parents during World War II or during hospitalizations, raised concerns about the impact of disruptions on children's attachments. The findings of Bowlby and Robertson (1953) echoed the earlier findings of Rene Spitz (1945). Children who experienced these disruptions were observed to go through predictable responses of protest, despair, and detachment.

When these observations occurred even in the presence of attention and offers of help from new caregivers, they challenged the notion that physical proximity alone was the goal of the child's behavior. Bowlby began to refine his theory to focus on the child's sense of security, based on appraisal of the primary caregiver's accessibility and responsiveness. This capacity for appraisal develops from the child's experience of the caregiver's accessibility and responsiveness. The child's sense of security then becomes the critical resource for the child as he or she encounters other experiences of distress. Bowlby's collaboration with James Robertson (1952), in the careful film documentation of children's responses to maternal deprivation, helped clarify the predictable pattern of phases that emerges when children are separated from their caregivers.

The first phase is *protest*, in which the child actively signals separation distress by crying, angry displays of distress, and careful attention to any sign of the caregiver's return. The dominant emotions are fear, distress, and anger. Efforts of other caregivers to soothe the child have limited success. The second phase, *despair*, appears to be marked by an increased sense of hopelessness that the caregiver will return. The overt expressions of distress and anger begin to diminish as the child moves into a period of grief and mourning. The diminished expression of distress and anger may be misinterpreted as the child's recovery from the loss. The third phase, *detachment*, is marked by a sense of giving up hope of the caregiver's return. Children in this phase may become more accepting of care from others, while some remain emotionally detached and joyless.

These three phases of attachment disruption are affected by the child's sense of *felt security*. This sense of security is grounded in three related cognitive processes: (1) belief that lines of communication with the caregiver are open, (2) the belief that physical accessibility exists, and (3) the belief that the attachment figure will respond when called upon for help (Ainsworth, 1990, p. 474). The child experiences distress in response to perceived threats of abandonment or loss by the caregiver. The degree of this distress is related to the perception of threat across the cognitive processes described above. Therefore, attachment-focused interventions "should focus on linking symptomatic expressions of fear and anger, to disturbances in attachment relationships . . . [to] help a child or adult experience and integrate painful experiences in order to gain control over symptoms" (Kobaks, 1999, p. 41).

Effects of the Caregiver's Attachment Style

Historically, the intergenerational transmission of patterns of attachment was understood more in terms of maladaptive parenting, especially maltreatment (Belsky, 1984). A significant change in this understanding emerged from the work of Mary Main in her development of the Adult Attachment Interview (AAI) (Hesse, 1999). To summarize, this landmark research found that when mothers are able to construct a coherent narrative about their own childhood attachment experiences, they are significantly more likely to have infants who are confident of, and able to seek comfort from, their mothers when needed. Thus, the mother's security of attachment predicted the child's security. Coherence in the narrative is marked by emotional openness and richness, as well as by resolution and acceptance. Therefore, it is not the mother's actual attachment experiences that are predictive, but rather her organization of these experiences as reflected in her internal working model (i.e., core beliefs about self, others, and the world), that predict her infant's attachment.

Similarly, mothers whose narratives depicted issues of insecurity were more likely to have infants whose behavior evidenced insecure patterns of attachment. For example, if a caregiver tended to avoid attachment topics in the narrative (dismissing style), her infant was more likely to demonstrate avoidant behavior with her (avoidant style). If a caregiver expressed unresolved anger and ambivalence in the narrative (preoccupied style), her infant was more likely to demonstrate highly aroused attachment behavior coupled with overt anger (ambivalent style). If a caregiver's narrative was marked by significant lapses, indicating intruding unresolved memories of fear (dismissing or unresolved style), her infant was more likely to demonstrate disorganized responses of fear, confusion, and prolonged freezing (disorganized style).

Subsequently, Dozier, Stovall, Albus, and Bates (2001) studied attachment patterns of infants who were removed from their birth homes due to neglect and abuse and placed with foster parents. They found that a shift from insecure to secure attachment occurred in these infants when they received consistent care from foster mothers with histories of secure attachments. On the one hand, two thirds of the infants placed with foster mothers who had an insecure pattern of attachment developed a disorganized pattern of attachment. On the other hand, two thirds of infants placed with foster mothers who had a secure pattern of attachment developed a secure pattern of attachment. This was after 8 months in placement, showing the power of the caregiver's own state of mind with respect to attachment on the developing child's pattern of attachment. This has major implications for child welfare policy and practice. This important research underscored that it is not just what the child brings to the relationship, but also how the caregiver's style influences the quality of the interactions. We recognize and support the centrality of the caregiver-child relationship as the core of attachment-focused therapy. Therefore, the caregiver's attachment style becomes an important part of what the caregiver brings to, and is able to provide in, the relationship with the child. For an excellent resource on this and other pertinent caregiver issues, please see the handbook *Hope for Healing: A parent's guide to trauma and attachment* (ATTACh, 2011), as well as Becker-Weidman (2010a, 2012) and Becker-Weidman & Shell (2010).

Attachment Patterns Versus Disorders

Attachment patterns (or states of mind with respect to attachment) are organized sets of expectations, beliefs, and behaviors that help a child effectively navigate the relationship with the caregiver. The child learns to adapt and accommodate to the caregiver's availability, emotional accessibility, and ability to provide support to the child. Attachment patterns exist within specific relationships; the child may develop different attachment patterns with different significant caregivers. However, usually by about age 5 years, the child will develop one pattern of attachment that is used in all relationships. As relationships change or new ones develop, the child will rely on the rules learned in previous significant relationships. Since these rules were created in experiences with the caregiver, new and different experiences can modify and change the rules, although this requires much repetition and also resolution of the initial traumas within which these earlier rules developed.

When the child continues to act based on an old set of such rules, regardless of how circumstances in the present have changed, this suggests that the problem may be more of an attachment disorder. Within the normal continuum of human experience are significant differences in degrees of security in attachment experiences. Insecure yet organized styles of attachment are common and can be functional for the parties in a relationship. Therefore, insecurity should not be equated with disordered attachment. Instead, disorders should be understood as chronic, pervasive, and rigid patterns of behavior that represent significant dysfunction across important domains of the child's life (e.g., interpersonal functioning, self-regulation, identity).

Overview of the Developmental Risks of Insecure Attachment

Longitudinal studies investigating effects of secure versus insecure attachment have found that a child's secure attachment to a caregiver increased that child's:

- Personal self-efficacy (Simmons, Paternate, & Shore, 2001)
- Resilience against stress (Ainsworth et al., 1978; Ford & Collins, 2010; Hanson & Chen, 2010; Mallers, Charles, Neupert, & Almeida, 2010; Masten & Coatworth, 1998; Pasco-Fearon & Belsky, 2004; Perrier, Boucher, Etchegary, Sadava, & Molnar, 2010)
- Advanced moral reasoning ability (Gillath, Sesko, Shaver, & Chun, 2010; Kochanska, 2002; Kochanska & Murray, 2000)
- Healthy cognitive development (van Bakel & Rikson-Walraven, 2002)
- Empathy and sensitivity (Lindsey, Caldera, & Tankersley, 2009; Mikulineer & Shaver, 2005; Zhou et al., 2002)
- Healthy emotion regulation (Barry & Kochanska, 2010; Braungart-Rieker, Hill-Soderlund, & Karrass, 2010; Maughan & Cicchetti, 2002; NICHD Early Child Care Research Network, 2004; Pauli-Pott, Mertesacker, & Beckmann, 2004)
- Positive affectivity (Borelli et al., 2010; Milan, Snow, & Belay, 2009; Paulussen-Hoogeboom, Stams, Hermanns, & Peetsma, 2007; Schuengel, Bakermans-Kranenburg, & van Ijzendoorn, 1999)

Insecure attachment may contribute to a child's risk of developing psychopathology. Insecure attachment alone is unlikely to cause psychopathology (Sroufe, 1990), except in cases where continued serious maltreatment accompanies the insecurity and the pattern that develops is the disorganized pattern. However, several important caveats must be considered. Development is a complex process in which it is likely that multiple factors contribute to the development of any specific disorder (Bernier & Meins, 2008). "The effect of a risk factor will depend on its timing and relation to other risk factors" (Greenberg, 1999, p. 472), and the risk factor can cause multiple outcomes.

The strongest associations between attachment and later psychopathology are seen in several areas. Children with ambivalent attachment patterns appear more vulnerable to developing anxiety disorders (Warren et al., 1997; Riggs, Cusimano, & Benson, 2011). Children with disorganized attachment patterns appear more vulnerable to developing dissociation (Carlson, 1998; Liotti, 1992). Additionally, disorganized attachment is often associated with a range of behavioral disturbances evidenced as controlling behavior with caregivers, aggressive and fearful peer relationships, internalizing and externalizing problems, and elevated psychopathology during adolescence (Liotti, 2011; Lyons-Ruth & Jacobvitz, 1999). It is the pattern most likely to develop into the psychiatric diagnosis of reactive attachment disorder.

Core Theoretical Principles of Attachment-Focused Therapy

In this section, we describe a few of the central principles of attachment-focused therapy. The reliance on intersubjective sharing of experience and attunement, are elements that distinguish this approach from other approaches to treatment. Other core principles are the importance of interactive repair and the co-creation of a coherent narrative. In summary, this treatment approach focuses on "the relationship" as the essential element in assessment and treatment (Becker-Weidman, 2010; Becker-Weidman, 2012).

Synchrony and Attunement

The concept of attunement came out of infant research by Stern (1977), Tronick (1989), and Beebe and Lachmann (1988). It was based on the synchrony, or "dance," within secure caregiver–infant dyads in which there is a complementary and jointly experienced emotional sharing. By tuning into every subtle shift in the infant's states, the caregiver feels with the infant instead of simply mirroring the infant's expression. As Siegel (1999) said, this helps the infant "feel felt" by the caregiver. This powerful sense of being known by and sharing one's reality with someone else forms the foundation of connection and trust. It helps the caregiver recognize and accentuate positive states of interest, pleasure, and joy, while simultaneously being able to minimize the infant's negative states of distress.

As clinicians and caregivers begin to attune to wounded children with serious attachment-related disturbances, they can better know the depths of the child's hurt, fear, and desperation. This understanding provides a way to appreciate how profoundly these hurts continue to shape children's perceptions, beliefs, and, ultimately, behavior. Their past hurtful experiences often have left them feeling rejected, alone, and even invisible. Consequently, the power of attunement is to offer compelling new experiences of emotional connection, recognition of their pain, and support for healing.

These new and "corrective" experiences thereby serve to powerfully contradict the earlier negative experiences, providing a catalyst to help children begin to rethink the conclusions they have drawn based on the past. Moreover, as the caregiver or clinician provides corrective experiences of attunement and feels with the child, the adult may be changed by that experience. This experience of attunement can help promote and evoke real empathy in the adult for these children, thereby providing the helper with a more complete sense of the child's experience to guide the interventions.

Similarly, clinicians attempt to raise awareness of the defensive and avoidant strategies these children use to cope with the hurts and traumas of their lives, so that new ways of coping and relating can be developed. This is easy to say and often very challenging to do. The challenge comes in finding the right pace and approach that balances exploration of these difficult issues with adequate support to help the child stay regulated and connected in the process. This starts with adequate experiences of attunement, so that the child can really "feel felt by," and so learn to recognize, the clinician and caregiver as resources of safety, trust, and help. The clinician and caregiver begin to put words to the child's past hurts and current struggles. The current struggles are framed in a way that honors the child's intention and ability to find a way to cope and survive hurtful and horrible past experiences and that avoids blaming or shaming the child.

To reach this point is a huge achievement, to be sure. However, it is ultimately just one side of attunement. It is, as Masterson (2005) wrote, attunement to the "false self." This false self is the defensive, learned maladaptive way of coping with maltreatment and profound loss. Its road map is the negative internal working model full of distorted beliefs about oneself, others, and the world (e.g., others are hurtful or untrustworthy; self is unlovable or bad; and the world is dangerous or chaotic). As clinicians and caregivers, if we miss this profound reality for the child, we miss that critically important opportunity to help the child feel felt by us.

It can be tempting to tell the child that the child really isn't as bad as the child might feel inside, to offer support and comfort. However, this creates a sense of not being known (or accepted) as the child really feels. Instead of feeling more connected or known, the opposite can happen. Therefore, the journey of healing must begin with attunement to this false self. This means that we first recognize that the child did not choose the negative beliefs, but rather that life has provided powerful experiences to create these beliefs. This is the child's reality; no one gives up their sense of reality easily. Once the child feels felt and understood, then the work of exploration and the creation of healing experiences can begin.

Recognition of, and attunement with, the false self also poses an important caveat. If we are overly attuned to the child's false self, we risk unintentionally reinforcing the beliefs of inadequacy and defectiveness. This can work against the child learning to trust in us or our ability to help, or, worse, can be seen as excusing the child's negative acting out. Thus, while attuning to the false self, we must never lose sight of the child's capacity for growth and health.

The journey to healing cannot be complete unless and until we find a way to begin to attune to, and help, the child imagine and experience a "real self." The real self allows intimacy, connection, spontaneity, and healthy coping. The real self is the source of hopes, dreams, and talents. To those of us with secure attachment experiences, it seems confusing that someone would not rush to embrace this self. But the child with serious attachment disturbances, born of hurt and heartache, is faced instead with a profound challenge. It is as if we are asking the child to step off the edge of the known world and trust that there will be something to catch the child, when the child has learned through powerful experiences not to trust self or others.

Efforts to attune to this real self will initially be experienced as profound challenges to the child's reality. Human beings in general do not respond well to this kind of threat. We defend our reality with all we have. And so it is with these wounded children. The more we connect to what we know as the real self, the more the child will feel compelled to prove to us, usually by unacceptable behaviors, that the child's true identity really is the false self, because it is familiar, and the unfamiliar is potentially frightening or dangerous.

Consequently, this attempt to recognize the fledgling real self will likely be perceived as a profound misattunement and rupture in the relationship with the child. Sensitive efforts to repair the rupture are critical at this point. If attunement is the salve of repair, to whom do we become attuned, the false or real self? This gets right to the heart of the challenges of our work. We begin with attuning to the false self so that we might bear witness to the hurts and honor the efforts to survive. We then sensitively and carefully begin to create a space for the real self to emerge. We do this by seeing the potential, believing in the possibility, and acknowledging the price paid by the false self in its efforts to cope and survive. We help the child begin to see through experience that other choices are possible. We begin to help the child (and caregiver) see the things that stand in the way of the real self showing itself and consciously attend to nurturing this fledgling new real self. We help the child and caregiver begin to clearly distinguish the false self from the real self. We help the real self find its voice, acknowledge its feelings, and own its right to be. We do this by creating experiences with the child and caregiver that are positive and therapeutic.

Interactive Repair

Achieving meaningful attunement and helping a child feel felt might all seem like lofty idealism in the face of the challenging behaviors that accompany children with attachment-disordered behaviors. That is why the notion of *misattunement* is equally important. Misattunement occurs when there are breaks in attunement.

For example, think of a toddler whose first steps elicit glee in the child and sheer delight in the caregiver. This powerful positive attunement will come to an abrupt end the minute the child teeters toward the stairs. The caregiver now may scream "no" and rush to scoop up the child for safety. The shared joy is suddenly interrupted as the caregiver's fear for the child's safety overrides the pride in the child's accomplishment. The child's glee is overridden by the negative feelings of being scolded, and the child experiences shame. This is a benign, and indeed necessary, example of misattunement. Clearly, maltreatment is a profound form of misattunement.

During the process of a child's development, it is not possible for any caregiver to be perfectly attuned to the child. Indeed, throughout our lives it is not possible to be perfectly attuned to another human being. Fortunately, development is also supported through helpful breaches in attunement, so long as these episodes are handled well. This is the notion of *interactive repair* that Tronick (1989) and Beebe and Lachmann (1994) have written about. Simply put, repair occurs when the caregiver recognizes the disconnection with the child due to misattunement and the child's negative feelings created by the disconnection. The caregiver then provides active assistance to help the child reconnect and reestablish the prior positive shared emotional state.

In the previous example of the toddler getting too close to the stairs, the sensitive caregiver would recognize the child's distress at having been scolded, offer comfort, and help redirect the child toward other positive behaviors. The child that was crying one moment ago is now quickly reengaged in a playful exchange with the caregiver. When these situations are handled in a consistent and empathic manner, the child learns several important lessons:

- Negative feelings can be tolerated because they do not last long.
- "It is what I do that is not accepted, but I am still loved and valued."
  Such experiences help the child move from shame ("I am bad") to guilt ("What I did is bad").
- Reconnection and repair in relationships is possible.
- Caregivers are valuable sources of help and assistance.

Children with attachment disturbances, sadly, have not had enough of this vital experience, and therefore have not had the benefit of learning these important lessons. Indeed, they too often have learned the very opposite.

Treatment becomes a critical new opportunity to teach the very basic experience of interactive repair as caregivers and clinicians navigate a minefield of often unknown trauma triggers with the child. In the course of normal parenting, breaks in attunement will occur with a child. For example, through the caregiver's appropriate limit setting (i.e., stopping the child from playing when the child is becoming reckless), the child may experience a profound rupture in attunement (e.g., thinking, "You just don't want me to have fun"). The child's reactions may seem excessive to the situation, such as extreme anger or aggression toward the caregiver, aggression toward self, or withdrawal.

However, the child's behaviors can make sense if the child has not experienced that relationships are, indeed, repairable. For example, a child may assume that such breaks are proof that the child is unlovable, unworthy, or defective, and the caregiver is hurtful, coercive, or mean. In these situations, the child needs the help of caregivers to reconnect, to improve emotional regulation, and to be able to reframe what happened so that the distorted beliefs can be changed.

Examples of Thought Reframing

Distorted belief: "My mom is trying to keep me from having any fun."
Reframe: "My mom is trying to help me keep from getting hurt when I am playing roughly."
Distorted belief: "I can't do anything right."
Reframe: "I just made a mistake. No big deal—I can still have fun."

When these experiences of misattunement are handled well, they provide critical experiences that support the development of affect regulation. When these inevitable events of misattunement cause distress states in the infant, the caregiver's moving in to repair the connection and comfort the child reduces the levels of cortisol and related stress hormones. As a result, the frontal cortex develops a greater concentration of glucocorticoid receptors that can help modulate stress responses (Schore, 1996). When there is little or no interactive repair, such as when the caregiver is abusive, neglectful, or continually misattuned, children may remain in chronically negative affective states (Skowron, Kozlowski, & Pincus, 2010). Such states can cause corticosteroid levels to be chronically elevated. This may then result in a reduction in the number of synapses or the death of neurons in the developing brain, according to Schore's hypothesis.

Internal Working Models

Bowlby hypothesized that the manner in which an infant was reared by the primary caregivers was a powerful influence on the infant's internal working model. An internal working model consists of mental representations a child develops, related to the way the child's primary caregivers have responded to the child's needs.

Internal working models are based on young children's expectations about the behavior of their attachment figures that develop into wider representations of themselves, interpretations of their experiences, and conclusions about how to interact with others. These models become interpretive filters through which children (and adults) construct their understanding of new experiences and relationships in ways that are consistent with past experiences and expectations, sometimes enlisting unconscious defensive processes in doing so. In this manner, internal working models constitute the bridge between young children's experience of sensitive and insensitive care, and the development of beliefs and expectations that affect subsequent experience in close relationships (Bretherton & Munholland, 1999; Johnson et al., 2010; McCarthy & Maughan, 2010; Newland, Coyl, & Freeman, 2008).

Bowlby first used the term *internal working models* to describe a set of representations or models an individual makes about experiences that help the person make predictions about future perceptions, beliefs, and actions. "They serve to regulate, interpret, and predict both the attachment figure's and the self's attachment-related behavior, thoughts, and feelings" (Bretherton & Munholland, 1999, p. 89). The internal working models develop from experiences a young child has with attachment figures. The internal working models therefore are complementary. For example, the young child who experiences the caregiver as consistently and reliably available, empathically responsive, helpful, and supportive of exploration and mastery will experience the self as lovable, worthy, and competent. Conversely, the young child who experiences the caregiver as unreliable, insensitive, or, worse, abusive and unsupportive of exploration and mastery, will experience the self (in varying degrees) as unlovable, unworthy, and incompetent. Internal working models can be thought of as the lenses through which the person perceives the world. Those lenses can be distorting of experience in the present if the experiences that created those lenses were damaging, maltreating, or distorting in some manner.

When a child is reared in a family environment where the child's needs for comfort, food, nurturing touch, and stimulation are met, the infant or child develops an internal working model which includes expectations that when the child cries due to discomfort or loneliness, an adult caregiver comes to the rescue at least most of the time, if not all the time. The infant begins to see self as worthy of this care and the primary caregivers as trustworthy in their responsiveness to the infant's needs. And since distress never becomes too painful, the child learns to tolerate distress, and develops greater impulse control, affect regulation, and behavioral regulation. If the infant, however, experiences a family environment where adult responses to cries for food, touch, stimulation, and comfort do not occur on a consistent basis, the child develops an internal working model that includes the belief that adult caregivers are not concerned about the child's needs and will not respond in a reliable or helpful manner. Bowlby (1969, 1980) believed that this internal working model acts like a blueprint for all future relationships in the child's life.

A person's internal working model assists in coordinating physiological, emotional, and behavioral strategies that assist the person in the fulfillment of attachment needs. Barnett and Vondra explained their understanding of internal working models, as proposed by Bowlby, as "unconscious mental representations of the availability of the attachment figure and of the efficacy and worthiness of the self in getting and having attachment needs met" (1999, p. 7). Based upon the treatment of the child by the caregiver, the internal working model could produce pro-social behavior that is moral and ethical, or antisocial behavior that is negative and potentially criminal (Crittenden, 1985; Dykas & Cassidy, 2011).

Thompson's (2000) analysis of earlier studies concluded that although a person's internal working model is an important precursor to the health or impairment of future relationships, internal working models can be altered and transformed both positively and negatively by later experiences. Resolution of a person's past trauma is associated with healthier parent-child relationship factors (Koren-Karie, Oppenheim, & Getzler-Yosef, 2008).

The beliefs on which the internal working models are constructed derive from experience with attachment figures. These experiences occur largely during early preverbal stages of development. Therefore these beliefs are developed experientially in the implicit memory systems. As such, they become largely unconscious and may be difficult to change (Kobacks & Sceery, 1988). Individuals cannot be talked out of these beliefs, but rather need to "experience their way out" of these beliefs to new beliefs.

Occasional lapses in the caregiver's provision of security are unlikely to have much impact on developing beliefs. However, as the pattern of interactions between the child and caregiver becomes more routine and predictable, both partners' reactions become more automatic. As this pattern of interaction becomes more habitual, the perceptions and beliefs central to it become less conscious and accessible (Bretherton & Munholland, 1999).

Understanding and working with a child's internal working models is considered a key foundation of attachment-focused therapy. Most children who present with serious attachment disorder behavior problems do not respond to traditional behavior modification approaches. Indeed, these approaches can have the unintended consequence of escalating the behavior instead of extinguishing it.

For example, traditional behavioral approaches might include responses such as ignoring bad behavior, removing the child to a "time out," and withholding special treats until a child has earned them. These interventions might work with a child who has a relatively secure internal working model. This child has had adequate experiences to trust that the caregiver acts out of a sense of beneficence (even if the actions are not liked by the child). This child may be better prepared to tolerate the negative feelings that arise, may be motivated to reestablish connection with and approval of the caregiver, and may consciously choose an appropriate corrective action.

However, the child who has not had adequate experiences of trust with the caregiver may likely respond in very different ways. This child may perceive the ignoring as a sign of the caregiver's indifference and lack of help, and perceive the time out as proof of the caregiver's lack of care and intention to abandon, shame, or reject the child. The child may also perceive the withholding of special treats as proof that the caregiver will be withholding and mean in the same way as previous abusive and neglectful caregivers were. The caregivers and other helpers who do not appreciate the critical role that perceptions and beliefs play in initiating and sustaining behavioral responses will likely experience that the child's problem behaviors escalate instead of extinguish. The caregivers or other helpers can then find themselves in an escalating control battle with the child.

Intersubjectivity

Intersubjectivity is the process of mutual interaction and engagement that promotes the child "feeling felt by" the primary caregiver (Siegel, 1999). It involves shared emotions (attunement), shared attention, and shared and complementary intentions. Through contingent communication, the primary caregiver begins to feel what life has been like for the child, and can help the child to put words to this experience. This process creates scaffolding for shared understanding in the moment. As the caregiver is better able to provide empathic supports to the child, the child can better access, rely upon, and learn to trust in the caregiver as a secure base and safe harbor. This process of intersubjectivity, or sharing of feelings, attention, and intention, promotes an increased capacity for attunement on the part of the caregiver, who can then employ it in subsequent encounters (Ginot, 2011).

Theory of Mind

Theory of mind (ToM), in general, refers to an individual's ability to interpret accurately what another person may be thinking or feeling. In caregiver-child relationships, ToM within the caregiver refers to the caregiver's ability to read the child's cues as accurately as possible, and to respond in a sensitive way to those cues. Fonagy and Target (1997) reported that ToM is a key determinant of self-organization in an individual's development, and has its roots in the child's earliest social relationships. A caregiver who is able to effectively communicate to the child the caregiver's understanding of the child's intentional stance will, in turn, stimulate the child's development of these skills. ToM also enables the development of the additional capacity of the *reflective function*, which refers to the ability to observe and then interpret one's own and others' behaviors in terms of mental states. Attachment with caregivers is at the root of this skill, which has an intricate role in the development of a child's healthy or untrusting internal working model.

For Fonagy and Target (1997), the development of reflective capacity, or the reflective function, results from the caregiver's understanding of the infant's internal state and the caregiver signaling that the child's behavior is intentional and understandable: "I get what you are feeling and I share your experience" (Bleiberg, 2001, p. 38). The infant can now internalize the attuned caregiver's reflective response and begin to know: "So that is what I am feeling!" (p. 38). This alerts children to their primary affective arousal and allows them to label their psychological experiences.

For this process to work, the caregiver is required to maintain moment-to-moment reflective functioning, through the use of attunement, while simultaneously attending and responding to the infant's day-to-day dysregulation or hyperarousal. This simultaneous attention and care to both the infant's internal and external needs helps convey that the caregiver can understand and handle the infant's internal state and behavior, while working to help meet the child's needs and restore the child to homeostasis. When the infant receives and participates in this ongoing process of positive affect regulation following a signal of distress, the child learns to be confident that the child can bring about a satisfying response from the caregiver. This person-specific, secure dyadic attachment subsequently leads to:

- More generalized patterns of relatedness and organization of behaviors, feelings, and coping strategies (Bouchard et al., 2008)
- The development of defensive adaptations, symbolic capacities (Walker & Murachver, 2011), and a sense of "I am me, the same that I was yesterday and am likely to be tomorrow" (Bleiberg, 2001, p. 61)
- The maturation of a triangular reflective perspective that supports the ability to simultaneously understand the individual perspectives of the self and other, as well as the shared perspectives of the dyad itself (Converse, Lin, Keysar, & Epley, 2008)
- The unfolding of an ideal self-representation; and, in adolescence, the development of a more autonomous identity
- Satisfactory self-esteem regulation

From a psychosocial perspective, *mentalization*, or reflective function, is the human capacity to make use of one's apprehension of other people's feelings, inclinations, intentions, moods, and wishes, or one's own. Acquired developmentally, it functions unconsciously, leads to the structuring of the psychological self, and enables the individual to test reality (i.e., to distinguish internal from external reality). Fonagy and Target (1997) argued that youngsters with "complex psychopathology" (severe disturbances in personality and behavior) lack this essential developmental achievement, either intermittently or pervasively.

Children with attachment-disordered behaviors have not developed the capacity for reflective function, described by Bleiberg as the "biologically prepared . . . capacity of humans, including very young humans, to interpret the behavior of all agents, themselves as well as others, in terms of internal mental states" (2001, p. 34). They lack the capacity to apprehend mental states, to attribute beliefs, feelings, or intentions to others, or to understand and respond to other people's behavior. They cannot tune into or "read" other people's minds, much less their own. They are "unable to preserve a psychologically grounded sense of self and others in the context of close human connections" (Bleiberg, 2001, p. 20). Hence, their treatment has to focus methodically on the imaginative unfolding and development of this subtle and vital capacity rather than on their disordered and dramatic behavior.

When feeling cut off from their capacity to create an integrated representation of the caregiver and from their own coherent sense of self-agency (lacking the ability to fight or flee), children will "escape" by inward flight or freeze (dissociation), and will detach threatening sensations from their other experiences. This fragments their perceptions into nonintegrated components and develops ultimately primitive psychological defense mechanisms, such as splitting and projective identification. Anger, irritability, or unstable moods give these children a fragmented sense of themselves and of others. Their ever-restless and changing behavior also generates or exacerbates chaos in their environment so that the caregivers are exhausted, and their severely challenged reflective function is further compromised.

To manage these mounting pressures to integrate contradictory perceptions of self and others, these children become increasingly demanding and rigid as they seek to coerce caregivers, siblings, peers, and teachers to mirror their ever-changing fragmented internal states, in an attempt to control their interpersonal relationships and regulate their affective experiences.

Coherent Narrative

Main and Goldwyn (1984) made a revolutionary contribution to the attachment field with the development of the AAI. The AAI is a semistructured interview that guides an individual through discussion of early attachment experiences and the effects of these experiences on current personality and functioning. One of the most important findings from this line of research was that a caregiver's "state of mind" regarding attachment is an excellent predictor of the security of attachment in the child. This is not merely a simple process by which the way a caregiver speaks and acts will influence the child to follow suit (Hesse, 1999). Rather, the evolution of research utilizing the AAI has helped elucidate how the language one uses to describe one's attachment experiences powerfully indicates the specific aspects of mental processes that represent potential capacities for emotional attunement, emotional regulation, and reflective capacity (Daniel, 2009).

There are several ways in which the language of clients is analyzed, but prime among them is how it reflects the "coherence" of their state of mind regarding their attachment history, and current beliefs and strategies for managing close relationships. Coherence is defined very precisely using H. Paul Grice's "maxims" (Neale, 1992), which define coherence in terms of quality of language or its truth, relevance, and quantity in relation to what is being asked, and the manner or clarity with which it is communicated. When these aspects of coherence are evaluated, they have been found to relate closely to the adult's, and the adult's child's, style of attachment (Steele & Steele, 2008).

Narrative coherence is therefore understood as the speaker's ability to access a range of attachment-related memories, and to discuss these memories through a developing flow of ideas and impressions. This discussion is coupled with a flexible ability to attend to the present, while also reflecting on the construction and narrative of past memories. The coherent narrative includes a richness that reflects an integration of both positive and negative events into a holistic story that makes sense of the experience.

The work of Main and others has demonstrated that as caregivers are supported in processing their memories to achieve greater coherence, they acquire greater attachment security, and their children's attachment styles, in response, shift toward greater security (Main, Kaplan, & Cassidy, 1985). This important work provides a useful blueprint for clinicians to support individuals and families in this process. In making use of this blueprint, trauma work, and attachment-focused therapy in particular, provide supports to help the caregiver increase attunement and reflective capacity. When this is achieved, the caregiver is better able to cocreate, with the child, a coherent narrative that makes sense of the child's experiences, the origins of negative internal working model beliefs, and the function of behaviors that have served as defensive strategies. This process represents the synthesis of all the guiding principles of attachment-focused therapy, and is the critical foundation for healing.

Safety

Complex trauma and the experience of relational trauma can result in the development of conditioned emotional responses in which the fear of the original maltreating caregiver is generalized to all subsequent caregivers, and even to any close interpersonal interactions (e.g., expressing emotions, physical closeness). The technical term for this process is *source attribution error*. The emotions and thoughts associated with the trauma, but not the explicit or episodic memory, are triggered. The person makes sense of these triggered feelings and thoughts by attributing the cause to the current situation and target. This can create a profound misperception that proximity to, and emotional connection with, another person (especially a new caregiver) is a source of fear rather than a source of safety and comfort, even in the presence of evidence to the contrary. The traumatized child continues to respond to new caregivers or significant others with the same defensive coping strategies used or attempted with the original maltreating caregiver, even when such strategies are unwarranted in the present. Without the sense of an available and accessible secure base, the child is left alone with the internal sense of a lack of safety from often overwhelming fears, anxieties, and distress that are fundamental to the traumatized child's chronic state of dysregulation.

Attachment-focused therapy actively works to promote and develop a greater sense of security with the current caregiver, so that the new caregiver can become a secure base for the child. As children feel safer in the external world, they can better access assistance in learning to regulate the emotions that compose much of their internal world. As this integrated sense of safety develops, the child is better able to process specific traumatic memories and reminders. Attachment-focused therapy seeks to restore the normal developmental process in which external supports and nurture provide experiences of self-regulation that become internalized and integrated in healthy development.

Limitations of the Theory

Attachment is only one of the core systems involved in human development (others include exploration and affiliation). Similarly, attachment disruptions cannot account for all distress, behavioral problems, or psychopathology. This is why the concept of complex trauma has important utility for clinical work: it focuses the clinician on a broad range of domains that may be affected by chronic early maltreatment within a caregiving relationship. Attachment theory and research can provide an important context for children who have experienced maltreatment by their caregivers, loss of relationships with caregivers, and multiple placements with different caregivers. These important life experiences are part of what shapes children with attachment-related traumas and may distinguish them from children with similar behavioral symptoms, yet whose attachment security has not been compromised.

CHAPTER THREE

Overview of Attachment-Focused Therapy

This chapter describes the core beliefs, values, and assumptions that inform the specific practice guidelines that are provided as part of the overarching framework for attachment-focused therapy. Attachment-focused therapies cover a range of different models and techniques. Various models may prioritize the principles of the treatment differently, and may incorporate a range of techniques and approaches in the service of these principles. The shared common feature of current models of attachment-focused therapy is the primary emphasis on increasing the child's capacity for regulation across emotional, behavioral, and interpersonal domains within a relational framework. The shared common approach to achieving this is to increase the child's sense of the caregiver being available and accessible as a secure base, and improving the caregiver's capacity to be that with the child.

Basic Assumptions

- Attachment is a fundamental building block of development. It is a foundational element that affects neurological, affective, cognitive, behavioral, and interpersonal functioning. If a child does not experience adequate security in the early caregiving relationship(s), then the child's capacity for basic trust can be severely diminished. Without adequate capacity for trust, the child may be unable to form the type of healthy reciprocal relationships necessary for successful functioning throughout life.

- Disrupted and frightening attachment experiences can place a child at risk of developing disorders of attachment, which can increase the risk of later developmental and psychological problems.
- In the work of healing attachment trauma in children, safety for all must be ensured. The child's sense of security must include safety from external threats of being retraumatized, as well as from internal threats of being overwhelmed by posttraumatic memories, emotions, and sensations.
- Sensitivity and compassion are required by both the caregiver and therapist and are essential to prevent retraumatizing the client in the service of healing.
- Relational trauma is at the heart of attachment trauma. It involves the profound failure of the early caregiving environment to provide adequate safety, security, and comfort to the child. The child's experience of losing or being deprived of a secure base or of being frightened by the same person who should provide safety may make the child more vulnerable to various other traumatic experiences. These negative experiences may cause vulnerability to developmental delays or deficits as the child is forced to navigate the various developmental challenges largely alone. In this way, relational trauma can lead to developmental delays (Becker-Weidman, 2009).
- Attachment-related or relational trauma means that the child has been wounded within the context of a caregiving relationship. This has deprived the child of the safety, security, comfort, and assistance that allow trust in a caregiver to develop. The conditioned emotional responses caused by maltreatment (Briere, 2002; Briere & Lanktree, 2011) may be seen in the behavioral responses of fight (emotional reactivity or aggression), flight (withdrawal or dissociation), freeze (emotional numbing or blunting), or appeasement (excessive compliance and hypervigilance regarding others, resulting in a loss of capacity to experience internal states). The conditioned emotional responses to the original caregiver, later generalized to others, can include the same behavioral responses and tension-reducing behaviors. The conditioning of these responses means that they are automatic and not consciously derived choices. They are examples of source attribution errors (Briere & Lanktree, 2011).

The conditioning process is not focused only on maltreatment experiences. This process conditions a broader set of experiences that includes the maltreatment along with many of the elements of context in which it occurred (e.g., images, smells, sounds, sensations). The traumatic memory may then be elicited years later through a whole host of reminders—even seemingly insignificant contextual details in benign and even positive experiences. Therefore, these conditioned responses can easily be transferred to others in the caregiving or helper role, and can lead to intense feelings of mistrust of others. In essence, it is the affect that is triggered, without the associated episodic memory components.

The child's conditioned responses can create profound challenges for new caregivers and helpers, whose benevolent intentions and compassion may be met by avoidance or rejection from the child. Avoidance and rejection occur because the child has experienced others as untrustworthy, hurtful, neglectful, or frightening. The child may appear resistant and controlling in an effort to try to be safe in an unsafe world. This process can then undermine the child's access to help by limiting and distorting interactions with current caregivers and can be a significant barrier to the formation of a therapeutic alliance. For this reason, a therapy focus on developing an alliance with the child and caregivers through the intersubjective sharing of experience is a vital first step in treatment (Becker-Weidman, 2010b).

- The primary focus of treatment is on current relationships: the caregiver-child relationship (for children), or client–significant other relationships (including the client-therapist relationship) for adults. In the treatment of children with disorders of attachment, it is important that the therapist support caregivers so that they can more easily function as a secure base. This provision of a secure base by the clinician allows caregivers to access support for managing their own emotional reactions to the child's emotions, behaviors, and perceptions. Caregivers are assisted in exploring the possible underlying meanings, perceptions, and emotions that are driving the child's behaviors. Often by the time caregivers seek specialized attachment-focused therapy for their children, they may be frustrated, hurt, discouraged, and exhausted. Before caregivers become a therapeutic secure base for the child, they will need encouragement, support, and understanding. In effect, whatever the therapist wishes the caregiver to do with the child, the therapist must be able to do or provide for the caregiver (Becker-Weidman, 2010b). It is through the intersubjective sharing of experience between the therapist and caregiver that the caregiver's capacity for attunement, sensitivity, reflectivity, and commitment can be enhanced. The therapist becomes the secure base for the caregiver in this challenging process of understanding and resolving difficult feelings, while also developing skills that may not come naturally.

Parenting children with disorders of attachment can challenge the caregiver's sense of competency. It can also profoundly challenge the beliefs and scripts that were shaped by one's own experiences during childhood. For example, caregivers may rely on traditional forms of discipline including spanking, believing that this experience was not harmful to them as children, or to other children they may have parented. When used with a child who has a disorder of attachment, however, the strategy may not work and will be counterproductive, causing greater reactivity, fear, or defiance. Consequently, caregivers of these wounded children must develop their capacity to provide empathy and attunement and engage in insightful, reflective, sensitive experiences with the child, which may be difficult to maintain in the face of a child whose distrust and fear continue to push the caregiver away. Parenting these wounded children can be challenging enough for the caregiver whose own state of mind with respect to attachment is secure, let alone for a caregiver whose attachment is insecure or disorganized. Therefore, there is a necessary parallel process in therapy, in which the therapist's provision of a secure base for the caregiver enables the caregiver to provide a more secure base for the child.

Infants and toddlers who have been moved to foster care are likely to develop a secure pattern of attachment only if their foster parents have a secure state of mind with respect to attachment (Dozier et al., 2001). It is likely to be even more difficult for older children with more complex histories of maltreatment and multiple caregivers.

- As the therapist creates a secure base for the caregiver, the caregiver will be more able to help the child increase capacities for trust. Caregivers must come to understand and appreciate that the process of healing relational trauma is fraught with resistance to the relationship itself, which is what the child has learned to do as a survival mechanism; it is an adaptive strategy. The deepening of the relationship that occurs as these adaptive strategies are amended may also be met with a conditioned response of increased fear as the child experiences new levels of vulnerability and need. The caregiver may understandably misinterpret these behaviors as indication that the child does not want a relationship after all, or that the therapy is ineffective, when instead these periods of regression are part of the normal ebb and flow in the healing process.
- Attachment-focused therapy is usually a family therapy approach to treatment. While the primary focus of treatment is on the relationship between the child and caregiver, it is important to recognize that children with attachment-disordered behaviors can have a powerful impact on the functioning of the entire family. Children with disorders of attachment may respond to the primary caregiver very differently than any other caregiver, creating the possibility of splitting. This can undermine the marital relationship and leave the primary caregiver feeling blamed by, and estranged from, the partner. Similarly, children with disorders of attachment can also have dysfunctional relationships with siblings. As the therapy progresses and the child experiences greater security with at least one of the caregivers, that security must then be integrated into healthier functioning within the larger family system.
- The broad range of problematic behaviors and dysregulated functioning associated with developmental trauma and disorders of attachment

argue for comprehensive assessments guided by special knowledge and expertise in both developmental psychopathology and child development. Assessments must be broadly focused to include psychosocial, interpersonal, psychological, cognitive, emotional, behavioral, clinical, developmental, and functional domains (for more on assessment, see Chapter 5).

- Evaluation and assessment should be multimodal so that collaboration of all providers is ensured, and information from various sources about the client is integrated.

- Attachment-focused therapy is driven by theory and principle; it is not a set of techniques. Whenever possible it should be grounded in empirical research. However, since there may not always be empirical research regarding a specific technique or methodology, solid grounding in theory and a well-formulated clinical conceptualization are essential.

- Secure attachment experiences foster healthy neurological development and regulation of a young child's brain. Conversely, the lack of such experiences can significantly increase the frequency of dysregulation, causing disruption of normal brain development (Schore, 2001). Neurodevelopmental research has suggested that traditional talk therapies may not adequately access implicit memories of trauma stored in the limbic system of the brain (Cozolino, 2010). Therefore, a comprehensive approach to therapy would likely include a variety of modalities to both access various pathways to these memories and provide opportunity for regulation and integration of neurophysiological functioning. For example, nonverbal strategies using music, expressive therapies, movement, yoga, or comforting physical presence to help calm the limbic region of the brain may be important before more cognitive strategies are employed (Perry & Szalavitz, 2006).

- One of the key goals of therapy is to address the underlying motivations, needs, perceptions, emotions, and beliefs expressed as symptoms and behaviors. This is accomplished through altering the child's view of self, others, and the world to include more positive, flexible, and constructive beliefs, while disconfirming fixed, negative, and distorted beliefs. By facilitating the development of a secure base, the clinician promotes an effective balance between the provision of security and comfort on the one hand and exploration of difficult feelings and memories on the other. The experience of a secure base provides a corrective emotional experience that supports healing and promotes resilience.

- The developmental effects of relational trauma can result in significant disparity between a child's chronological and functional age (Becker-Weidman, 2009). Provision of corrective experiences of a secure base, coupled with support for exploration that follows, increases the chance that the child will be able to learn skills that promote effective functioning. The younger the child, the easier it is to provide nurturing experiences that address earlier unmet needs. The efforts to meet these needs must always sensitively balance the child's actual chronological age with receptiveness to nurturing, so that these efforts are experienced as meaningful and not shaming to the child. This can be challenging to do effectively with young children, and becomes even more challenging with older children.

For example, a traumatized preschooler may easily be engaged in playful interactive games that forge emotional connections with the caregiver. Older children may yearn for that kind of connection and yet be unable to let themselves explore these feelings. For example, a 10-year-old whose developmental age and needs are younger may be difficult to engage in interactions that are responsive to the child's attachment and developmental needs. Indeed, a 10-year-old may appear to be so resistant to, and dismissive of, nurturing that it is difficult for the caregiver to meet these responses with empathy and attuned caregiving, yet this is exactly what the child desperately needs. That is why attachment-focused therapy remains an individualized approach guided by corrective experiences of intersubjectivity that continually seek to build trust, develop greater emotional regulation, and forge a secure base for the child. For this reason, a strictly manualized approach with a specific number of sessions in a defined sequence is not adequate for this group of children (Briere & Lanktree, 2011). Rather, a more flexible and individualized approach that takes into account caregivers' capacities to be sensitive, reflective, insightful, and attuned as well as their relationship histories and the history of the child and the child's developmental needs must be used. This approach may use a loosely defined "manual" of approaches, processes, and phases that can be tailored to the specific family situation.

- As noted above, many children who have experienced relational trauma exhibit uneven development. They are particularly likely to be developmentally younger than their chronological age in the areas of social and emotional functioning (Becker-Weidman, 2009). When caregivers, therapists, and other helpers fail to take this discrepancy into consideration, they may assume that the child's resistance or behavioral acting-out is purposeful defiance rather than a reflection of the child's developmental age. However, if the discrepancy between chronological and functional age is considered, it can become easier to recognize reactions as evidence of the child's developmental functioning.

For example, a typical 10-year-old child may be expected to make appropriate apologies for misbehavior. Yet a 10-year-old with a history of attachment-related traumas may lack the prerequisite skills of affect regulation and perspective taking necessary to support an age-appropriate apology. When this child is expected to deliver an age-appropriate apology and instead becomes dysregulated, angry, and defiant, this reaction may be the result of shame at not being able to meet the parent's expectations because the child is developmentally younger than the chronological age. Therefore, interventions should be targeted to meet the child at the child's developmental level, recognizing functional inabilities (delays or deficits) and strengths, and to have developmental age-appropriate expectations for the child.

- Treatment is grounded in the intersubjective sharing of experience coupled with interactive repair. Therapy is not something "done to" the child; rather, it is an interactive process in which the caregiver and child, with support from the therapist, explore their feelings, perceptions, and intentions as they are revealed in present experience—the intersubjective sharing of experience in which there is shared emotion (attunement), shared attention, and shared and complementary intentions. Through treatment there is a collaborative process of making new meanings from these experiences within the safety of the present relationships in the treatment setting and in the home. The core corrective emotional experience of this form of therapy is the provision of empathic, sensitively attuned, and supportive interventions to help the child and caregiver engage in accessing assistance at becoming better regulated and developing enhanced capacity for social-emotional skills.

- The process of finding new meanings for the child's behaviors and experiences includes continuous attention to reframing both the child's and the caregiver's experiences, perceptions, intentions, and behaviors. The therapist provides a valuable resource in modeling recognition of "kind attributions" (Marvin, Cooper, Hoffman, & Powell, 2002) , a way of reflecting the underlying intentions and needs instead of judging the explicit reactions or behaviors. This supports a more constructive way of understanding and reframing difficult behaviors and reactions by both caregiver and child. This is essential since pervasive shame and fear are at the root of many symptoms and behaviors. The therapist's modeling of this type of reframing sets a tone of acceptance and positive valuing of the efforts of both child and adult.

Safety Principles

Some forms of attachment therapy were historically associated with the use of highly confrontational and even coercive methods. It is important that any attachment therapist be well informed about the risks of such methods in retraumatizing children. Such methods are not appropriate nor are they grounded in attachment theory, empirical research, or current thinking regarding the neurodevelopmental impacts of experience. It is the therapist's responsibility to ensure the child's safety (psychological and emotional, as well as physical) in any form of treatment as well as that of the caregivers. This section describes some of the important safety principles that should be used when treating families with a traumatized member. These principles apply to both clinicians and caregivers in their work with traumatized children.

The touchstone that underlies all the safety principles we are advocating is "do no harm." The following principles suggest how this fundamental axiom would be applied. These principles do not represent an exhaustive list, but are presented to provide the clinician or caregiver with guidelines for the multitude of individualized situations that might arise.

- The essential guiding principle is that safety is always and at all times the overarching prerequisite for any attachment-focused therapy. The provision and maintenance of safety refers to physical, emotional, and psychological safety.
- The therapist and caregivers must work together to maintain sensitive attunement to the child's cues and respond in a sensitive and therapeutic manner. This shared responsibility and collaboration will help ensure that effective steps are taken to adjust, suspend, or terminate an intervention process when there is any indication that the child's sense of psychological or physical safety is threatened and that dysregulation may occur. The therapist maintains parallel attention to the caregiver's feelings and reactions to support the caregiver in the provision of the secure base for the child. The therapist will then similarly adjust, suspend, or terminate an intervention process if the caregiver's sense of psychological or physical safety is threatened and headed toward dysregulation.
- The use of coerced holding or forced eye contact for treatment purposes is expressly contraindicated as it may retraumatize the child. Holding against a child's will may be appropriate only as a last-resort safety measure (see text on use of restraint below) to protect a child from harming self or others; however, this is not therapy. It is a protection from harm. Further, comfort with developmentally appropriate forms of physical and emotional closeness (e.g., ability to make eye contact) may be a goal of therapy, but should not be a forced technique of treatment. Such closeness is better supported by gradual desensitization, through playful encounters that do not overwhelm the child's coping and unintentionally reinforce his defensive responses. The clinician should keep in mind the importance of staying within Briere's "therapeutic window," which is a useful guideline to avoid coercive practices (Briere & Scott, 2006).

The use of touch may be included in some forms of therapy. However, if touch is used, it must be done cautiously, sensitively, and always in accordance with informed consent, congruence with the therapist's professional code of ethics, and in alignment with a collaborative treatment plan. It remains the responsibility of the therapist to ensure that any use of touch is in the client's best interest, without exploitation of the client's vulnerabilities, and is not coercive or dysregulating.

Physical restraint is not treatment and should only be used under the following conditions:

1. To prevent a person from harming self or others, or committing serious property damage.
2. As a last resort after other, less intrusive methods have been attempted and have failed to calm the person.
3. By persons who have received appropriate training in the safe use of physical restraint.
4. In a manner that monitors and ensures that there is no interference with the restrained person's basic life functions such as breathing, circulation, temperature, and so on.
5. In accordance with any laws or regulations in the specific jurisdiction that address the use of physical restraints or therapeutic holds.

If the child's safety cannot be ensured during a restraint according to these requirements, then additional help should be sought from other adults or backup resources such as a mobile crisis team or the emergency services number in that jurisdiction.

- No form of shaming, demeaning, or degrading interaction is ever acceptable as a therapeutic intervention.
- Children with disorders of attachment may become dysregulated even with very compassionate and sensitive interventions. Dysregulation occurs when the child's coping is overwhelmed due to intense emotional reactivity that precludes, or seriously interferes with, the capacity to maintain constructive engagement in the processing of emotional material. If a child becomes dysregulated, then the clinician must act immediately, decisively, and purposefully to help the child regain regulated functioning. Over time the clinician helps the caregiver perform this critical function so that the provision of support and protection can generalize beyond the therapy and become integrated into the parent-child relationship.
- A goal of attachment-focused therapy is to resolve dysregulation from earlier trauma and help the child heal so that the child may more easily accept and access help and support from the caregiver. Therefore all interventions should be guided by this dual focus. To maintain sensitive attention to this dual focus, clinicians must assess possible interventions according to the following criterion: The clinician must provide effective treatment interventions that may bring up difficult memories and exper-

iences with their attendant feelings, memories, and sensations, while at the same time maximizing the well-being and safety of everyone involved in the intervention process (Briere & Scott, 2006).

Attachment-focused therapies cover a range of different models and techniques. In this book we do not endorse any one model of intervention. Rather, we seek to provide guidance on the core concepts and elements that should be part of any best-practice approach for attachment-focused therapy. The primary purpose of this book is to provide a framework for the overarching principles that guide such models. Various models may prioritize these principles differently, and may incorporate a range of techniques and approaches in the service of these principles.

The diversity of these approaches is important for two reasons. First, this is an evolving field, in which innovation and creativity support the ongoing refinement of effective strategies. Second, the complexity inherent in the children and youth who present with attachment-disordered behaviors clearly argues for a comprehensive continuum of approaches, interventions, and adjunctive therapies.

Core Concepts

The framework for the overarching principles is grounded in several important concepts underlying any attachment-focused treatment approach.

Attachment-focused interventions are based on a relational model of change. If children have been wounded physically and/or psychologically through relational trauma, then a safe, supportive, and well-attuned relationship with a caregiver provides a critical foundation for safety. Providing the child with emotional, physical, and psychological safety is a critical foundation and essential prerequisite for trauma resolution work and healthy development.

Increased security in the caregiver-child relationship is central to positive therapeutic outcomes. As psychologically wounded children experience greater security, they can more effectively recognize, challenge, and resolve negative and distorted thoughts and beliefs. As these thoughts and beliefs change, their behavioral problems will resolve or may be more amenable to other interventions. While serious behavioral problems typically accompany attachment-related difficulties, the focus, at least initially, is more often on understanding and resolving the roots of the behavior than on behavior management strategies alone.

Treatment focuses on increasing the child's capacity for regulation of emotions, behavior, and interpersonal functioning. These social and emotional domains are often the most negatively affected by early relational or developmental trauma experiences. This developmental remediation of core self-regulation skills occurs within the context of the secure base provided within therapy and increasingly by the caregivers.

One of the central components of the therapeutic process and a critical corrective developmental experience is the provision of sensitive and empathic attunement to the child within the intersubjective sharing of experience. Attunement is a process in which the clinician and caregiver pay close attention to the child's reactions and more subtle cues, strive to empathically understand the nature of these reactions, and attempt to acknowledge and respond to the underlying feelings and needs. Attunement is one element of the intersubjective sharing of experience, which is a central therapeutic agent of treatment. One of the primary common factors found in treatment outcome research (Lambert, 2004) is the primacy of the therapeutic relationship, unconditional positive regard and acceptance, and empathy.

Another of the core components of the therapeutic relationship is the development of increased "reflective capacity" (Fonagy & Target, 1997). Main (1991) and Fonagy (1996) have both argued that sensitivity from the caregiver alone is not sufficient to develop security in attachment. Rather, sensitivity becomes a pathway for the caregiver's capacity to understand the difference between actual experiences and how these experiences are then represented as mental states. Recognition of these mental states enables the caregiver to understand and appreciate the differences between the actual experience itself and how the child thinks or feels about it.

A caregiver who can make this kind of distinction is better able to understand that people may respond differently to the same experience and that these mental states are capable of changing. This capacity then enables the caregiver to shift perspective between the child's emotional state and the cause of the distress. The caregiver's ability to hold these two different mental perspectives in turn provides a model for the child to begin to understand the difference between the child's own current emotional state and how the child might think about and understand that experience. This experience then provides a critical platform for the child to become aware of the child's own mental states and intentions. Therefore it is central to treatment that the clinician help the caregivers develop and enhance their reflective function.

In addition, caregiver insightfulness is related to the reflective function and another core dimension of treatment. The caregiver's capacity to be insightful allows the caregiver to achieve greater understanding of the child's and the caregiver's experiences and how these affect perceptions, emotions, and behavior (Oppenheim, Goldsmith, & Koren-Kari, 2005; Oppenheim & Koren-Kari, 2002; Oppenheim, Koren-Karie, & Sagi, 2001).

The development of reflective capacity comes from the caregiver's understanding of the child's internal states and signaling to the child that the child's behavior is intentional and understandable. As a result of this attuned intersubjective sharing of experience the child will experience efficacy. The child will feel able to influence the world and effect responses from the world, which is a primary basis for motivation and persistence.

Attachment-focused therapy seeks to increase the caregiver's reflective function, so that the caregiver can better understand and respond to the child with empathy and active support, even in the face of serious behavioral problems. The development of the reflective function typically occurs in a parallel process in treatment. As the clinician facilitates and supports the caregiver through empathic understanding, the caregiver becomes better able to do the same for the child. As the caregiver is better able to provide empathic supports, the child can better access, rely upon, and learn to trust in the caregiver as a secure base and safe harbor. This process of empathic connection then can promote an increased likelihood of greater sensitivity to and receptivity toward attunement in subsequent encounters, which begins to reduce the patterns of learned avoidance.

Another core component of the therapeutic process is how attunement and reflective capacity combine to support intersubjectivity. It begins with the provision of sensitive attunement to the child and develops into a process through which the caregiver and child come to share the same emotions and understand the emotions through this shared experience. As the caregiver both feels what life has been like for the child and begins to help the child put words to this experience, the process creates scaffolding for shared understanding in the moment. The shared experience of attention, emotion, and intention between the caregiver and the child are at the core of intersubjectivity, and provide at an early preverbal stage a burgeoning way for the child to discover and come to know the self (Trevarthen, 1993). As the caregiver is better able to provide empathic supports to the child, then the child can better access, rely upon, and learn to trust in the caregiver as a secure base and safe harbor. The experience of intersubjectivity then also promotes an increased likelihood of greater sensitivity to, and receptivity toward, attunement in subsequent encounters. The intersubjective sharing of experience is a central therapeutic element in attachment-focused treatment.

- Another core component of the therapeutic process is the development of a coherent autobiographical narrative, which is the ability to make sense of one's life experiences; integrate both positive and negative experiences into a more holistic understanding; and resolve negative and distorted conclusions to allow for more constructive and helpful beliefs about oneself, others, and the world. Enhanced reflective capacity grounded in experiences of emotional support and shared meaning making promotes the building of a coherent narrative.
- Relational trauma can take a toll on children's development across multiple domains. Therefore, specific attention must focus on recognizing and addressing these developmental deficits, especially in the social and emotional areas of functioning.

Goals and Objectives of Treatment

A primary goal of therapy is to increase the child's security of attachment to the caregiver as well as to increase the caregiver's capacity to create a secure base for the child. This is a challenging task because children with significant histories of trauma and attachment-disordered behaviors typically have learned from experience to fear and mistrust adults and relationships, which creates a vulnerability to misinterpreting the intentions of adults who try to protect and assist them. Therefore, it is important to recognize that there is a necessarily iterative process in the gradual development of a child's sense of a secure base following a history of attachment-related trauma.

Some degree of safety must be established before there is any therapeutic progress. In other words, treatment begins by creating and then maintaining an alliance. An initial and very tentative sense of safety can usually be achieved through the above-described core components of the therapeutic process. These core components provide powerful opportunities for corrective developmental experience that can challenge experientially based beliefs stemming from earlier trauma. As these beliefs are challenged by new and different experiences, there is an opportunity for a deeper level of safety to be felt. As greater levels of safety are achieved, greater exploration and challenge of the negative beliefs is possible, which creates an even greater level of perceived safety leading to deeper exploration, integration, and healing. This continued, gradual, sensitive process leads in time to a greater sense of security, which in turn facilitates the therapy itself and makes subsequent goals possible.

Another goal is to resolve the impact of attachment-related trauma on the child's development to support healthy functioning in the present and continued healthy development in the future.

The specific objectives of therapy depend on the individual needs of the caregivers, family, and child as they relate to the above goals. Listed below are objectives for the child, family, and caregivers that are typically involved in this form of therapy:

- Improved ability to recognize and express feelings in constructive ways (e.g., child is able to cry when sad instead of isolating self; child learns to verbalize angry feelings instead of hitting)
- Improved ability to reflect on behavior as connected to underlying feelings and thoughts (e.g., "When I start feeling like no one could really love me, I start pushing people away.")
- Increased ability to smoothly self-regulate affect and regain emotional equilibrium without destructive extreme expressions or protracted periods of extreme distress
- Improved ability to recognize and challenge negative and distorted thoughts by weighing evidence to the contrary (e.g., "It feels like I never can get what I want, but sometimes I do get what I want, like I got what I wanted for my birthday. My mom always feeds me. I am safe. Maybe this really is just about not getting to go to the mall and isn't about everything.")

- Improved ability to tolerate and accept appropriate physical and emotional closeness from a caregiver
- Improved ability to seek comfort, help, and assistance from a caregiver when distressed
- Increased ability to show a range of self-regulatory behaviors including impulse control and other age-appropriate executive functions
- Improved ability to engage in interpersonal problem solving with caregiver and significant others to find mutually acceptable solutions, as appropriate
- Improved ability to tolerate and accept limit setting and discipline from authority figures
- Improved reflective capacity, evident in both the ability to reflect on one's own feelings and behaviors and the ability to take the perspective of others
- Improved ability to understand the state of mind of another, accepting that others may have different feelings, intentions, and thoughts
- Improved capacity for healthy self-esteem based on an ability to assess oneself in a balanced way that appreciates both strengths and limitations
- Improved ability to take pro-social actions such as apologizing and making amends, or volunteering to help others
- Improved peer relationships and capacity to engage in pro-social and cooperative age-appropriate play
- Closer agreement between the child's academic achievement and aptitude and ability
- For caregivers:
    a. Increased capacity to engage the child in the intersubjective sharing of experience
    b. Increased reflective function
    c. Deepened commitment
    d. Increased attunement with the child's emotional and mental states, resulting in fewer states of dysregulation in the child
    e. Increased insightfulness into their own emotions, reactions, and behaviors and those of the child
    f. In some circumstances, resolution of past traumas that are interfering with parenting capacity
    g. Increased ability to see the emotions and perceptions driving symptoms and act on what is driving the behaviors rather than focusing on the surface behaviors

The Process of Therapy

While the practice of attachment-focused therapy varies among differing approaches (e.g. Theraplay, attachment-focused narrative therapy, or dyadic developmental psychotherapy), the process of attachment-focused therapies share a few common elements, as described below. Broadly speaking, these elements involve the importance of relationship as the vehicle for healing—in other words, the creation and maintenance of a therapeutic alliance.

The process of therapy should include the following elements:

- In attachment theory terms: An alliance creates the secure base necessary for exploration. Exploration leads to integration. Integration creates healing. This occurs in a cyclical and iterative process. Developing and maintaining the alliance allows for exploration, which leads to integration and healing. This strengthens the alliance and allows for deeper exploration and further integration and healing (Becker-Weidman, 2010b).
- The caregiver and therapist must form a strong therapeutic alliance that supports empathic exploration and collaborative understanding of the nature of the child's difficulties (history and current functioning), underlying reasons for the behaviors, and potential for healing, as well as the caregiver's feelings and needs.
- The caregiver and therapist then begin to provide an initial preview of the therapy to the child that minimizes blame of the child, reduces shame, addresses the positive intentions of the adults, and clarifies the desired aims in relational as well as behavioral terms (e.g., the child's ability to feel safe with and supported by the caregiver, as well as a resolution of the child's self-injurious behavior).
- The therapist then leads the caregiver and child in a collaborative and sensitive identification of specific key areas of difficulty (relational, emotional, behavioral, psychological), coupled with beginning exploration of the meaning and source of these difficulties and the needs and beliefs underlying the behaviors.

Examples of the above elements in understanding the child

The child who is described as having chronic problems of lying is now seen as a child whose past experiences showed that telling the truth resulted in brutal punishment, and that by figuring out what the adult wanted to hear, the child had a greater chance of safety.

The child who smears feces believes self to be profoundly disgusting due to early experiences of emotional abuse and abandonment. The child fears abandonment and reenacts experiences that reflect the child's sense of self.

The child who hoards food has experienced that food is only occasionally available and so hoards it to avoid the pain of hunger.

The child who acts in sexually seductive ways toward adults was sexually abused by a caregiver in the past. This child assumes that such behavior is expected and is part of all such relationships. The child may at times want to feel some control instead of the vulnerability of being the victim, and thus initiates sexual activity. The child may also feel ambivalence about this and consider it the only way to feel close to someone and cared about. Or, sexual acting-out may be a tension-reduction behavior. Some trigger evokes the emotions associated with early trauma and the behaviors reduce the tension associated with the evoked emotions.

- The caregiver and therapist provide empathic, well-attuned experiences of intersubjectivity to identify specific areas of difficulty (e.g., feelings, beliefs, behaviors) as they emerge in the present, in interaction with the caregiver and therapist. These therapeutic experiences help put words to the child's earlier experiences of attachment-related trauma and begin to make sense of how past experiences connect to current functioning.

Example

An 8-year-old boy and his adoptive father begin therapy. The child will not make eye contact with the adults, mumbles one-word answers to questions, and hides his head under his coat. Instead of asking the boy why he does this, or demanding that he sit up straight and participate, the parent and therapist take a different approach. Instead of viewing the child as defiant or defensive, the father understands his son's behavior as evidence of shame or fear. How we view or understand another's intentions and behavior affects how we feel about the person and how we then respond to the person. This is why it is so important to have kind attributions as these are more likely to lead to better therapeutic responses (Becker-Weidman & Shell, 2010). The father may begin a conversation, trying to put words to what it must be like for his son to feel scared about what they will do in therapy. The father or therapist might even point out how discussion of behavioral problems could make the son think he is bad, or that his dad is mad at him or thinks that he is a bad kid. The father might then explain his reasons for seeking therapy, such as that he loves his son and sees the hurt in his heart that sometimes comes out as anger, and that he wants to help his son learn to let love into his heart instead. The father may talk about how he wants a better relationship with his son and that the therapy is to help them both. The father may then share some of the things he especially loves about his son. The therapist and father might talk about how hard it must have been in the past when another caregiver hurt the son, so he learned not to show his feelings or talk about things. The therapist and father watch for subtle nonverbal clues as to whether the boy is relaxing (e.g., perhaps he has lowered his coat so that he can peer over the edge and make brief eye contact), instead of asking him how he feels. Perhaps later in the session the boy will sit up and begin to share some thoughts or feelings. If the therapist or parent then asks a question that is too difficult for the child to answer directly, he might again hide his face. The therapist, perceiving that some level of connection had been reached earlier, might ask the child to signal yes or no to the question instead of having to answer verbally.

- The child is supported in the identification, expression, and greater regulation of emotions. This process involves empathic sharing between the child and the adults. It also requires active comforting and explicitly accepting the child's feelings by the caregiver and therapist. Within this process is the developmental remediation of emotional skills such as learning to label feeling states, understanding ways to constructively take care of feelings, and learning to reflect on how others may have similar or different feelings.

Examples

A child may respond that she feels "nothing" or that a traumatic experience did not have any effect. The therapist might acknowledge that not feeling was probably a good way to survive something that is hurtful and even overwhelming to most people. The therapist may wonder with the child, "How do you make yourself feel nothing?" "What's it like not feeling?" Then the therapist might ask the child to reflect on what another child at that age might have felt or needed, if that child did feel something. A child who has learned to dissociate from feelings may be able to access some of those feelings by having the feelings identified and normalized through comparison to those of other young children in similar situations.

Another child might have problems with explosive outbursts of anger and rage. The therapist might sensitively explore the triggers for these outbursts with the family by consistently responding to them with comments such as, "Let's see if we can figure out what was so hard for you then" or "What happened just before you got so upset?" These messages seek to reveal the primary source of the reaction and help the child learn that anger is the secondary reaction when the primary need is frustrated.

Another child might have real difficulty tolerating any feelings of sadness. As soon as those feelings begin to emerge, the child responds with anxiety and excessive activity or even aggression. The therapist might begin to wonder about how sadness can feel so scary that it has to be chased away. The therapist and caregiver might then look for ways to help the child recognize, label, express, tolerate, and manage sadness.

Another child may be extremely reactive and respond in unpredictable ways that do not make sense to those around the child. The therapist may help the child and caregiver understand the role of conditioned triggers and source attribution errors in trauma, how reenactments of the trauma continue, and how tension-reduction behaviors, while adaptive, are hurtful. The therapist can then enlist the child and caregiver in an active process to "tame" the triggers so that the child can more accurately assess current threats versus conditioned fears.

- The child is also supported in the identification and processing of the core elements of the negative internal working model (e.g., feelings about self, others, and the world) and the experiences that created those beliefs. This can be accomplished by using the therapist-caregiver, caregiver-child, and therapist-child relationships to identify moments when reactions are indications of the underlying internal working model beliefs, and look for chances to challenge and resolve these negative and distorted beliefs.

Example

PARENT: I told him he couldn't go on that Boy Scout trip, because. . . . **CHILD (interrupting):** It's not fair. I hate you!

THERAPIST: Wow, you are really angry.

CHILD: Yes, I am. She never lets me do anything.

THERAPIST: So when your mom said you couldn't go, maybe you felt like that was proof that she didn't want you to have fun, or maybe thought you didn't deserve that?

CHILD (shrugs): I don't know. I don't care.

THERAPIST: How do you make yourself not care?

CHILD: I don't want to care!

THERAPIST: When your mom says no, it seems like it might feel like it did when you were little and didn't get much of what you needed and you were trying to take care of yourself a lot. That probably feels pretty scary and makes you mad. I wonder why your mom said no this time.

PARENT: I said no because it is an overnight camping trip. Last time you went to an overnight, you had an accident and wet the bed. The other kids teased you and your feelings were really hurt. I was afraid that if something like that happened you would be far away and wouldn't be able to call me to go get you.

CHILD: So you think I am stupid.

THERAPIST: What I heard your mom saying was that she was trying to protect you and make sure you were okay and ready to handle such a big step. But when she tries to help you or take care of you, maybe you think that means she doesn't think you can handle things or maybe you did something bad. Maybe it seems really hard to trust that a mom would be trying hard to protect and take care of you.

- The caregiver provides corrective experiences of interactive repair, in which the caregiver recognizes the child's feelings, provides empathic attunement, models active efforts at comforting the child, and provides assistance to facilitate repaired connection.

Example

An 11-year-old girl comes in from school and her mom greets her, saying that she got a call from the principal that the girl had been in trouble at school. Immediately, the girl becomes angry and starts blaming the other child. The mom tries to redirect her, repeating what the principal said. The girl yells an obscenity and the mom, in frustration, yells at the girl that she is always getting in trouble and sends her to her room. The mom calms down and goes in to talk to the girl:

Mom: I'm sorry I yelled. That didn't help things. Clearly you are upset and I don't really know why. I didn't listen to you and I am sorry. Can you tell me what happened today?

Girl: Why should I? You never believe me. You always believe them.

Mom: I am sorry that I may have done something to make you feel that way. That must really hurt to feel like I never believe you. I want to believe you. Sometimes it is hard because I don't know what really happened. Sometimes I know it is hard for you to tell me what really happened. But you know, I can't help you if I don't know what happened and why. Can you tell me in your own words? I want to help you. I will listen to you; I love you.

Girl: But I didn't do anything. It was the teacher's fault.

The girl then explains that the argument started over a substitute teacher telling the girl she had to go to the bathroom alone, when the plan with the regular teacher was for the girl to go with another girl. This plan was developed because the girl had once been assaulted in a public bathroom and was fearful of being in such places alone. However, the substitute teacher did not know this plan and enforced the solo trip to the bathroom for all the students. When the girl refused to go alone, she became increasingly argumentative, resulting in her being sent to the principal's office. At that point the girl was focused on her anger with the substitute and was unable to explain to the principal the reasons for the other plan. The girl was then given a detention and had to stay in the office during the lunch period.

Mom: I'm sorry, honey, that you had such a rough day. It must have been really hard for you that the substitute didn't know this, and it can be really hard to tell a stranger about how scared you are.

Girl: She wouldn't have cared anyway.

Mom: Well, we don't know that for sure. What I do know is that I wish I had been able to help you with this when it was happening. It must have been really upsetting to be in trouble, but unable to explain what you were feeling you needed. Then you come home and right away I start in on you and we end up yelling at each other. I didn't realize how hard this was for you. Again, I am sorry.

Girl: It doesn't matter.

Mom: Yes, it does matter, and you matter to me. How can I help you fix this?

Girl: I don't know. It probably can't be fixed. They will just think I am that bad girl who gets in trouble all the time.

Mom: It doesn't have to be that way. How about if I call the principal and explain it to him for you? Let's put our heads together and think of some ways we can make sure this doesn't happen again and while we are at it, let's find some ways to help you be able to let others know what you are feeling instead of just reacting in anger. Angry behaviors can get you in trouble and people miss what is really going on.

GIRL: Okay, Mom.

This example indicates that the caregiver takes the initiative to go to the child when there has been a rupture in the relationship, instead of assuming that a child should be able to figure this out alone. The caregiver offers empathy, models interactive repair, and tries to help the child rectify the situation, so the child can regain a state of positive feelings and regulation.

- Reframing is a process of modeling "kind attributions" (Becker-Weidman, 2010b; Marvin et al., 2002), while looking beneath the behavior to reflect on and recognize the possible intentions and needs the behavior serves.

Reframing with kind attributions clarifies the child's motivations, for example:

1. "Resistance" to accepting help from the caregiver may represent the child's profound distrust that anyone could ever care or the child's fear of being hurt.
2. Anger in response to seemingly simple requests may represent the child's profound sense of shame at not being able to do what is asked or fear that the request will result in something bad or hurtful happening to the child.
3. "Manipulation" may represent the child's lifetime of learning that the child's needs don't count and won't be met, so the child had better get what the child can no matter how.
4. Emotional coldness may represent the child's profound lack of experience with empathy (and not being able to give what the child has never had).
5. Opposition and defiance may represent the child's distrust of the adult's intentions and motives; the child may believe the adult is hurtful and does things to make the adult feel good but not the child.
6. Deliberately hurting others may represent the child's belief that since hurt is always inevitable, it is best to hurt others before they can hurt you.
7. Cutting and other tension-reduction behaviors may function to reduce the stress associated with trauma triggers.

Similarly, the caregiver's motivations may be reframed:

1. Anger and negativity may represent the caregiver's profound hurt at not being able to connect with and help the child.

2. Demands and even criticism of the therapy or system may represent the caregiver's desperation and anger that no one has been able to help the child and family so far.
3. Numbness may represent the caregiver's exhaustion and hopelessness.
4. Hopelessness may represent the caregiver's fears that the caregiver cannot help this child.

The clinician then provides empathic attunement to both the caregiver and the child to uncover the underlying intention or need. This creates a new opportunity to make sense of these feelings, behaviors, and reactions in a different way than the likely negative attributions they had previously drawn. This is not a one-time conversation, but rather an ongoing and iterative process in making sense of experiences and reframing those experiences. The ongoing support of enhanced security within the caregiver-child relationship in the therapeutic process provides repeated opportunities for feelings, perceptions, and reactions to be explored in this way.

This process supports acceptance of all feelings, reflection on their meanings, and reconsideration of the conclusions previously drawn. The goal is to find a way to integrate these experiences into a more helpful understanding of how the past shapes who we are and how we respond, while still promoting increased opportunity to be able to choose to respond differently in the present. As the caregiver is supported in better "feeling what the child feels" and understanding the source of the child's behaviors, the caregiver's responses become better attuned to what the child needs. This promotes an increased ability for the caregiver to put words to the child's internal experience, create an alliance with the child so that the underlying needs are better met, and forge a more secure base for the child so that the caregiver becomes a constructive resource for the child and deeper exploration can lead to further integration and healing.

As the child has a greater sense of feeling felt by the caregiver and receives more well-attuned responses, the child's frustration and shame can begin to diminish. This, in turn, helps support greater regulation, so that the child can be more receptive to efforts of support and guidance.

Thus, in experiencing each other differently, the previous negative and distorted beliefs begin to shift, as new experiences create opportunity for new perceptions and beliefs. In this way, the early, often preverbal, beliefs born of profound negative attachment experiences can be resolved and hopefully replaced with more positive and helpful beliefs. The development of a coherent narrative is, then, an experientially based approach that emerges out of increased security in the caregiver-child relationship, as coached and supported by the clinician.

- As attachment-related memories and trauma are explored, the therapist applies the concept of the "therapeutic window" (Briere & Scott, 2006) or "window of tolerance" (Siegel, 1999). This means that exploration sensitively seeks to keep the level of arousal generated by the exploration at an optimal level. It is not always possible to gauge the optimal level, as this will vary between children given their age, development, and coping abilities and resources. The optimal level for a given child or caregiver may also vary given changing circumstances, such as the current level of stress, developmental stage, or perceived security. The optimal level for the resolution of traumatic memories is dependent on two conditions. First, the feelings associated with these memories must be activated so that the child has meaningful access to the memory and is not in a state of avoidance. Second, the level of arousal and affect generated by the memory must be manageable. If the level of arousal is too great, then the child will become dysregulated and unable to process the experience.

Example

A caregiver is discussing the family's upcoming trip to Disney World and remarks that the child seems ambivalent about this. Upon further exploration, this seems to possibly fit with the child's earlier experiences in foster care of looking forward to visits with the birth mother, yet being disappointed that she would frequently fail to show up. She also often made promises to the child that she failed to keep. As the therapist proceeds to explore this further, several reactions are possible in the child.

First, the therapeutic window may not be reached. The child maintains that "it didn't matter" in the past when the birth mother did not keep promises. The child continues to talk about times the birth mother did keep her word or about other peripheral things associated with the visits (e.g., how the social worker let the child play on the social worker's computer) in a manner lacking affect. This indicates that the traumatic memories are not accessed due to avoidance and defense.

Second, the therapeutic window may be missed due to overarousal. The child begins to talk about visits with the birth mother. Soon the child is very upset and begins kicking the furniture, yelling, "I hate her" and "I hate this stupid therapy. I want to go home now!" Attempts to calm the child are met with more aggression and cursing. At this moment the therapeutic window has been "overshot" and the child is in a dysregulated state, demonstrating potentially dangerous behaviors. It is not possible to process the memories evoked because of the dysregulated state. The therapist must stop the exploration, provide attunement and interactive repair (with the parent or caregiver joining in) to reinforce the child's sense of an available secure base, and make explicit that this memory is still very painful for the child. The therapist, as part of the interactive repair process, accepts responsibility for causing the dysregulation by saying, for example, "I am sorry. I didn't realize how upsetting this would be for you. I should have stopped this sooner. Should we stop talking about this now and talk about something else?" If the child can regain regulation with these supports, then further exploration may be initiated at that point or at a later time.

The therapist and caregiver acknowledge that this is a painful memory and encourage the child to continue expressing (e.g., talking about, drawing, enacting) feelings associated with these memories. The child persists in disclosure of thoughts and feelings associated with the memories, perhaps occasionally seeking comfort and reassurance as needed. The child may cry or hide the child's face or even become angry, but is still able to remain engaged in the process, so that the disclosure and feelings run their course and the child is able to regain a state of calm as the caregivers provide comfort and support.

The therapist and caregiver remain engaged in the process with the child, providing emotional support and assistance in making meaning of the experience. By the end of the therapy session, the child has either emotionally regrouped to a positive state, or is effectively accessing ongoing support from the caregiver, so that the child is not alone in the aftermath of the feelings, but feels connected and validated.

This chapter has provided the reader with an overview of attachment-focused therapy. The elements and principles described are general and apply to the large variety of attachment-focused therapies. We began by describing the basic principles of attachment-focused therapy. The effects of early developmental trauma on later development can be profoundly debilitating. This chapter describes an approach to treatment that focuses on relational healing factors for relationally-based trauma. Treatment and parenting are focused primarily on "the relationship," on the intersubjective sharing of experience that allows for revisiting and revising early trauma and associated narratives into a more coherent and integrated experience.

CHAPTER FOUR

Core Concepts of Trauma & Trauma-Focused Therapy

The purpose of this chapter is to describe elements of trauma-focused therapy, which complements attachment-focused therapy. The elements of trauma-focused therapy described in this book are subsumed within an attachment-focused therapy approach. In other words, attachment-focused therapy may be applied to a variety of problems, including the treatment of complex trauma, and is a broad approach to treatment. Trauma-focused therapy is a more narrow set of principles, concepts, and approaches.

Introduction to Trauma Theory

Although the term *trauma* has become a part of our common language, trauma's comprehensive nature and significant consequences can be overlooked and underestimated. Trauma has two parts: (1) the experience or event itself (traumatic stressor(s)), which involves an overwhelming threat to safety for individuals or someone close to them, leaving them unable to cope; and (2) the immediate response, aftermath, and long-term effects to the individual (acute stress, PTSD, or complex trauma; Courtois & Ford, 2009; McFarlane & Girolamo, 1996; Weathers & Keane, 2007), which is the more useful construct and the one we will use in this text.

PTSD and Complex or Developmental Trauma

Trauma can be differentiated into two categories according to its qualitative and quantitative nature. First, trauma is a single or an unexpected occurrence, such as a severe accident, witnessing a crime or school violence, the sudden death of a loved one, a single episode of abuse or assault, or a natural disaster. The effects or symptoms of trauma range from an acute stress response to meeting the criteria for PTSD.

Post-traumatic stress disorder became a formal psychiatric diagnosis in the development of the *DSM-III* (American Psychiatric Association, 1980). It is conceptualized as an anxiety disorder in adults in response to a discrete trauma. The symptoms of the disorder are primarily anxiety based. Further, individuals diagnosed with this disorder typically have explicit memories of the trauma that they are able to relate to some degree, so that the symptoms in the present can be connected to the trauma of the past. In addition, in order to meet the criteria for PTSD, the person must have "experienced, witnessed, or have been confronted with an event or events that involve actual or threatened death (American Psychiatric Association, 2004, p. 427) However, the reality is that many children with histories of trauma do not easily fit the criteria of this disorder, and so the impact of the trauma may be overlooked or minimized. PTSD alone is insufficient to describe the reactions, symptoms, and impairments of complex trauma.

Complex trauma (Cook et al., 2003, 2005), also called developmental trauma disorder, involves multiple traumatic experiences, such as ongoing physical, emotional, or sexual abuse, abandonment by the caregiver, chronic or severe neglect, domestic violence, or death or gruesome injuries as a result of community violence, terrorism, or war (Ford, 2005; Terr, 1991).

Complex trauma's defining factor is that it involves chronic early maltreatment (e.g. physical abuse, neglect, or failure of protection) within a caregiving relationship. When trauma is perpetrated by the caregiver, there is a convergence of the maltreatment itself, the loss of the caregiver as a safe base, and the overwhelming distress with which the child must cope and navigate the various developmental challenges, largely alone (Main & Hesse, 1990; Schore, 1994). That the maltreatment occurs within the caregiving relationship is one reason that its effects are so damaging and pervasive. In addition, because the events are chronic and occur early in life, they further erode and damage a child's normal developmental pathways.

Complex trauma places a person at risk for recurrent anxiety, in addition to interruptions and breakdowns in the most fundamental outcomes of psychobiological development: the integrity of the body; the development of healthy identity and a coherent personality; and secure attachment, leading to the ability to have healthy and reciprocal relationships (Cook et al., 2005; van der Kolk, 2005). This profoundly shatters children's sense of security, leaving them feeling betrayed and shameful, helpless, terrified, and vulnerable in a dangerous world.

Complex trauma can cause impairment in seven domains: attachment, biology, emotional regulation, behavioral regulation, defenses, cognition, and self-concept. In fact, because complex trauma can result in such pervasive impairments, the result is often that the range of behavioral and emotional symptoms of the trauma is conceptualized under other diagnoses. The difficulty is that each problem may be treated as a discrete problem, rather than viewing the broad range of difficulties as all related to one primary underlying cause. Complex trauma is a clinical construct that captures the pervasive effects of relational trauma much more fully than does the psychiatric diagnosis of reactive attachment disorder or PTSD.

Reactions to and symptoms of trauma can vary according to the child's age, developmental level, stage of dependency, temperament, inherent resiliency, and learned coping mechanisms as well as the type, severity, and duration of the trauma experienced (www.nctsn.org; Levine & Kline, 2006).

One of the most important considerations for clinicians to remember when working with trauma is that the sensitivity to the presence and impact of trauma can best be understood when one attempts to look at it through the eyes of the child at the time the trauma occurred. Fundamentally, this means that there can be no objective standards that define whether an experience amounts to traumatic stress for the individual. Trauma is always about the subjective emotional experience of the person involved (Siegel, 1999).

Trauma and Memory

Among the most common symptoms of unresolved trauma is that the person may reexperience the trauma mentally and physically in unpredictable ways in the face of reminders of the earlier traumatic experience (often called "triggers" or "conditioned emotional reactions"; Briere, 2002). When traumatic memories are triggered, they may be reexperienced through repeated intrusive thoughts, nightmares, flashbacks, and other symptoms of anxiety. These symptoms are a sign that the body and mind are actively struggling to cope with and ultimately master the traumatic experience. Consequently, the individual learns to avoid trauma reminders.

A core issue in trauma is that time does not heal these wounds. Rather, the individual becomes consumed by the inability to process or integrate the reality of these particular experiences. This occurs because during a traumatic event, ultrahigh levels of stress hormones stop the hippocampus from working properly. Consequently, explicit memory logs an inaccurate time frame of events in a jumbled order with significantly missing steps and without registering when the trauma ended. The individual attempts to make sense of, and end, the trauma experiences through repetitive replaying of the trauma in images, behaviors, feelings, physiological states, and interpersonal relationships (van der Kolk, McFarlane, & Weisaeth, 1996, p. 7).

The processing of more typical, nontraumatic experiences involves the transfer of important facts to long-term memory and the corresponding process of deletion of insignificant components of experience. These important memories are stored in a more integrated manner in which the events remain mostly connected with the time and context of the memory itself as well as with the affective elements of the experience. This process is fundamentally interrupted in trauma.

Implicit traumatic memories, on the other hand, may become accessible through more unconscious channels such as the emotions or other sensory information (e.g., image, smell, sound, or physical sensation) associated with the traumatic experience. The disruption of the normal processing may result in a significant disconnection and fragmentation between the factual components of the memories and other elements such as the time and context in which they occurred. Therefore it may be difficult, if not impossible, to place the specific memory correctly in time and context.

In addition, "source attribution errors" (Briere & Lanktree, 2011) may also occur. The trigger in the present evokes emotions and thoughts associated with the past trauma. The person then attributes these emotions and thoughts to the current experience and others present. So, for example, a touch on the shoulder by a foster parent may evoke the fear and anxiety associated with prior abuse. Those feelings are then experienced as being caused by the foster parent, and the child reacts with fear or aggression as if this foster parent is the abuser.

This can lead to the original traumatic experiences being relived in the present, which impedes the individual's ability to gain perspective on and effectively process the experience. The result is that unresolved traumatic memories can produce the seemingly contradictory response pattern that is emblematic of complex or posttraumatic stress reactions. This pattern involves prolonged periods of acute hyperarousal followed by periods of physical and mental exhaustion, which in turn can lead to withdrawal, avoidance, and even numbing.

In time emotional exhaustion may set in, leading to distraction, and clear thinking may be difficult or impossible. Emotional detachment, as well as dissociation, or numbing, can frequently occur. Dissociating from the painful emotion includes numbing all emotions; consequently, the person may seem emotionally flat, preoccupied, or distant. The person can become confused in ordinary situations and experience problems with concentration and memory (Briere & Scott, 2006). The person may also engage in tension reduction behaviors such as substance abuse, sexual behaviors, cutting and self-mutilation, and various eating disorders (Briere & Lanktree, 2011).

Physiology of Trauma

Fundamentally, trauma can be understood as thwarting or interrupting the normal biological response to threat, which prepares us to attempt survival through fight, flight, freeze, or appeasement (Levine, 1997; Minton, Ogden, Pain, & Siegel, 2006; Rothschild, 2000). When a threat to one's survival is perceived, multiple mechanisms in the body automatically prepare it for action and create a significant buildup of energy to make that action possible. Most typically, this action is seen as fight or flight. If the threat itelf is too overwhelming, fight or flight may not be possible, even for capable adults. Certainly for children facing attachment-related traumas, truly fighting back or fleeing is rarely possible. When one cannot fight or flee from an overpowering threat, the body may default to other biological responses, which are freezing or appeasement.

If the threat persists and the body is unable to respond as needed (e.g., to complete the action and return to a relative state of equilibrium or calm), then the result is a highly activated, yet incomplete or thwarted biological response to threat. If this occurs chronically, then the state of activation becomes a "trait" and the person is left in a chronic state of feeling threatened. If this response is never effectively completed, then it can remain frozen in time as a physiological response waiting for its chance to be processed and resolved.

Instead of serving as the intended acute response to extreme stress, these incomplete autonomic and corresponding neuromuscular responses become chronically dysfunctional because the feedback systems can no longer work to achieve equilibrium. When this occurs, the individual can become stuck in a state of chronic vulnerability to alarm and hyperarousal, which may alternate with a similarly chronic state of exhaustion and numbing.

The amygdala and limbic system of the brain are involved in the conditioning of trauma (LeDoux, 1999). In fact, input from the eyes and ears reaches the amygdala before it reaches the cortex and enters conscious thought. Once the amygdala has responded to a particular threat, it can become increasingly sensitized to reminders of the threat. This process can result in conditioning of both the explicit components of the trauma itself (e.g., abuse) and a range of contextual elements (e.g., the sensory components).

The individual's processing can then be hijacked into a conditioned overarousal or underarousal set of responses, instead of being more fully processed at a conscious level via the prefrontal cortex and related brain structures. This has great value as a survival mechanism, but such automatic reactions without full processing also have important liabilities. For example, the individual who is triggered will continue to respond in an unconscious, automatic manner appropriate to the past traumatic experience, even in the absence of an immediate threat in the present.

Therefore, it is necessary to remember that some trauma is not consciously remembered, but rather is literally relived in the body. This reliving is not merely a reexperiencing of disturbing emotions or sensations. Rather, it is a reliving of the original fear-inducing experience, coupled with the pent-up physiological survival response associated with it. The painful reality is that this reaction continues even when present external conditions change. Consequently, these overt behaviors and reactions of the traumatized individual may seem unpredictable and unwarranted in the present circumstances.

In traumatic reactions, fear states become conditioned, relived, and reinforced. The result is that these states can become conditioned as traits, persisting without resolution (Perry, Pollard, Blakley, & Vigilante, 1995).

As human beings, we innately seek mastery of these experiences to return us to a state of equilibrium. This can lead to unconscious reenactments of the earlier experiences in an effort to master and resolve the fear experience. However, the chronically ineffective response patterns of unresolved trauma create both lasting arousal and vulnerability to reminders, along with impediments to accurate recognition and processing needed for resolution. Consequently, these reenactments can then be seen as chronic patterns of sabotage or other hurtful actions toward the individual or others.

One of the more damaging elements of complex trauma is that the trauma occurs within the primary caregiving relationship. Complex trauma has wide-ranging effects on a variety of domains. One set of effects comes from the maltreatment itself. Children may become highly sensitized to, and fearful of, expressions of anger, sudden movements, and even touch. Yet the contextual conditioning of trauma does not stop there. Other contextual elements can become conditioned as well, although these may be less obvious to others. One such component is the context in which the maltreatment or loss occurred, which may include a broad range of things including time of day and season, as well as a host of sensory elements (e.g., sights, sounds, smells). In addition, an important component is the relationship with the caregiver itself (e.g., being fearful of close relationships, strong feelings, dependency, and vulnerability).

Child Trauma Versus Adult Trauma

It is important when assessing the presence of trauma to consider the differences between children and adults. Both are physiologically wired to respond with fight, flight, freeze, or appeasement responses. Adults, as more competent and autonomous individuals, can be traumatized, but may also be able to escape or mediate the severity and duration of some traumas by employing various coping responses or defensive measures. Adults have more advanced cognitive skills and capacities and also have greater autonomy and efficacy than children do. Children are, by nature, dependent and vulnerable. When they respond to traumatic experiences with the fight, flight, freeze, or appeasement reactions, they are less able to carry out defensive measures, lack well-developed independent coping strategies, and may very well be frightened by their actual physiological responses. In addition, when trauma occurs within the caregiving relationship, a necessary and vital source of security, safety, and comfort is unavailable, further damaging the child's capacity to effectively cope.

Child maltreatment in the form of physical or sexual abuse is easier to understand as traumatic for the child than are neglect by and loss of a caregiver. Yet, when one assesses the situation through the eyes of the child, it is easier to empathically connect with the terror the vulnerable child may experience. Young children are dependent on their caregivers for their very survival. Consequently, the inability to access the caregiver's attention, protection, and care is terrifying for the child and can signal danger to survival. Threat to survival is at the core of what makes a situation traumatic. Neurobiological and neurodevelopmental research reveals how threats to survival in relational and attachment-related trauma disrupt the normal psychological and biological foundations necessary for development.

Children who experience this type of trauma shift the core processes of the brain and body focused on learning to processes focused on survival. Instead of growing and acquiring new knowledge through exploration and play, children must remain hypervigilant to what is and is not safe (Courtois & Ford, 2009). The survival brain relies on the stress response system for survival responding (Nuemeister, Henry, & Krystal, 2007). However, the stress response system supersedes and reduces the functionality of brain systems that are necessary for attention and learning, emotion regulation, distress tolerance, personality formation and integration, narrative memory, and relationships. In addition, the stress response system potentially compromises the immune system's ability to fight off disease and promote healing (Courtois & Ford, 2009).

Fear and Attachment Security

Children who experience attachment-related traumas have often experienced profound and chronic fears that have not been acknowledged and resolved. The fear may be due to experiences of being hurt by maltreatment, loss of a caregiver's protection and support, the caregiver's frightening actions directed either at the child or toward another as in domestic violence, neglect, or overwhelming negative affective states that the child is left to manage alone. The fear may also be due to some combination of these experiences.

A child's behaviors may appear on the surface as defiance, oppositional behavior, anger, and even rage. However, it is important to understand that such displays of anger are commonly triggered by underlying fears of vulnerability, shame, difficulty trusting that the adult will care for the child, and loss. These profound feelings, when repeated and reinforced without resolution, can create and perpetuate patterns of automatic survival responses such as fighting, fleeing, freezing, or appeasing.

Fear is a normal response to frightening stimuli. Children with a secure pattern of attachment have benefited from the comfort, protection, and support for understanding their feelings provided by a responsive, attuned, committed, reflective, and empathic caregiver. Caregivers with insecure attachment styles are less effective in responding to their children's fear. Instead, they may respond in ways that ignore or minimize the child's feelings, may act in unpredictable and inconsistent ways, or may respond in negative and coercive ways. Consequently, these caregivers are less able to help their children resolve fearful states. Unresolved states can become traits (Perry et al., 1995). The caregiver's own frightened or frightening responses to the child can be a significantly disorganizing influence on the child's developing state of mind with respect to attachment.

Core Concepts for Intervention

Provision of "Disparity"

Healing is promoted by both the absence of danger and the provision of positive experiences that are the antithesis of danger. Therefore, it is not just the absence of maltreatment, abandonment, or loss that is necessary for increased security, but rather the provision of corrective emotional experiences marked by security, attunement, empathy, comfort, and shared joyful and positive emotional communication. It is the disparity between the triggered traumatic response and the supportive and healing immediate experience or environment that leads to a lessening of the conditioned response (Briere, 2002; Briere & Lanktree, 2011). This allows the child to experience feeling protected and felt by the caregiver and clinician in the present, making exploration of past painful and frightening experiences possible. Traumatic triggers and negative internal working models must be addressed with sensitivity and compassion, so that the child receives empathic assistance in identifying, challenging, and overcoming the feelings and beliefs of the past. In this way, the child can challenge distorted and negative beliefs and in turn becomes better able to discriminate the present from the past.

Focus of Treatment

Attachment-focused therapy is by its very nature a trauma-focused treatment. Specific work on the child's traumatic memories and reactions is important to decrease symptoms and change patterns of coping. Symptoms may include significant behavioral problems, emotional dysregulation, and interpersonal functioning deficits. Many self-destructive behaviors, such as cutting, stealing, and sexual acting out, among others, can be seen as tension-reducing behaviors. People use such behaviors to reduce tension because their capacity to regulate affect and tolerate distress is limited. Attachment-focused treatment is primarily concerned with addressing the child's current functioning and development, rather than explicit reworking of past traumas. However, specific traumatic memories may arise during treatment and are then addressed in ways that support greater security in attachment. Attachment-focused therapy is fundamentally about altering the child's views of self, others, and the world to increase capacity for positive, constructive beliefs while disconfirming and resolving rigid, negative, and distorted beliefs. This is achieved by creating experiences that are, by their very nature, therapeutic. It is through the intersubjective sharing of experience that healing can begin to occur. Behavioral interventions alone are rarely sufficient to effect change at the level of core beliefs, and therefore, problematic behaviors may persist. So, in attachment-focused therapy, specific attention is paid to the child's core beliefs, or internal working models, as evidenced in the child's thoughts, feelings, behaviors, perceptions, and interactions. This approach is usually necessary to produce lasting change in negative behaviors.

These core beliefs, especially those based in profound shame experiences, can be potent triggers for traumatic reenactment. The child's coping responses to the unresolved trauma may be evident in avoidance (e.g., being withdrawn, daydreaming, avoiding other children) and physiological reactivity and hyperarousal (e.g., anxiety, sleep problems, behavioral impulsivity).

Exposure and Consolidation

The balance between exposure and consolidation is increasingly recognized in effective trauma treatment (Briere, 2002; Briere & Lanktree, 2011). Typically, children's posttraumatic reactions to relational trauma are overdeveloped avoidance strategies regarding their own traumatic memories, feelings, and thoughts, as well as interpersonal interactions. They may rely on self-destructive tension reduction strategies that put them at risk of additional trauma (Briere & Lanktree, 2011). Avoidance encompasses both the experience and the use of coping strategies in attempts to evade the trauma. Exposure, a technique used to counter avoidance, increases arousal by confronting those aspects of experience, behavior, and sensation that are being avoided, while simultaneously preventing the use of maladaptive coping strategies (Beutler & Clarkin, 1990, p. 273). This must be done in a sensitive and attuned manner. The therapist will want to evoke affect but not too much; dysregulation is not therapeutic and must be avoided, and if it occurs, active steps must be taken to remedy and repair. The concept of the "therapeutic window" captures this balance (Briere & Scott, 2006).

Exposure is a technique used to activate elements of traumatic memories and affect to integrate implicit and explicit memories so that the child can develop access to a range of appropriate coping responses, especially those that include using a secure base as a source of support and comfort. A traumatized child's lack of affect regulation skills can easily result in the child becoming overwhelmed in the process of trauma work. An overwhelmed child will likely feel threatened instead of safe, and will resort to familiar avoidance strategies and tension reduction behaviors.

Progress toward strengthening the child's sense of security will be undermined if the child feels threatened, which can derail the therapy. Therefore, effective interventions must sensitively and repeatedly assess and monitor the child's capacity for affect regulation and distress tolerance as the therapy unfolds, to ensure that the child and caregivers have the skills necessary to cope with feelings generated by the therapy. If affect regulation capacities appear to be limited, the focus must then shift to increasing distress tolerance and affect regulation capacities before further exposure, integration, and healing can occur. The caregiver should be the primary source of safety, comfort, security, and assistance when possible. In other instances the therapist or others may have to act this this capacity.

Exposure needs to be balanced with consolidation. Consolidation or integration is the process that helps the child develop distress tolerance and affect regulation capacities, as well as new perceptions and beliefs, so that the child can begin to experience increased security, trust, and competency in the present. These new experiences provide the scaffolding for further exposure (exploration) and resolution (integration and healing), by increasing the child's sense of trust in the process and hope for the future.

Effective attachment-focused therapy seeks to selectively arouse, confront, explore, and diminish the child's fears, while simultaneously identifying, reinforcing, and generalizing the child's strivings for healing, connection, and resilience. The important balance is increasing affect regulation and distress tolerance capacities, on the one hand, with reducing triggers and distress, on the other hand. The caregiver should be present and active in the therapy to provide comfort, assistance, and support to help reach this goal.

Therapeutic Window or Window of Tolerance

Children learn best when they are in a calm and receptive state. The learning brain is more active in this state. The "learning brain" refers to the state of the brain in which executive functions are more active and the taking in and processing of new information is possible. In this state certain brain structures are more active (for example, the hippocampus and prefrontal cortex). When in a state of distress, the survival brain is more active, which impedes learning, exploration, integration, and healing. The "survival brain" refers to the state of the brain in which survival is paramount. In this state the limbic system and the stress-response systems are most active. Extreme stress impedes the process of maintaining attention and focus on anything other than immediate survival, increases defensive reactions, and decreases behavioral flexibility and the activity of executive functions that are largely higher brain functions of the cortex. Therefore the goal of attachment-focused treatment is to stay within the range in which the child can be most receptive to processing, integrating, and resolving conditioned reactions—the therapeutic window (Briere 2002; Briere & Scott, 2006) or the window of tolerance (Siegel, 1999). This is an ongoing process since the child's receptivity will be determined by a multitude of factors, including the significance of the stimulus, the child's overall functioning on a particular day, relative level of stress and coping ability, and the available safety and support provided by primary caregivers.

This range exists between two boundaries of affect arousal. On one end is the boundary of too little arousal, in which the child's well-developed avoidance strategies continue unchanged. On the other end is the boundary marked by too much arousal, when the child is overaroused to the point of being overwhelmed by intense affect and is unable to tolerate or regulate the affect. When a traumatized child is overwhelmed, there is greater chance that the child will feel forced to resort to the very defensive responses of withdrawal, avoidance, or dissociation, which the therapy is seeking to resolve and change.

Children are not always able or willing to communicate their discomfort with the therapeutic process. The following clues may indicate that the child is having difficulties with the subject (U.S. DHSS, 1994):

- Behavior changes, including distracting or avoidant behavior
- Changes in affect, including shame, sadness, irritability, and anger
- Attempts to change the topic of conversation
- Somatic complaints
- Complaints of boredom
- Dissociation

Consequently, the therapeutic experience can be organized so that it does not overwhelm or exhaust the child. Some ways in which the therapeutic session can be structured are as follows:

- Examine one aspect of the abuse at a time
- Create cycles of work and rest or play
- Break the discussion into small increments that provide a sense of accomplishment at completing a task
- Incorporate esteem-building experiences into the therapy session
- Differentiate between past and current experiences
- Allow the child time to reflect and think about new information
- Allow the child to choose and discuss emotionally manageable subjects

Identifying and attending to life experiences that were not abusive or neglectful is also an important part of therapy. This helps the child place the harmful experience in context and shows that maltreatment is only one of many factors or experiences that impacted his life. The child then can identify skills and areas that the child is competent enough to manage or master.

Focusing on both positive and negative experiences can enhance the child's sense of self. Attending to life experiences that do not include being abused helps the child expand the child's sense of self and identity. This allows the child to integrate the experience into an overall sense of self that is not based solely on victimization and shame. It also initiates the grief process that many children need to experience in order to let go of old images, expectations, behaviors, and feelings.

Many children with histories of attachment-related trauma may initially be highly reactive to a range of triggers, so that the therapist or caregiver unintentionally overshoot the window of tolerance. These episodes are important as a model for how the therapy itself will progress. First, the therapist and caregiver must learn to become attuned to shifts in the child so that states of dysregulation can be recognized and responded to quickly. Over time the attunement of the therapist and caregiver will increase so that the child's states are more closely monitored and dysregulation will be avoided. Second, the episode must be acknowledged quickly and sensitively so as to begin the process of interactive repair. The adult must accept responsibility for causing and then repairing the dysregulation. Third, the therapist, caregiver, and child begin to collaboratively recognize, honor, and make sense of the triggers. This creates the scaffolding for further exploration, integration, and healing (consolidation).

Arousal Modulation, Affect Tolerance, and Regulation

An important element of trauma and attachment-focused therapy is that conditioned emotional responses to traumatic memories are resolved so that they no longer exert influence on the traumatized individual in the present. These conditioned emotional responses are typified by increased physiological arousal. The state of physiological arousal in the context of threat is a normal survival response that triggers the person to respond. However, in chronic forms of trauma, the child is unable to escape and so this physiological warning system loses its survival value. Instead, states of arousal can become conditioned as more permanent traits (Perry et al., 1995) that persist even in positive circumstances and relationships and that can be triggered by benign events that may be only vaguely similar to the original trauma. For example, a child who has witnessed extensive domestic violence may be triggered by current caregivers raising their voices during a heated discussion.

Trauma resolution and healing requires that the internal world of the traumatized child become more effectively regulated. Appropriate affective regulation would allow increased capacity to feel and flexibly express a range of feelings (both positive and negative), as well as transition from states of upset back to states of calm.

Affect regulation is achieved when internal states begin to be "befriended" (van der Kolk, 2007). For children with histories of attachment-related traumas, their profound feelings of insecurity, distrust, and fear make sense in the face of traumatic experiences and the lack of a secure base in the past. "Befriending internal states" first means recognizing their value and meaning. The second step is promoting an increased recognition of the intended transitory nature of these states, so that once their meaning and value are recognized and addressed, the individual can transition back to a state of calm.

This awareness, coupled with help in learning to transition from the presumed trait back to a state, is an important experience of seeing one's internal world as being capable of change. This creates a sense of hope, so that chronic feelings of fear and loneliness can begin to give way to feelings of calm and connection.

The process of befriending internal states (van der Kolk, 2007) can be most effective when the child has assistance in controlling, tolerating, and then regulating the intensity of internal arousal. Optimal arousal promotes increased self-observation and reflection. Observation and reflection allow greater access to changing distorted perceptions and beliefs. Optimal arousal can be more effectively maintained when the clinician utilizes specific techniques that reduce distress and creates an experience of safety and regulation, prior to the purposeful use of selective arousal. For example, coaching on breathing control, relaxation techniques, attention to somatic sensations, mindfulness (Briere & Lanktree, 2011), and cognitive control strategies can help the child begin to develop increased capacity to tolerate negative affects and transition back to more positive affects.

Arousal can also be reduced to manageable limits through the use of various interventions, which might include such techniques as ventilation, reassurance, relaxation and distraction, healthy physical activities, reflection, advice and teaching, use of pleasant imagery, breath control and diaphragmatic breathing, focusing on sensations, and counter conditioning (Beutler & Clarkin, 1990, p. 274).

Individuals with attachment-disordered behaviors often have distorted internal working models that perceive threat even in benign and helpful circumstances. This perception of threat can increase the level of arousal and interfere with effective treatment. In such situations, there may be a need for more evocative or nondirective approaches. By using relatively nonintrusive interventions such as playfulness, acceptance, curiosity, empathy, encouragement, restatement or reflection, and the use of metaphor and analogy, the clinician may be able to help the child reduce the level of resistance. As increased trust in safety and support emerges, the clinician may be able to increase the use of structuring, asking direct questions, clarifying feelings, setting limits, and providing guidance and advice. Intense and probing interventions should only be utilized when significant security has been established and there is a strong alliance between therapist and client (Becker-Weidman, 2010b).

Resistance

According to *Treatment for Abused and Neglected Children* (U.S. DHHS, 1994, p. 48):

> Many behaviors that are initially perceived as resistance are really behaviors that are geared to monitor and manage anxiety generated by recall of the abuse experience. Fidgeting, fooling around, interrupting, asking inappropriate questions, and straying from the topic or task all need to be considered as possible coping behaviors that help a child disengage from his/her painful feelings and thoughts generated by the abuse.
>
> The ego defenses or defensive maneuvers that a child uses to protect him/herself from overwhelming stimuli or memories related to the abuse experience need to be acknowledged and used so the child feels validated, capable, and able to survive in the best way he/she knows how. A child seldom lets go of a defense mechanism, a defensive shield, or protective maneuver simply because he/she is told to do so. Tailoring interventions that facilitate the child's ability to process the experience and manage the anxiety and stress that are generated are important. A child will change his/her behavior when he/she feels capable of managing his/her world without that behavior. Most children will often do this at their own pace.
>
> It is important to note, however, that not all resistant behavior means the child is unwilling to participate in therapy. Furthermore, the child may not understand what is expected of him/her within the therapeutic relationship. The child will benefit from clear descriptions of the purpose and benefits of therapy as well as clarification of how to think about and respond to questions, including the options of "not knowing" or "not wanting to say" (yet).

From Dr. Bruce Perry (www.childtrauma.org):

> When a child, particularly a traumatized child, feels that they do not have control of a situation, they will predictably get more symptomatic. If a child is given some choice or some element of control in an activity or in an interaction with an adult, they will feel more safe, comfortable and will be able to feel, think and act in a more "mature" fashion. When a child is having difficulty with compliance, frame the "consequence" as a choice for them—"You have a choice—you can choose to do what I have asked or you can choose something else, which you know is . . ." Again, this simple framing of the interaction with the child gives them some sense of control and can help defuse situations where the child feels out of control and therefore, anxious.

Goal Sequence or Phase Approach

The goal sequence, or phase approach, refers to recognition that processing traumatic memories must occur in increments in order to provide a framework that allows the child's coping skills to be developed and solidified. This provides support for processing deeply distressing trauma memories, as opposed to forced exploration and cathartic expression. "Pacing the exploration of the maltreatment, loss, and other traumas over a period of time, and placing those experiences in the context of the child's overall life experience, is more therapeutic than listing all the details and memories in one or two sessions" (U.S. DHHS, 1994, p. 58). The principle is: safety and coping before trauma exploration. The therapist must first create an alliance and then maintain that alliance for exploration, integration, and healing to occur (Becker-Weidman, 2010b).

Attachment-focused trauma therapy often involves understanding how past experiences shape the child's beliefs and perceptions, as they are often the cause of the current behavioral and relational difficulties. The focus is on resolving the negative and distorted beliefs and perceptions, so that the child can learn to behave and relate differently in the present without the distorting influence of past traumas being triggered. The content of past traumatic experience is important in helping the child create a more coherent autobiographical narrative. It is important to remember that a child who does not feel some relative sense of safety in the present cannot be expected to process traumatic material. Children who are currently experiencing a lack of security may be unable to access and process memories of past trauma, which is why working to increase the child's sense of a secure base with the current caregiver is deemed essential in this approach. The alliance must be developed, nurtured, and maintained in order for exploration to occur. The alliance is what creates the secure base in treatment.

Since attachment-focused trauma therapy is focused on resolving developmental trauma, each step in the process will likely include exploration of the difficult behavior or feeling, coupled with new experiences of support, comfort, and assistance. This can help facilitate the development of important emotional, cognitive, and social skills that were underdeveloped or thwarted by the earlier trauma. The process of therapy should include exploration, followed by integration of a greater sense of security, along with the development of the new skills and perceptions (a new narrative) gained by access to a secure base through the intersubjective sharing of experience. These new skills, once acquired, may need a period of practice and integration before the child is ready and able to proceed with more exploration. This process proceeds in a cyclical manner. The alliance allows for exploration. Exploration leads to integration and healing, which strengthens the alliance and allows for deeper exploration (Becker-Weidman, 2010b).

Development of a Coherent Trauma Narrative

The development of a coherent narrative is important in resolving attachment security. Similarly, the development of a coherent narrative is another important element of trauma and attachment-focused therapy. Two narratives that facilitate the development of an integrated and coherent narrative are the "claiming" or attachment narrative and the "trauma" narrative; the story of the maltreatment. In treatment of attachment-related traumas, the two narratives are inextricably connected. The attachment narrative involves the individual's ability to access a range of attachment-related memories, perceptions, and emotions, and to discuss these memories in a manner that reflects an integration of both positive and negative events into an integrated story that makes sense of attachment experiences. The trauma narrative involves the specific experiences of relational trauma and the meaning that is ascribed to them. In the development of a coherent narrative of the trauma, it is important to identify and support the methods or strategies that the child used during and after the experiences of maltreatment or loss. This is done to honor the survival strategies adopted by the child and recognize that those survival strategies were, in that past environment, adaptive strategies. The point is to help the child recognize that these efforts were the best that the child was capable of in a difficult, frightening, and hurtful situation. This supports the child's attempts at managing an unmanageable situation and allows the child to hear that these attempts were important and worthy of recognition. This will reduce the child's shame and inappropriate sense of having been responsible for the maltreatment.

Such recognition and acknowledgment is the first step in reframing, which is where the intersection between the attachment and trauma narratives occurs. Typically the child begins therapy because of behavioral difficulties. Many of these problematic behaviors have their roots in the survival strategies employed by the child during earlier stages of development, which can include a range of behavioral expressions of the fight, flight, freeze, and appeasement responses that may result in tension reduction behaviors. These attachment-disordered behaviors may cause a range of difficulties across multiple domains of the child's life (e.g., family relationships, peer relationships, development, academic achievement). Feedback about the child from peers, schools, and even the community can be very critical, negative, and hopeless. Therefore, the attachment-disordered behaviors then serve to create ongoing negative feedback loops that reinforce the child's sense of being bad, defective, unworthy, and unlovable. Further, the frustrated and angry responses of others can similarly serve to reinforce the child's beliefs that others are hurtful, untrustworthy, uncaring, coercive, and dangerous and that the world is a scary and chaotic place.

The resolution of the trauma through the development of a coherent trauma narrative primarily helps the child understand that the behaviors have their roots in early survival strategies and, as such, were not "bad." Second, the child may begin to understand that these survival strategies no longer make sense in the changed circumstances of the child's life, and, indeed, that the continuation of these strategies will have important negative consequences.

Often by the time the caregivers seek attachment-focused therapy, their negative beliefs have also been reinforced. The cumulative effects of the frustration with the child's behavior and the inability to find effective parenting strategies, coupled with the inability to connect with the child in a meaningful emotional way, leave many caregivers doubting their competency and fearing only negative outcomes for the child.

The child and the caregiver need compassion and sensitivity in recognizing the painful and alienated places in which they find themselves. The reframing process inherent in this approach to treatment begins by looking beneath the behavior to reflect on, and recognize, the possible intentions and needs the behavior serves.

CHAPTER FIVE

Assessing Children With Attachment Issues

> Note: Attachment-focused therapy is based on improving the relationship between the child and the caregiver, so that the caregiver can be a resource to the child. A comprehensive assessment must include an assessment of the child and the caregiver's capacity to be insightful, responsive, sensitive, reflective, and committed, and their state of mind with respect to attachment. An assessment is not complete or adequate if it does not include both caregiver and child.

A clinical assessment of a child who has a disturbance or disorder of attachment is a complex task for a variety of reasons. Important developmental and other psychosocial historical information may be missing or inaccessible. Information from different sources may conflict, and it is often difficult to determine what is most accurate. Prior assessments may have focused more on symptoms than on causes, resulting in a plethora of conflicting diagnoses. In addition, previous assessments may have been narrow in focus and may not have considered the various domains of impairment that chronic early maltreatment can engender. The child may present with signs and symptoms indicating a range of possible comorbid diagnoses. Given these many challenges, assessments should be multidimensional and cross-contextual, and should include a range of methods such as clinical interviews, psychometric instruments, and data gathered from other sources.

The need for a multidimensional, cross-contextual assessment is also fundamental because an attachment disturbance does not exist in the child alone; rather, it is a phenomenon that develops and is expressed within a relational context with primary caregivers. Therefore, adequate assessment of a child's attachment issues must include an assessment of how these issues are manifested in the child's significant relationships and how the significant others respond. Parents who bring these children for treatment may perceive that assessment of the relationship, either explicitly or implicitly, unfairly blames them for the child's difficulties. Clinicians must address these reactions within a context of psychoeducation that addresses two critical components: first, how attachment styles develop and become largely unconscious templates for future significant relationships; and second, how attachment-related traumas, as a form of relational trauma, can make the child vulnerable to conditioned interpersonal reactions that have more to do with the past than the present. In addition, parents' own history, patterns of attachment, and related issues affect how they experience and respond to the child. These issues go to the core of informed consent for the parent or caregiver: in this form of therapy, caregivers are the critical agent of healing; they are the keystone of good treatment outcomes. In many ways, the best predictor of treatment outcome may not be the degree of disturbance in the child but, rather, the parent's insightfulness, sensitivity, pattern of attachment and attachment history, commitment, and reflective function. Consequently, the parent must be willing and able to actively function as a therapeutic support for the child. This can pose real challenges when the child appears to be resisting, if not defying, the parent's help, emotional support, and guidance. Thus, the struggle to navigate this challenging process, while supporting healing, profoundly affects both the child and the caregiver. A comprehensive assessment of what all family members bring to this struggle can help the clinician more effectively provide the supports, information, and guidance needed to increase the chance that the treatment will be effective.

Another important challenge in this work is that many children with complex trauma and disordered patterns of attachment are in foster and adoptive placements, and as a result it is often very difficult to collect accurate detailed histories on the child (developmental histories, placement histories, and even where the child lived and why the child was moved). Consequently, when a child is assessed early in his or her stay in a family, caregivers may not be aware of the child's history of behavioral and developmental challenges. In these cases, it is essential to realize that any initial evaluation can only provide preliminary diagnoses and clinical formulations. Similarly, if a child with an attachment disorder is still in the birth family, there may be other barriers to collecting comprehensive data. For example, birth parents who have maltreated the child may not be able to discuss the difficult attachment history without minimizing or ignoring certain events for fear of repercussions. Some of these parents may also be unaware of what happened to the child because of their incapacity or absence.

When we are assessing children early in their stay with their current family, we must be aware that behaviors change over time, and that the current family may not yet be familiar with the range of behaviors the child may express. When histories of physical and sexual victimization and aggression are unknown, the sudden eruption of such behavior often leads to the child being removed from the home. Frequently, the children themselves are reluctant to recount their histories accurately because they may be only too aware of the possibility of loss or they may have repressed such painful and terrifying memories. Other times, trauma occurred prior to verbal memory, and the child may simply not have words to explain what has happened, or the memories may be hidden behind a dissociative barrier.

Goals of Assessment

- To begin to organize the complex array of information from the psychosocial history into a coherent understanding that can generate hypotheses about the sources or causes of specific behaviors, in order to guide treatment priorities.
- To establish a preliminary differential diagnosis (although any diagnosis is subject to ongoing review).
- To determine the capacity of the current caregivers to participate in their child's treatment, and whether they will need additional preparation or treatment of their own before effective treatment of the child can begin. Capacity may refer to a variety of factors. Specific areas to consider are the caregivers' attachment history and pattern of attachment, insightfulness, commitment, sensitivity, and reflective function (Becker-Weidman, 2010a; Becker-Weidman & Shell, 2011). The best predictor of placement stability is the caregiver's commitment (Dozier & Lindhiem 2006).
- To develop an understanding of child, parent, and family functioning.
- To establish a collaborative working relationship (an alliance) between the clinician and the family in exploring and making sense of the reactions of both the child and the caregivers. This provides the context for treatment.
- To discuss treatment expectations and set realistic goals for the work.

Screening, Intake, and Referral

Assessment begins with the initial screening, intake, and, where appropriate, the referral process. The screening process focuses on determining issues of client safety and the appropriateness of the provider's services. It sets the stage for a thorough assessment, which is essential before beginning treatment. The purpose of the assessment is to determine the causes of the difficulties presented by the family, since it is causes that are the focus of treatment.

An initial assessment of risk is important to make decisions about whether to accept the case or whether other more appropriate referrals, such as to a higher level of care, are needed. The following questions are important to consider:

- Is outpatient counseling the appropriate level of care at this point? Are there imminent risk factors that indicate the need for a higher level of service (e.g., imminent risk of danger to self, others, or property, suicidal or homicidal ideation or actions, other current dangers, ongoing abuse, domestic violence), or other factors that might interfere with treatment (e.g., untreated substance abuse, significant medical issues)? If yes, then referral to another resource may be indicated.

- If outpatient counseling is appropriate, what frequency is anticipated to maximize effectiveness?
- If outpatient treatment is appropriate, what level of support (e.g., telephone support or emergency sessions) may be necessary?
- Does the clinician have that availability and can the clinician provide that level of support?
- Can the family afford services?
- Is timely initiation of services possible?
- If timely initiation of services is not possible, is referral to other providers advisable? In other words, is there another provider who can meet the family's needs?

An initial assessment of the fit between the family's stated needs and the clinician's approach and level of expertise is also important to consider.

- How well does the prospective client or family's needs mesh with the clinician's approach (e.g., individual versus family or conjoint therapy)?
- What are the prospective clients' expectations of the therapy and its likely outcomes?
- How well does the clinician's level of expertise meet the stated needs of the prospective client or family?
  1. Is the presenting problem beyond the scope of practice, expertise, or control of the clinician? If yes, then what is the process for referral and connection to another treatment provider or level of care?
  2. Given the lack of specialized attachment-focused therapy resources for families around the country, a clinician may feel it necessary to try to work with a family whose needs are beyond the current expertise level of the clinician. In such cases, the clinician should clearly discuss this with the caregivers and share the plan in place for supervision, consultation, additional training, and crisis management.

Authority to Consent for Treatment

It is also important to determine whether the person calling has the authority to consent for treatment. The clinician needs to know the laws and regulations of the jurisdiction where the service is provided. Laws and regulations can vary on such issues as the age at which a child must consent to treatment, whether one or both parents or caregivers must give consent, and what, if any, documentation (e.g., copy of custody order) should be maintained in the client record.

Overview of the Assessment Process

The ultimate purpose of an assessment may vary. Some assessments are sought to determine or corroborate a diagnosis for a child. This type of initial evaluation can often be completed in three or four clinical interviews with the caregivers, the child, and a combined one with the caregivers and child (Becker-Weidman, 2007). Additionally, such an evaluation should include a review of records, the administration of various psychometric instruments, and a session to review the results of the assessment and treatment recommendations with the caregivers and others, such as social services staff and other agencies involved in the child's care and treatment (Becker-Weidman, 2007, 2010a, 2010b; Becker-Weidman & Shell, 2011). Assessments that are the initial phase of therapy will typically involve many of the same components. The difference is that the findings are utilized to develop the initial treatment plan and clinical formulations, which then become modified over time by developments that occur in the course of the therapy. For example, as the caregiver is able to provide reparative experiences of a secure base for the child, the child may reveal additional content (e.g., explicit traumatic memories or distorted beliefs, as well as reactions to implicit memories). This content then becomes part of the ongoing assessment of the child, as well as a specific focus of treatment interventions. In this manner, developing and strengthening the therapeutic alliance allows for greater exploration, which leads to further integration and healing (Becker-Weidman, 2011). Assessments for purposes of termination of parental rights, custody decisions, and other legal questions will require a more extensive assessment and additional meetings. In such assessments it is critically important to determine the validity and reliability of conclusions derived from observation, material from multiple and diverse perspectives, standardized testing, and clinical interviews since the information will be utilized for a specific decision with significant lasting implications, versus the working hypothesis that guides ongoing therapy.

Regardless of the type of assessment, it is important to recognize that an assessment, particularly in regard to the development of a clinical formulation, is an ongoing process that informs treatment. The assessment of attachment-related traumas is no different from that of other traumas: as the individual experiences increased safety, the client is more likely to be able to have access to traumatic material, so disclosure can be an ongoing and iterative process.

Looking Beyond Symptoms

Behaviors can have a variety of causes. Since it is the underlying cause, motivation, or dynamic that is the focus of treatment, a comprehensive assessment must attempt to determine the causes of the various symptoms and behaviors expressed. In recognition that difficult behaviors frequently represent a child's coping skills developed in response to previous adverse situations, it is important that the clinician frame questions about difficult behaviors in terms of adaptive coping in a maladaptive setting. Attachment-related traumas can have significant impacts on multiple areas of a child's development. Specifically, the National Child Traumatic Stress Network and other prominent researchers (Cook et al., 2005) have suggested that when children experience early, chronic maltreatment within a caregiving relationship, the domains of impairment may include attachment, biological processes, affect regulation, behavioral control, cognition, defensive functions (dissociation), and self-concept. These seven domains of impairment must be addressed within a comprehensive assessment (Becker-Weidman, 2007). It is not that the therapist must be an expert in each area. However, the therapist must have some way of assessing functioning in each domain and then, when appropriate, make referral to the relevant professional for further assessment (e.g., neuropsychologist, occupational therapist certified in sensory integration, developmental pediatrician, neurologist). With such wide-ranging impacts on a child's functioning and development, it is essential that assessment be a comprehensive process that involves clinical observations of the child and of the child and caregivers together, data collection from the caregiver and the child, reports from the school and other professionals involved with the child, and a review of previous records, reports, and evaluations.

One benefit of developing a multidimensional, multisource assessment of the child and family is that identifying patterns of behavior across contexts increases the likelihood that the clinician will accurately identify behaviors that are characteristic of the child and family in general, and not simply in one setting. The use of multiple samples of data over time from multiple sources helps provide a detailed picture of strengths and weaknesses and potential foci of intervention.

When the Child Is in the Family of Origin

Much of this chapter may leave the impression that we are discussing only children who have had to leave their parents to live in foster or adoptive homes. In fact, for a number of reasons, children still living in their family of origin might suffer from a disorder of attachment. This may be because the child has experienced intractable pain as the result of a medical condition during the first few years of life. Infants know that their caregivers are there to make things better, and their experience of unrelieved pain may seem to show them that the parents failed in this important job. In that way, a medical illness or major injury may be experienced by the young child as no different than being abused. Other infants may have the misfortune of having a parent with a chronic illness, either psychological or physical, or parents may need to leave their infant for long periods of time, as is often seen in single-parent military families. The resulting unavailability or inaccessibility of the parent can be experienced as a significant loss and even abandonment for the child and in severe cases may result in unintended neglect of the child. We now understand that neglect has developmental ramifications equal to abuse. Of course, a child may also lose an attachment figure to death or divorce in the first years of life, which may also cause attachment strains or, in some cases, an attachment disorder.

Other children may remain with or are returned to parents who have abused or neglected the child. This does not preclude the parent's ability to help the child heal, but this shared negative experience can become a powerful barrier if not effectively addressed. When abuse or neglect has occurred as a result of a parent's problems with substance abuse, mental health, domestic violence, or another significant stressor, that stressor needs to be addressed and resolved to a degree that it does not pose the same risk to the child and parent before reparative work can effectively be done in the parent-child relationship. A child and parent must feel and actually be safe in order to process past traumas. The process of rebuilding trust is a fragile one; relapse by the parent may be experienced by the child not as a transient state of regression but as further confirmation of the parent's lack of trustworthiness. Parents who have maltreated their children in the past may need to get help in resolving their own attachment injuries and past traumas so that they can become the sort of parents that they wish to be. Therapy in these cases must include parents taking responsibility for hurting the child, and discussions of what they have done to ensure that this does not happen again.

In all these instances, birth parents who seek to help their children heal from past attachment-related traumas must have the capacity to act in therapeutic ways to support their children. This is a challenge for any parent, but can be even more complicated when the parent is the source of the child's hurt. Consequently, these parents may need even more help and support than other parents to assist their birth children in resolving attachment injuries.

Diagnostic Considerations

First of all, it is important to recognize that the behavioral symptoms of many disorders significantly overlap. The same behavior may have different causes and, therefore, receive different treatments. For example, the symptom of emotional reactivity may derive from developmental deficits, psychological trauma, chemical imbalance associated with mood disorders, organic disorders, or head injury. Taken alone, reactivity cannot indicate the true cause of the difficulty. The process of differential diagnosis is to systematically consider similarities and differences among and between symptoms to derive a coherent and scientifically supportable hypothesis that can direct the treatment. Reactive attachment disorder, which is narrowly defined in the *DSM-IV-TR* (American Psychiatric Association, 2000), has little to do with attachment (Zeanah, 1993) and is hardly related to what is more popularly known as attachment disorder, with its long list of behavioral characteristics spanning many diagnoses. It is important for clinicians doing attachment-focused work to be familiar with diagnostic criteria and assign diagnoses only when the specific criteria are met.

The *DSM-IV-TR* is a diagnostic system built on symptom clusters and behavioral symptoms. It is important for clinicians to appreciate the limitations of such a system in that it does not always acknowledge or address the causes of symptoms and disorders. A clinician doing attachment-focused treatment must also consider the potential causes since attachment-related difficulties derive from developmental experiences. Many diagnoses in the *DSM-IV-TR* or *ICD-10* (Buck, 2010) that might seem appropriate are very difficult to apply to young children. It is frequently true that children with histories of early trauma in the caregiving setting show a complex set of symptoms that are poorly captured by independent diagnoses such as reactive attachment disorder, PTSD, ODD, ADHD, conduct disorder, bipolar disorder, and so on. In addition, these children often have impairments in many other domains of functioning, which further complicate accurate diagnosis.

Some promising research has indicated that a new diagnostic category, called complex trauma, or developmental trauma disorder, may more fully capture the range of difficulties we frequently see in the children we treat (Cook et al., 2003, 2005). However, at this time that category has not been accepted by the *DSM* or *ICD* committees and so is best considered a clinical formulation rather than a psychiatric diagnosis. There are also some useful diagnostic conceptualizations in the *Diagnostic Classification 0–3* (Zero to Three, 2005). But, again, while conceptually useful, these categories of diagnosis are not widely accepted. At present, it is necessary in many situations for the clinician to use the *DSM* or *ICD* nomenclature, while framing the clinical conceptualization in broader, more useful terms, such as complex trauma.

Another important diagnostic issue is that many children meet the criteria for a given diagnosis, but this diagnosis may not be primary, or the etiology of the child's condition may justify a different interpretation of the child's clinical condition and a different diagnosis. This issue may arise, for example, with the diagnosis of ADHD. Children with histories of trauma and abuse often show many of the attention and hyperactivity symptoms of ADHD, but the more appropriate diagnosis may be PTSD, an anxiety disorder, sensory integration dysfunction, prenatal exposure to alcohol or drugs, or traumatic brain injury. A child who is hypervigilant will have a difficult time attending to a teacher's instructions or focusing on schoolwork, but the hypervigilance is related to the child's trauma history. Of course, it is possible that children with histories of trauma may also have ADHD, and only a comprehensive assessment will enable the clinician to distinguish between the two or determine if they are comorbid conditions.

For many reasons, it is also possible that a clinician will not hear the whole story from the child or family during the initial assessment. It is not unusual in treating clients with histories of trauma that their reporting of symptoms and experiences changes over time, corresponding to their sense of safety and trust in the relationship with the clinician and family and the treatment process. Additionally, there may be periods when trauma-related symptoms intensify as exploration of traumatic memories occurs. Dissociation may also be stronger or weaker depending on other events in the client's life. Therefore it is especially important that trauma symptoms be reassessed and reviewed on a regular basis.

The remainder of this chapter is organized in three sections, reflecting the comprehensive nature of the assessment process: Assessment of Caregivers, Assessment of Child, and Assessment of Family. The three sections include a description of the purpose of that part of the assessment, critical elements to be included, an overview of the clinical interview, and structured assessment tools.

Assessment of Caregiver

Because the caregiver-child relationship is the focus of treatment and a necessary vehicle for change, it is essential that caregivers are willing to consider how their own parenting styles, internal working models of attachment, and history of trauma or loss can be either strengths or impediments to their ability to parent a child with attachment disturbance. In many respects, the capacity of the primary caregivers is a better predictor of treatment outcome than how disturbed the child is. Many clinicians find that it is useful to start seeing caregivers alone to determine what their parenting strengths and challenges are and to help them understand the deep personal commitment and specialized skills required to be part of a therapeutic team helping a hurt child. Some caregivers may benefit from a course of therapy themselves before they are ready to provide the type of help their child needs. This is especially true if they themselves have histories of unresolved trauma or maltreatment. Important elements to be considered in the caregiver assessment are:

- State of mind with respect to attachment
- Commitment
- Insightfulness
- Reflective function
- Sensitivity

The purpose of the assessment of caregivers is:

- To identify caregivers' strengths, challenges, insightfulness, commitment, state of mind with respect to attachment, and reflective abilities.
- To develop a preliminary understanding of caregivers' inner working model of attachment, including their thoughts, beliefs, feelings, and perceptions of themselves as individuals and as caregivers of their child.
- To explore caregivers' level of commitment to and degree of empathy for their child.
- To identify the level of stress present and supports utilized and needed.
- To identify the presence of any barriers to caregivers' capacity to effectively participate in treatment. Such barriers may include overwhelming current

stressors (e.g., domestic violence, impending separation or divorce, physical illness, financial problems, and other stressors) whose effects may limit caregivers' capacity to make the treatment a priority. Other barriers may include caregivers' unresolved issues with mental health or substance abuse, or their own relationship traumas, which also may limit their capacity to be emotionally available to the child in a sensitive and attuned manner. Another barrier could include the presence of serious psychopathology, such as current affective, anxiety, or personality disorders, especially as it might affect the ability to provide parenting necessary to meet the child's attachment-related needs.

Critical Elements

The following elements must be included in an assessment, with an understanding that only a preliminary assessment of several of these elements can be attempted during an initial evaluation:

The personal history of each caregiver, including, as relevant, but not limited to the following:
1. Strengths including resiliency
2. Caregiver's attachment history and current status
3. Caregiver's trauma history, including significant losses, and current status
4. Other significant life events
5. Current and past significant relationships
6. Medical and psychological history, diagnoses, and treatment
7. Current psychological functioning
8. Family history and relationship history

Parenting relationship, if relevant, including but not limited to the following:
1. History of the relationship
2. Strengths
3. Decision to parent
4. Infertility issues, if relevant, including the frequency with which these issues surface, the triggers, and the pervasive feelings present
5. Degree of commitment to the marriage or partnership
6. Degree of intimacy
7. Level of conflict and conflict management patterns
8. Degree of commitment to parenting

Shared parental roles:
1. The amount and type of interaction with the child
2. Where caregivers agree or disagree in terms of parenting
3. What makes them feel successful as parents

4. If relevant, spirituality and how it guides parenting
5. Values and beliefs about discipline
6. Support systems and extended family

Caregivers' current stressors and nature of support system:
1. Quality, extent, and accessibility of support from natural supports (e.g., family, friends, neighbors, and others)
2. Experiences with formal supports (e.g., therapists, social workers, schools, medical providers, support groups, and others)
3. Quality, extent, and priority of self-care

Resiliency of caregivers:
1. Ability to identify and willingness to share one's own hardships and process of managing or overcoming these hardships
2. Sources of self-esteem (internal and external)

Perception of strengths of the child:
1. Special skills, personality style, intelligence, resiliency, and other positive strengths
2. Strengths that have come from the child's history and prior experiences

Perception of the quality of the caregiver-child relationship:
1. Similarities and dissimilarities with the child
2. Levels of closeness with the child
3. Primary sources of conflict with the child

Caregivers' insight and reflective capacity:
1. Ability to think about thinking and feeling instead of reacting
2. Ability to recognize that people (including self and child) may have different thoughts and feelings about the same events and circumstances
3. Ability to consider that the child's behavior may have different causes and meanings
4. Willingness to try different responses to the child's behavior
5. Capacity to reflect on how their own past experiences may affect their response to the child; for example, recognizing that when another "pushes their buttons," it is the caregiver's button and the caregiver's responsibility to disconnect that button in order to create a more positive relationship

Special considerations for foster or adoptive parents:
1. Expectations of the child before placement and now, and differences between the child they have and the child they imagined
2. Degree of preparation for parenting this particular child
3. Adoption issues or themes that have emerged, where relevant, including

loss, grief, identity, entitlement, control, unmatched expectations, ethnicity, cultural issues, family adaptation to a child with special needs, intimacy, rejection, or guilt and shame

Expectations for treatment.
1. Goals to be achieved
2. Behaviors to be increased and decreased
3. Desired outcomes and changes in relationships among family members

Clinical Interview

After interviewing the caregivers about the child and the presenting problem (see Assessment of Child, below), it is important to learn more about the caregivers themselves.

The clinical interview is the opportunity to begin to establish the degree of trust and working relationship necessary for attachment-focused therapy to be successful. An alliance is necessary for exploration for effective treatment. Parents of children with attachment-disordered behaviors may feel misunderstood, alone, and even blamed for the child's problems. Therefore, it is important that the clinician consistently provides empathetic, strength-based and supportive responses to the caregivers so that they experience that the clinician genuinely understands the problem and its severity. It is also important to acknowledge what the caregivers have done well and to acknowledge the successes of the child and family as their story unfolds.

The content of this interview process is outlined above under Critical Elements. While the content is important in helping the clinician assess the caregiver's capacity to be a therapeutic agent in the child's treatment, the process of the interview becomes a way of modeling how the therapy itself will progress. The clinician seeks to provide a secure base for the caregiver from the very beginning of the contact. This creates and maintains the alliance that is necessary for exploration, integration, and healing. This means that the interview is marked by empathic acknowledgment of the caregiver's struggle and related feelings. This acknowledgment is then coupled with gentle exploration that helps create a context in which the intentions, not just the behaviors and reactions, of both the caregiver and the child can begin to be considered more fully. Indeed, how the caregiver thinks about these things is more important than what is thought. Therefore, the process of interviewing becomes a framework to support the development of empathy for the child. This collaborative process of exploration can be quite different from the more traditional question-and-answer process of initial interviews used in other forms of therapy in which the assessment and treatment phases are treated as distinct. This becomes an iterative process in which the exploration and resulting integration create a stronger alliance and allow for further and deeper exploration (Becker-Weidman, 2010b).

Assessment of Child

A thorough assessment of a child's emotional, psychological, and relationship functioning must occur within the context of the child's current and past relationships. In addition, the assessment should gather data from various sources and be multimodal (e.g., individual, parent-child, and family interviews; record reviews, clinical interviews, behavioral observations, and standardized instruments). Standards for assessing the child's caregivers and family are addressed in this book. The assessment of a child must be comprehensive and address a variety of issues and domains, which are described below. As previously mentioned, children who have experienced complex trauma may have difficulties in seven domains, each of which should at least be screened.

The assessment process for the child begins with a clinical interview or series of interviews with the caregivers, initially focused on the presenting problem. The clinical interview is an opportunity not only to gather information but, equally important, to provide information as the first step in increasing caregivers' understanding of their child and building empathy, both of which lay the groundwork for treatment.

As information is gathered about the child, the clinician provides a contextual framework for the caregivers that can assist them, if necessary, in shifting their view of the child's behavior to a strength-based framework and help them focus on the drivers of behavior rather than on merely surface symptoms. This may help a family's view of the child change from seeing the child as manipulative and choosing to misbehave to a more insightful view of the causes of the behavior, and can provoke a more empathetic response to the child. One way in which to facilitate this is to discuss with parents the information you gather with and from them about the child's history. The clinician can ask and capture the information from their responses to questions such as these:

- Considering your child's history, what are the various losses the child has experienced? (Probe for concrete losses like parents, pets, teachers, and so on, and more abstract losses like a sense of security, control, or concept of family)
- What messages might you expect the child to have internalized about life, parents, adults, themselves, and so forth?
- What feelings would you expect to emerge as a result of this history?
- What behaviors would you expect to see as a result of this life history?

Purposes of Evaluation

- Developing a differential and multiaxial diagnosis
- Developing clinical formulations to guide treatment planning

As previously described, assessment should focus on the underlying causes of behavior, not merely surface symptoms, since the same behaviors can have multiple and varied causes, each of which may require different treatments. The focus includes developing an understanding of the child's inner working model of attachment, a formulation of how current maladaptive behaviors developed as adaptive responses to various circumstances, and how the child's life experiences and development are affecting the child's current relationships and functioning in various domains, thoughts, feelings, and behaviors.

Critical Elements

- Child's history: Some of these elements may not be known. For example, for many children adopted internationally, early history is unknown. However, it is important to consider the following issues and what protective and hurtful experiences may have occurred.

  1. Prenatal care and prenatal environment including family stressors, maternal substance use history, family trauma, and exposure to environmental toxins. Cultural issues may be an influence. For example, children adopted from the predominantly Muslim former republics of the Soviet Union are less likely to have been prenatally exposed to alcohol than children adopted from Russia.
  2. Birth (including prematurity and neonatal intensive care, if any).
  3. Achievement of developmental milestones, and whether any of these were earlier or later than expected.
  4. Chronology of separations, moves, and placements, the quality of relationships, and the reasons for each move. Include any time periods living with relatives other than birth parents, even if parents were still officially custodial.
  5. Specific history and chronology of maltreatment, whether known or suspected, including neglect, medical neglect, and malnutrition, if relevant. History of medical or pain issues that were not abusive but may have caused relational difficulties, such as surgeries and hospitalizations. Included in this section is a history of legal issues, permanency decisions, and related issues. It should be determined whether each aspect of maltreatment history has been reported to the authorities, or whether the clinician must report new material.
  6. Description of all primary caregivers (e.g., birth family, institutional staff, current family), including birth family health, mental health, and substance abuse histories.
  7. Educational history, special education history, Individual Educational Plan (IEP) and 504 plans, academic performance, behavior in academic settings, results of standardized tests, and behavior reports.

8. The results of psychological testing.
9. Previous treatment history including previous diagnoses, inpatient and outpatient treatment and results, medication history, previous evaluations, and social histories.
10. Other critical events and experiences, whether suspected, reported or confirmed.

• Review of records:

Previous evaluations, social histories, adoption summaries, legal documents, police reports, protective services investigative reports, treatment summaries, and other documents as available.

• Current functioning:

1. Nature and quality of current relationships with caregivers, siblings, other family members, and peers.
2. Adaptive functioning (communications, daily living skills, socialization, motor skills) and developmental functioning. Are there differences between the child's chronological age and the child's developmental age in various areas of adaptive functioning? If so, what may be the factors underlying these delays and what are the likely implications of these delays? Are there times when the child regresses in adaptive functioning, and what are the triggers for those times?
3. Cognitive functioning, including screening of neuropsychological functioning; the possible effects of prenatal exposure to alcohol and other substances; executive functioning including planning, judgment, initiation, self-monitoring, impulse control, attention shifting, and verbal and nonverbal information processing; and current academic functioning with IEP and 504 status.
4. Cultural or ethnic identity and issues related to it. This is especially important when child is adopted internationally or is of a different race or culture than the parents.
5. Sensory integration issues and occupational therapy.
6. Speech and language issues.
7. Physical health, including, if relevant, malnutrition history and exposure to environmental toxins such as lead.
   • Biological processes including sleeping and eating patterns, chronic illnesses, and medications.
   • Alcohol-related neurodevelopmental dysfunction and lingering effects of prenatal exposure to chemicals and environmental toxins.
8. Psychological and emotional status.
9. Affect regulation.
   • Responses to stress and threat

- Factors that contribute to dysregulation
- Expression and management of emotions
- Ability to tolerate frustration and stress

10. Behavioral regulation.
11. Dissociation and other psychological defensive strategies as adaptive mechanisms.
12. Mental status.

- Complex trauma domains and issues and functioning in:
    Attachment
    Behavioral regulation
    Emotional regulation
    Cognition
    Defensive functions
    Biology
    Self-esteem
- Self-concept: identity, sense of self and self-concept, and cultural, religious, and racial identity issues.

Components of the Evaluation

- Records: including protective service reports, police reports, court documents related to termination of parental rights and permanency issues, adoption summaries, international records, school records, previous treatment records, evaluations, and medical records.
- Clinical interview with the parents to gather history and current functioning, and assess parents' capacity and commitment (see previous section for details).
    - Clinical interview with the child to assess current functioning and to establish a relationship. Depending on the age of the child, the clinical interview may allow the clinician to assess current level of functioning, self-concept, and understanding of past and current relationships, and to begin assessing the child's state of mind with respect to attachment.
- Assessment of caregiver-child relationship, which may be accomplished by formal or informal observational methods. The nature and quality of the attachment relationship may be explored through a variety of means, depending on the methodology used and the age of the child.

Assessment of Family

In addition to child and caregiver assessments, it is important to attempt to assess the current family as a whole. Without a clear understanding of the problems, capacities, and strengths of the entire family, it is difficult to develop a treatment plan. In the case of an adopted or foster child, it is helpful to learn as much as possible about the birth family as well, and other families in which the child has lived, as well as any institutional placements. The general purpose of a family assessment should be to acquire a more complete understanding of the pattern of relationships among family members and of the child within the living environment. This assessment includes gathering information about the family's values and experiences, manner of managing differences, conflict, intimacy, expectations, and related issues. Additionally, because one of the primary outcomes of the assessment process is the identification of problems, strengths, needs, and capacities, the caregivers (and family as a whole) reflect the most important resources for these characteristics for the child. Finally, through a family assessment, the clinician has the opportunity to examine the caregivers and assess their abilities and challenges. If there are issues of racial or cultural differences between the child and family, these also need to be assessed, along with the ways in which the family plans to integrate these differences into its traditions and history.

Critical Elements

- Assessment of family functioning, including information on birth family, if different, and other families the child has lived in.
- Observations of parent-child and sibling interactions (e.g., roles, alliances, use of defenses, complementary strengths, conflict resolution strategies).
- Composition of all families, including relationships with child, current quality of relationships among all members of the family, and special needs of other family members, present and past.
- If relevant, spiritual base of family, and whether it differs from that of past families or the child.
- Racial or cultural identification of families, including, if child is not of same race or culture as current family, how these differences are managed.
- Nature and quality of social support for family.
- Pets and animals.
- Safety concerns.

Standardized Instruments

When clinical interviews are supplemented with standardized instruments, the clinician can often begin to make better sense of the complex set of symptoms presented in a more comprehensive and integrated manner. Standardized instruments also provide an opportunity to screen caregivers for psychopathology that may interfere with treatment. These instruments can provide an opportunity to corroborate clinical impressions developed from review of the history and the clinical interviews. Indeed, an assessment approach that integrates clinical interviews and standardized assessment tools has the potential of supporting clinical judgments that have greater validity than those obtained through the use of either procedure alone.

The use of standardized instruments can help the clinician learn about a whole range of symptoms in both the child and the caregivers that might take much longer to identify in the course of therapy. They also can provide information from caregivers, teachers, and the children themselves, and thus offer a sense of the similarities or discrepancies between these sources. Because they are standardized, these tools can also help the clinician get a better understanding of how severe the problems are when compared to those of other children or adults, which is a critical factor in developing an individualized treatment plan. Finally, and perhaps most important, when there is a convergence between what is identified as critical in both the clinical interviews and standardized instruments, the clinician can be more certain that the clinical judgments about how to proceed are correct.

Different clinicians will choose to use different tools for the assessment process. This decision should be based on the age of the child, the nature of the presenting problems, and the purpose of the assessment. Additionally, the specific requirements for the use of psychometric instruments are governed by the test publisher, and tests should be used only by those with the proper training and credentials to use and interpret them. Validity and reliability of tests should also be considered when selecting instruments and can usually be found in published material by the test publisher or by consulting the Buros *Mental Measurement Yearbook*, published annually and available in many libraries (Geisinger, Spies, Carlson, & Plake, 2011). The following tests and questionnaires have been found to be useful by many clinicians, although others may be equally valid. The listing is included for illustrative purposes only and is not meant to be prescriptive.

The Parenting Stress Index (PSI)

The PSI identifies stress in parent-child systems that could lead to ineffective parenting as well as behavioral problems on the part of the child. The PSI assesses both general parent and child-specific domains. The instrument is a 120-item questionnaire completed by caregivers of children ranging in age from 1 month to 12 years. It yields several scores and has a validity scale. It has good reliability and validity and is a very useful instrument to use in the parent assessment component of an evaluation. The Child Domain includes the following subscales: Distractibility/Hyperactivity, Adaptability, Reinforces Parent, Demandingness, Mood, and Acceptability. The Parent Domain includes the following subscales: Competence, Isolation, Attachment, Health, Role Restriction, Depression, and Spouse.

The Stress Index for Parents of Adolescents (SIPA)

The SIPA identifies stressful parent-adolescent systems that could lead to ineffective parenting as well as behavioral problems on the part of the adolescent. The SIPA assesses adolescent, parent, and adolescent-parent relationship domains. The instrument is a 112-item questionnaire completed by the parent or parents of adolescents ranging in age from 11 to 19 years. The Adolescent Domain includes the following four subscales: Moodiness/Emotional Lability, Social Isolation/Withdrawal, Delinquency/Anti-Social, and Failure to Achieve or Persevere. The Parent Domain includes the following four subscales: Life Restrictions, Relation With Spouse/Partner, Social Alienation, and Incompetence/Guilt. The SIPA yields three additional scores: Adolescent-Parent Relationship Domain, which measures the perceived quality of this relationship; Life Stressors, which indicates the number of stressful events the parents have experienced in the past year; and the Index of Total Parenting Stress, which represents a composite of all domains and indicates the total stress experienced as a function of parenting a particular adolescent.

Beck Depression Inventory (BDI)

The BDI was designed to measure depression and its severity. It can be useful in children over the age of 13 and with caregivers. It is self-administered and has 21 items, with good reliability and validity.

Beck Anxiety Inventory (BAI)

The BAI is a 21-item scale designed to measure anxiety in those aged 17 to 80 years. It measures subjective, somatic, and panic-related symptoms of anxiety. It has good reliability and validity.

Vineland Adaptive Behavior Scales–II

The Vineland is an individually administered measure of adaptive behavior for ages birth through 90 years. There are three versions: (1) A survey edition that is administered in an interview format by the therapist, (2) a parent/caregiver edition that can be completed by the caregiver, and (3) a teacher edition. Domains measured by the scales are communication skills, daily living skills, socialization, motor skills, and maladaptive behavior. The Vineland is especially useful for children who have experienced early neglect and abuse to assess whether their skills in different areas are consonant with their chronological age, or whether there are areas of functioning that may be significantly below expected age level. The instrument is well validated and has excellent reliability and validity.

Child Behavior Checklist (CBCL)

This checklist is also known as the Achenbach. There are parent-, teacher-, and youth-completed versions. Ages include 1.5–5, 6–18, and adult. All the Achenbach questionnaires have good reliability and validity.

The scales for ages 1.5 to 5 include parent and caregiver forms. Scales called From Each Informant, Internalizing, Externalizing, and Overall Problem are generated, as well as cross-informant scales including Emotionally Reactive, Anxious/Depressed, Somatic Complaints, Withdrawn, Attention Problems and Aggressive Behavior, and Sleep Problems. In addition, there are scales indicating likely *DSM-IV-TR* diagnoses.

The CBCL 6–18, filled out by caregivers, the Teacher Report Form 6–18, and the Youth Self-Report 11–18 each yield competence scales in the areas of social skills and activities, as well as problem scales including Internalizing, Externalizing, and Total Problems. There are also cross-informant scales, as well as *DSM-IV-TR*–oriented scales to suggest specific diagnoses.

Behavior Assessment System for Children, Second Edition (BASC)

This assessment system includes parent rating scales, teacher rating scales, a structured developmental history form, parenting relationship questionnaire, and a student observation system, as well as a self-report of personality. Scales are designed for three age levels, ages 2–5, 6–11, and 12–21 years. Rating scales cover both adaptive (6 scales) and problem behaviors (10 scales).

Behavior Rating Inventory of Executive Function (BRIEF)

This questionnaire allows one to assess executive function behaviors in home and school environments. It is an excellent screening tool to determine whether or not a formal neuropsychological assessment by a board-certified neuropsychologist is indicated (Mattson, 2010). Executive functions include Inhibit, Shift, Emotional Control, Working Memory, Plan/Organize, Self-Monitoring, and so on. There are parent and teacher report forms and a preschool version. There are clinical scales, two validity scales, and two broader indexes—Behavioral Regulation and Meta-cognition. The preschool version is for children aged 2 years through 5 years 11 months. The standard BRIEF is for children aged 5 to 18 years. The instrument has excellent reliability and validity.

Trauma Symptom Checklist for Children (TSCC) and Trauma Symptom Checklist for Young Children (TSCYC)

Caregiver-completed test for ages 3 to 12 years (TSCYC) and self-report for 8–16-year-olds (TSCC). It is designed to assess trauma-specific impairments. It has two validity scales and nine clinical scales including Anxiety, Depression, Anger, Posttraumatic Stress, Dissociation, and Sexual Concerns. While both have excellent reliability and validity, the TSCC often produces scores that significantly underreport trauma symptoms since it is a self-report instrument. Often, later in treatment, children are able to more accurately report symptoms and so it may appear that there has been an increase in the severity of symptoms. For this reason, the TSCYC is often a better instrument to use.

Conners Rating Scales–Revised

These scales can be used for the assessment of ADHD and related problem behaviors in children aged 3 to 17 years. There are parent, teacher, and adolescent self-report versions. While the reliability and validity of this instrument are good, it is primarily a measure of symptoms and not underlying causes. Therefore, it may overdiagnose ADHD. Children who have attention difficulties caused by sensory integration difficulties and other non-ADHD causes will still score in the clinical range on this instrument, even though their attention problems are not caused by ADHD.

Beery-Buktenica Developmental Test of Visual-Motor Integration
This is a test of visual-motor integration for clients ages 3 years to adulthood (Beery, 1997). It has subtests for the visual and for the motor portions of visual-motor integration. It has excellent reliability and validity.

Projective Measures
These measures provide useful information about the content of a child's thinking. They must be administered by testers who have received training in their administration and interpretation.

House-Tree-Person (HTP)
This clinician-administered projective test used with clients over the age of 3 years is designed to elicit information about how an individual experiences the self in relation to others and to the home environment. The HTP provides information that can reveal an individual's general conflicts and concerns regarding social relationships, sense of self, and body image, as well as specific aspects of the environment that the person finds troublesome. It has been found to have good reliability and validity (Bucks, 1995).

Child Apperception Test
This is a clinician-administered projective test for children from 3 to 10 years of age, measuring personality traits, attitudes, and psychodynamic processes.

Marschak Interaction Method
The Marschak Interaction Method is a videotaped, structured interaction between each caregiver and child. It is taught as part of training in Theraplay and should be used only by those who have such training. It can help the clinician identify strengths and problem areas of the caregiver, the child, and the interaction between the two. It is also used to plan treatment. It does not have standardized reliability or validity scales.

Standardized and Semistructured Assessment Tools
Research-based attachment assessments such as the Strange Situation Protocol, Adult Attachment Interview, and story completion instruments can provide very useful clinical information.

Strange Situation Protocol
This protocol involves eight episodes, 3 minutes each, designed to measure a young child's (infant to about 3 or 4 years of age) pattern of attachment with the child's

primary caregivers (Ainsworth et al., 1978). Each episode is increasingly provocative, designed to evoke attachment-related behavior. The separation and reunion episodes are particularly significant. The procedure takes about 30 minutes to administer and can provide a significant amount of useful clinical information.

Adult Attachment Interview

This research-based instrument has been found to provide a wealth of clinical information (Cassidy & Shaver, 2008; Hesse, 1999; Main & Goldwyn, 1984; Steele & Steele, 2008). It is a semistructured interview of 21 questions and a number of probes. It takes between 45 and 90 minutes to administer. It can be used with clients from about age 16 into adulthood.

Attachment Story Completion Test

This is a story stem completion test designed to assess a child's state of mind with respect to attachment (Bretherton, Ridgeway, & Cassidy 1990). Each stem is increasingly provocative and is designed to evoke attachment-related thinking. It can be used with young children and teenagers.

CHAPTER SIX

Treatment Planning

A collaborative treatment planning process with the family will be the best approach to addressing the identified problems. The process engages the family in identifying what changes they want, strengths, and tools that will best support and sustain achievements in therapy. The family participates in developing a treatment plan based on both needs and strengths, including the following:

- Identification of problem focus
- Goals and objectives
- Strategies for obtaining the goals and objectives
- Time frames for achievement and monitoring of progress
- Roles and responsibilities

Children and youth with attachment-disordered behaviors often have some degree of mistrust of others, coupled with beliefs that they are bad, unlovable, and to blame. Indeed, some research has shown that children and youth with significant histories of maltreatment can misperceive neutral, and even positive interactions, as threatening (see "hostile attribution bias," Dodge, 1985). While children in general do not typically understand the potential benefits of therapy, these children and youth in particular are especially unlikely to perceive treatment as helpful at its onset. Indeed, they may likely interpret needing treatment as confirmation of their being bad or defective or blamed for family problems. Psychoeducation and informed consent are important considerations in the preparation of these children and youth for treatment. Often the "treatment plan" may be a simple statement such as, "We are all here to help the family become a happier place." This idea is not pejorative, does not cast blame, and reflects the fact that often everyone in the family has some degree of unhappiness with how they are all getting along, and everyone has some role to play in helping effect change.

The poorer the child's coping at the onset of therapy or the less able the caregivers are to be insightful, sensitive, reflective, and committed, the greater the importance of preparation. Children with attachment-disordered behaviors may have high levels of avoidance and behavioral disruptions, coupled with lack of trust in others. On the other hand, caregivers' negative histories, previous unsuccessful attempts at treatment, and other difficulties may lead them to feel unsure of treatment, defensive, and not fully engaged. Therefore, a therapeutic alliance is challenging to establish and maintain. Indeed, resolving this difficulty with interpersonal relationships should be considered a significant treatment focus and goal, instead of a prerequisite for treatment.

While some models of attachment-focused therapy generally lack established empirical evidence for their effectiveness, there are a number of empirically-supported and evidence-based treatment approaches (Craven & Lee, 2006). Please refer to the discussion of this topic in the introduction. While such empirical evidence is the highest standard of best practice, it is also important to remember that ethical standards of clinical work require that clinicians always have, and can always articulate, a clear rationale for their approach, and interventions grounded in theory and research. Generally speaking, the clinician should favor the use of evidence-based approaches over those without any peer-reviewed publications or support.

Anticipated Outcomes

Treatment goals should be established collaboratively between the clinician, caregivers, and child. Goals must be individualized to fit the assessment of needs, strengths, developmental level of the child, and caregiver capacities. These goals typically focus on improvements in the following areas:

- Enhanced security in the caregiver-child relationship, as evidenced by the child's willingness and ability to access comfort, help, and assistance from the caregiver, so that the caregiver can become a more normalized source of support for the child.
- Enhanced affect-regulation skills in the child, as evidenced by the child's ability to identify, express, and tolerate a range of both positive and negative emotions, be able to stay engaged and regulated, and manage emotions constructively.
- Enhanced cognitive skills in the child, as evidenced by the child's ability to identify negative thoughts, seek evidence to determine if they are still accurate in the present, challenge distorted thoughts, and strengthen positive thoughts in the present.
- Enhanced developmentally appropriate self-efficacy, as evidenced by a more balanced global sense of self-esteem (ability to accept strengths

and weaknesses), capacity to organize self toward achievement of developmental goals, and acquisition of more chronologically appropriate behaviors.

- Enhanced interpersonal skills, as evidenced by ability to more accurately read social cues, manage interactive repair with others, act in empathic and pro-social ways toward others, and demonstrate age-appropriate moral development.
- Enhanced caregiver capacities to be insightful, reflective, sensitive, and committed to the child. This can be seen in the following: less critical, blaming, or negative attributions regarding their child; the use of more accepting and less pejorative language in discussing the child; more empathy for the child; and more consistent use of attachment-facilitating parenting methods (Becker-Weidman & Shell, 2010).

General Principles, Roles, and Responsibilities

- Individualized treatment is determined by the needs of the child and family, as identified in the assessment process.
- It is clear that children with histories of attachment-related traumas may not connect their current behavioral problems with their trauma histories (Perry et al., 1995). Similarly, these children do not typically seek treatment voluntarily for these problems. Therefore, the clinician often begins the planning with the caregivers, but continues to actively seek to engage the child (see the section on informed consent in Chapter 9) in this process.
- Treatment is in line with the standards of practice as outlined in this text.
- The caregivers and, ideally, the child may sign the treatment plan along with the clinician or at least indicate some degree of agreement verbally. Children (especially older children and adolescents) with serious attachment-disordered behavior may initially refuse to sign the treatment plan. This should not be a barrier to beginning therapy. Rather, the initial phase of treatment should focus on engagement strategies to begin to develop an alliance with the family and promote more active participation as the therapy progresses.
- Unlike other child therapies in which the primary therapeutic relationship is between the clinician and child, attachment-focused therapy is primarily a family therapy treatment approach and may be described as attachment-focused family therapy. This approach recognizes that the primary focus of the treatment is on the caregiver-child relationship. The primary caregiver has the critical role in provision of corrective experiences for the child. Therefore, it is vital that the clinician have a strong therapeutic alliance with the primary caregiver to be able to support the caregiver in well-attuned, empathic, and constructive responses to and experiences with the child.
- Research has found that maltreated children do not typically have

well-developed vocabulary skills necessary to label or describe their internal states, compared to other children of the same age, IQ, and basic vocabulary ability (Rogosch, Cicchetti, & Aber, 1995). Children who have experienced complex trauma do not typically associate current behavioral problems with earlier abuse (Perry et al., 1995). Therefore, when these issues are coupled with a general tendency to mistrust adults and misperceive intentions of others as hostile, these children often have significant difficulty in knowing what to say or being able to put experiences into words. This can be misinterpreted as resistance and defiance. Instead, attachment-focused clinicians are urged to view this clinical presentation as more of a skill deficit (i.e., to consider that likely the child "can't" do this, instead of automatically assuming the child simply "won't" do this). In addition, children with trauma and attachment difficulties often have expressive levels of communication that are significantly above their receptive levels (Becker-Weidman, 2009). Expressive communication refers to verbal expression while receptive communication refers to understanding verbal expressions. Since we usually speak with a person at the level on which they speak to us, this can lead to a situation where a child is not doing what the child is asked. While this may appear to be defiant, it may be because the child does not understand.

- Clinicians and caregivers need to be sensitive and careful in categorizing and reacting to the child's experience or feelings before the child has had a chance to express that experience. Often the child will need help doing so and may need the clinician to speak for or about the child. Forcing the child to respond may confuse the child or even elicit a response the child feels is expected by the clinician or caregiver, instead of an authentic feeling. It is often more productive to ask the child to describe what happened and how the child felt about the experience. The clinician and caregiver can then help the child come to the child's own estimations of the experience by asking if it was helpful or hurtful, happy or sad, scary or pleasant, or any combination that helps the child identify and express honest feelings. The clinician and caregiver can ask, "How do you feel about that?" or "Do you ever feel angry about what happened?" For children who can't put this into words for themselves, it can be helpful to ask, "What would you say to another child who was in that situation?" The clinician and caregiver can also help the child talk about the experience by asking, "What is the most frightening thing that ever happened to you?" or "When was a time that you felt strong and powerful?" In this way, the clinician can get a sense of the child's inner world and gain some insight into the child's thoughts and feelings (U.S. DHHS, 1994). And the therapist or caregiver may sense the child's experience and put that into words for the child by asking, for example, "Can I pretend I'm you and talk for you? If I get anything wrong, will you just correct me?" Then speak for the child, periodically checking with the child: "Did I get that right?" In this way, the therapist or caregiver reflects back to the child what the therapist believes is the child's experience, and the child can come to better understand the child's own internal experience.

- Clinicians and caregivers who work with abused and neglected children need to use words and terms that accurately describe abuse and neglect. Words and expressions that either minimize or overdramatize the experience can create the impression that the clinician and caregiver just do not understand the child's situation. Exaggerated statements, such as, "Well, you survived abuse, so you can survive anything," or "I'm so mad at your dad for doing that to you," say more about the adult's reactions than about the child's experience (U.S. DHHS, 1994).

- All clients have the right to ask questions about their treatment and receive answers that make sense. This allows them to experience an appropriate sense of control in the therapeutic process, something they did not experience while being maltreated. This means speaking a language that children and caregivers understand when discussing symptoms and effects of abuse, and refraining from using therapeutic jargon or terminology that is not familiar to most clients. Children need to have their symptoms described to them in developmentally appropriate language. Often, metaphors or examples are helpful for explaining the repercussions of abuse or neglect. Clients need to have a clear answer to their questions, and clinicians can fulfill this need by asking children or caregivers if the answer was helpful to them (U.S. DHHS, 1994).

- Children and caregivers have the right to be treated as individuals who have issues and experiences that are unique to them. By making assumptions or telling clients how they feel, the clinician may overlook a client's need to be treated as a special person. Asking clients to confirm or deny a hypothesis helps them feel that they are part of the discovery process. Mentioning that some other people have felt a certain way about what has happened to them can give children permission to consider feelings that they may not have acknowledged or have been afraid to share. To assume that because a child has been maltreated that the child must feel or think specific things is to respond in a presumptuous manner that decreases the child's sense of integrity and individuality (U.S. DHHS, 1994).

Monitoring and Evaluating Progress

The initial treatment plan is a beginning conceptualization of the clinical and other issues that need to be resolved in order to support improved functioning. It is important to remember that this process represents a series of hypotheses about what the underlying issues are, what interventions will be most effective in resolving these issues, and what goals are important to the child and family. The clinician then systematically works to ensure that each session and intervention relates to the treatment plan.

The recovery process inherent in healing attachment-related traumas is an individualized, iterative, and cyclical process. One can think about phases rather than stages. The phases repeat and build on each other: developing an alliance, maintaining the alliance, exploration, and integration and healing (Becker-Weidman, 2010b, 2011, 2012). This means that each step in the process includes attention to safety (physical and psychological), exploration through well-attuned interaction, and support for consolidation of new information into understanding and different behavioral responses. This process supports an ongoing, interactive testing of the various hypotheses about the underlying issues and how to best resolve them through caregiver-child interactions. Therefore, the monitoring and evaluating of progress is a vital and dynamic part of the therapy itself.

The formal treatment plan itself is monitored periodically through review with the caregivers and child. Reviews may occur more or less frequently as indicated, especially as new information is shared. These reviews can be formal and written, or more informal and verbal. In any event, the treatment record should reflect that some review of progress and status has occurred. This is common in treatment of complex and attachment-related trauma. Treatment plans should be adjusted and modified as needed, and these changes documented in the case record.

It is also important that steps toward healing be recognized and celebrated. Success builds both the foundation for, and the belief in, continued progress. Exploration leads to integration and healing, which deepen the alliance and allow for deeper exploration and further integration and healing. In the difficult process of altering distorted core beliefs, it is easy for children to discount, minimize, or fail to recognize steps in the process. Therefore, it is important in treating these children to identify, acknowledge, and celebrate successes. Such positive responses may not be easily accepted by the child and may lead to temporary regression if the positive encounter is experienced as too powerful, or is a direct challenge to a long-held negative belief (e.g., "I don't deserve this"; "I'm afraid they will keep expecting this of me and I'll let them down"; "Good things never last, so I'll stop it before some else spoils it"). This is why relapse prevention strategies, and recognizing that progress ebbs and flows and is not linear, are important in the treatment planning process. Otherwise these episodes of regression can be viewed as treatment failure and reinforce hopelessness on the part of the caregiver and child. Correctly implemented, they can serve as important insights into how powerful and tenacious the distorted core beliefs are for the child.

Safety Planning

Given the very real dangers often inherent in attachment-disordered behaviors (e.g., physical aggression, self-injurious behaviors, and serious risk taking), it is important that the treatment planning process clearly address safety measures such as safe containment strategies, crisis plans, and available resources and sources of help such as crisis services.

Treatment planning must also address the safety needs of the child as well as other family members, and pets in the home, as appropriate. It is important to handle this planning in a sensitive and respectful manner, so as not to shame the child. Further, given the child's likely distorted perceptions of the intentions of others, it can be helpful to explicitly state the intentions of such safety measures. For example, the caregiver might explain, "Good parents are supposed to keep their kids safe. That is why I am making sure that the gate stays locked. I don't want you to get hurt in the street." Therapists should explain that the use of safe containment strategies, such as restraint, are used only as a last resort and "to keep everyone safe so no one can get hurt."

Inclusion of Family Support Network

Children with significant attachment-disordered behaviors may exhibit a range of problematic defenses such as denial, blaming, and splitting, which can further fragment a vulnerable family's access to support. Therefore, education of and co-ordination with others who interact with the child and family becomes vitally important to the overall success of treatment.

Treatment planning should address education about the unique challenges and dynamics inherent in attachment-disordered behaviors, such as:

- Predicting and previewing splitting as a common psychological defense and how triangulation can undermine the efforts to support attachment between the caregiver and the child.
- Explaining the role of traumatic triggers in behavioral problems versus oppositionality and defiance.
- Explaining how chronic dysregulation from unresolved trauma can be misinterpreted as ADHD.

Additionally, coordination of care with other service providers (e.g., psychiatrist, school, probation officers, primary care physician) is important so that a unified approach prevents helpers from working at cross-purposes. Treatment planning should address education and coordination among the family's natural support system (e.g., relatives, friends, neighbors, and faith community) to help reduce isolation of the family. Isolated families struggling to manage children with severe attachment-disordered behaviors can be especially vulnerable to child abuse, out-of-home placements, adoption disruptions or dissolutions, and other breakdowns. Planning may also be needed for respite and other supports. This is important not just for the immediate course of therapy but to build meaningful and lasting supports that will sustain the family after treatment.

Psychiatric Consultation and Medication Evaluation

The complexity of symptoms and the range of possible comorbid diagnoses associated with attachment-disordered behavior may make a psychiatric consultation and evaluation for medication an important part of treatment planning. Typically children are referred to an attachment-focused therapist following several other courses of treatment that have not been optimally effective. So it is frequently the case that children come to therapy already having acquired a list of diagnoses and a corresponding assortment of medication. In those cases, the therapist may need to work with the prescribing provider to assess whether, as greater regulation is obtained through the therapy, some (or all) of the medications can be tapered, if not discontinued. In addition, the thorough and detailed assessment previously described may lead to consideration of different causes of behaviors and of ending or changing certain medications. For example, if it were determined that a child's attention problems were primarily a function of sensory integration dysfunction and not ADHD, then it might be appropriate to discontinue ADHD medications.

Reactive attachment disorder is not treated with medication; it is primarily a psychological and emotional disorder, not a biochemical imbalance. The etiology of this diagnosis is deemed to be an environmentally caused disturbance from pathogenic care and, therefore, it lacks the biological etiology associated with other medication regimens. The level of emotional and behavioral dysregulation typically associated with attachment-disordered behavior may call for medication support, at least initially. It is helpful if the therapist develops a collaborative relationship with a child psychiatrist who is experienced in working with developmentally based as well as biologically based disorders. This interdisciplinary approach can be very helpful in identifying and medicating possible comorbid diagnoses as needed.

Neuropsychological Evaluation

Children who have experienced complex trauma and disorders of attachment may also have significant neuropsychological impairments (Mattson, 2010). In addition, prenatal exposure to alcohol, drugs, or environmental toxins can lead to notable impairments in executive function and other neuropsychological functions. Referral to a board-certified neuropsychologist for an evaluation can provide important information that affects treatment planning. Behaviors grounded in neuropsychological impairment rather than psychological, emotional, or interpersonal trauma and functioning require different treatment approaches. Often neuropsychological impairments call for more environmental modifications. In addition, a neuropsychological evaluation can be very helpful in working with the educational setting and developing an Individual Educational Plan or 504 plan that addresses all the child's difficulties and strengths.

Regression and Relapse Prevention

Treatment planning should address the chronicity of the attachment-disordered behaviors by including focus on relapse prevention strategies. Understanding these strategies helps the caregiver recognize how difficult change can be, and how likely temporary periods of relapse might be. Helping families reframe such relapses as further information about unresolved memories or beliefs, or unrecognized developmental challenges, is especially important as future developmental stages or other life experiences may serve as triggers in the future. Trauma recovery is not a simple, linear process. Indeed, as the child or youth reaches greater levels of security and is better able to reflect on and share internal experiences, the processing of other traumatic material may become possible. Reexperiencing traumatic feelings, sensations, or memories is common and expected, and can result in periods of regressive behaviors. This is a normal reaction and should be previewed for the caregivers and child in a way that helps them understand these phases, without losing hope that healing is progressing. Hopefully, at each such phase, there is a greater resource for coping both in the individual child and in the relationship with the caregiver.

Treatment Interventions: Rationale for an Integrated Approach

Attachment-focused therapy is an individualized, relational approach with a specific focus on enhancing the security of the child's attachment with a primary caregiver. That security is sought in order to resolve the child's "compulsive self-reliance" (Bowlby, 1980), in which the child steadfastly and resolutely is unable to use the support of significant others in coping with life. Resolution of this chronic response allows the child the ability to accept and seek comfort as needed, to be supported in developmentally appropriate exploration (of both internal feelings and external normative life experiences), and to resolve negative and distorted beliefs that undermine self-esteem, social connectedness, and prosocial behaviors.

Treatment approaches should be drawn from a variety of sources, including increasing parental sensitivity to promote attachment security, helping children develop better social problem-solving abilities, enhancing children's emotional understanding, and improving interpersonal functioning (O'Connor & Zeanah, 2003).

Children with attachment-disordered behaviors and symptoms typically benefit most from an individualized treatment plan that will nearly always include work with the family to help them create greater security in attachment. A family treatment focus is essential because the family environment contributes to the origin and maintenance of the child's difficulty. If the caregiver was the source of the child's relational trauma and is now rehabilitated, specific attention must be provided to help the child process traumatic memories and reactions from the earlier experience, so that greater attachment security can be possible. New caregivers (e.g., foster or adoptive parents) may not understand their role in treatment if they did not participate in the earlier trauma. However, the attachment-related traumas of these children are often stored in implicit memory systems and may still be triggered and acted out in new relationships. Therefore, the healing of relational trauma requires a healthy relationship that provides new corrective emotional experiences and support for mastery of social and emotional skills.

The individualized treatment approach is based on a process of ongoing assessment of the child's functioning across multiple domains, including attachment security, affect regulation, cognitive functioning, behavioral control, self-concept, and interpersonal functioning. Structured assessments are used initially and may be repeated periodically throughout the treatment. However, assessment of this complex phenomenon is never static. It is constantly informed by observations within the caregiver-child relationship. This relationship is the key to providing the child with experiences that counter the early ones of relational trauma. It provides supports in the present for the child to master behavior related to the above domains, as evidenced within the child's relationship with the primary caregiver and then extended to relationships with others.

The field of developmental psychopathology includes the principle of *equifinality* (Cicchetti & Rogosch, 1996), which means that many pathways lead to the same behavior. Since the above multiple domains are themselves affected by a range of factors (e.g., genetic, prenatal, developmental, traumatic), there are multiple pathways to the development of specific symptoms. These symptoms provide evidence of deficits, delays, or distortions in the areas of physiological arousal, affect regulation, neurological and cognitive functioning, self-concept, and interpersonal functioning.

Likewise, there are multiple pathways to healing. Given the complexity of attachment-disordered behaviors and insecure attachment, coupled with the relative newness of clinical approaches to these problems in older children, there are a variety of different approaches. What we have done in this book is to present a set of principles that serve as a framework for attachment-focused therapy. In summary, we believe that attachment-focused therapy must be well grounded in theories of attachment, trauma, child development, and resiliency. Specific interventions must be congruent with a general framework that includes the following:

- Relational experiences of empathy and intersubjectivity
- Assistance in the resolution of dysregulated states and conditioned emotional triggers and reactions
- Supports for enhanced capacity for affect regulation
- Supports for enhanced capacity for reflection and development of coherence in making sense of one's life (the development of a coherent autobiographical narrative and the cocreation of new meanings)

- Supports for disconfirmation and resolution of negative internal working model beliefs
- Supports for exploration and opportunities for mastery of skills, especially in the area of social and emotional functioning

Coercive techniques are specifically contraindicated as they are likely to retraumatize the child. Attachment-focused therapy is premised on the creation and maintenance of physical, emotional, and psychological safety for the child. Interventions or responses by either the clinician or caregiver that negatively impact the child's holistic sense of safety will likely result in the child's dysregulation and thereby interrupt the therapeutic process (please see Appendix A for further discussion).

While touch can be an important tool in helping develop attachment security, many new approaches and models can be utilized without reliance on touch. Cradling is now considered a possible position for specific interventions (e.g., a young child may choose to sit in a caregiver's lap, or an older child might sit next to a caregiver for comfort, while discussing troubling memories or dreams). Physical proximity, touch, and holding are never forced as part of the therapeutic intervention. Increased comfort with physical proximity and touch are now viewed as outcomes of effective attachment therapy.

> Note: Therapeutic holds or restraints are for safety only and require specialized training and implementation. See Appendix A for further discussion.

Mutual and continuous gaze is correlated with emotional connection. Developmentally appropriate levels of eye contact should be considered as an outcome measure of the effectiveness of treatment, instead of being a required and coercive part of intervention. Forcing eye contact will likely be dysregulating for children with traumatic histories and is coercive. While infrequent or averted gaze may indicate lack of involvement, it may also indicate discomfort and dysregulation due to profound shame reactions. Therefore, it is important to remember that selective changing gaze is normative in regulating the flow of communication (Beutler & Clarkin, 1990).

One of the most important developments in attachment-focused therapy derives from advances in the neuroscience of trauma. This research has helped clarify how fear is the core affective experience of trauma (LeDoux, 1999). Developments in the field of trauma research have shown how well-dosed activation of traumatic memories, coupled with active assistance in reestablishing regulation and consolidating understanding, are effective and therapeutic (Briere, 2002). Defensive strategies such as avoidance, resistance, and dissociation must be understood as adaptive strategies or coping efforts on the part of the child to survive the maltreatment or losses that are at the root of the attachment disturbance. These adaptive strategies can change only as new, more constructive coping strategies are developed in the new home.

For many decades, therapists working with children have disagreed about whether directive or nondirective approaches should prevail. Reasonable professionals still disagree. Our experience working with posttraumatic reactions in children has shaped our collective beliefs and led us toward specific approaches. Researchers in the treatment of trauma in children (Cohen et al., 2006) found that while both the nondirective and directive approaches may have positive effects, in cases of trauma the sensitive use of exposure can have a significantly more positive treatment outcome. We emphasize the critical importance of sensitive, well-dosed exposure, coupled with active assistance in helping the child regain and maintain regulation. As the trauma literature has made increasingly clear, successful treatment involves directly addressing the underlying trauma in a sensitive, well-dosed manner and in a phased approach that supports consolidation of improved functioning.

Our focus on developmentally appropriate practice derives from the work of Bessel van der Kolk (2005) and Bruce Perry (2001), which continues to articulate the real impact that trauma can have on children's development. It builds on the importance of relational approaches and the power of intersubjective experiences to heal (Hughes, 2007). We recognize that children's development may represent diverse levels of functioning in consistent patterns or in patterns of specific conditioned emotional reactions. We do not assume that a child of a certain chronological age is the same as a child of a younger developmental age, but rather that the possible differences in functioning between these two "ages" needs to be considered when planning and assessing interventions (Becker-Weidman, 2009). Generally, children should be treated in a developmentally sensitive, appropriate, and responsive manner that takes into account the child's developmental age in specific domains.

Emotionally disturbed children, who may function within emotional and social realms in immature ways, may lack critical coping and cognitive skills that an older child may be presumed to have developed. For example, a chronologically "normal" 10-year-old may be presumed to have the skills to cope effectively with a time-out. However, another 10-year-old child with less developed coping and cognitive skills may not be able to soothe himself and begin to reflect on his behavior. For this child, the enforced separation, without assistance in coping, may recapitulate earlier experiences of maltreatment and unintentionally set the child up for a triggered negative response. Such a child may also not have received adequate experiences of empathy and interactive repair. Without these experiences, he may be poorly equipped to take the perspective of the other, understand the impact of his actions, or really know how to take steps to repair the breach in the relationship. Indeed, for many of these children, experience has taught them that relationships are not repairable. Therefore, the use of time-out in this case is not an effective strategy, and instead may have unintended consequences of reinforcing the child's distorted beliefs that he is bad and others are rejecting and abandoning. We want to help caregivers and clinicians recognize why such common strategies may not be effective, and assist in the development of other interventions that are responsive to the child's level of functioning and needs.

Many of the children we treat demonstrate significant difficulty with any emotional and physical closeness due to conditioned responses of fear and defensiveness caused by a history of relational trauma. We seek to provide sensitive, positive, and even playful exposure to experiences of physical and emotional closeness that would be expected in the event of a more secure attachment. The purpose of this is to support the development of a more positive caregiver-child relationship so that the child can more easily access the caregiver for support, assistance, or comfort as needed. We recognize that across healthy development, children's approach to, and needs for, these resources do change. Yet, while we believe that healthy children have choices about how and when they use such resources, children with histories of relational trauma often do not even perceive that such a choice is possible.

As Alan Schore (1994) has stated, attachment is supported through the "amplification of positive affect." Children with histories of maltreatment, especially when compounded by relational trauma, often demonstrate a significant constriction in range of affect and may indeed be biased toward affective expressions of fear, anger, and sadness. We draw on the work of Tronick (1989) and Stern (1977) in an effort to provide developmental models of *parental sensitivity*. Parental sensitivity is critical to helping caregivers learn to read and respond to the child's cues, especially when they may be difficult to discern due to the child's distorted, frozen, or dissociated expressions. Many of these children react in a fearful manner or attempt to rebuff or reject the caregiver's mere presence, even at times when the child is most distressed and in need of comfort, support, and guidance. A caregiver's increased ability to read the child's cues as potentially generated by profound insecurity instead of anger, defiance, or rejection may help counter the caregiver's feelings of rejection and in turn support more consistent responses of empathic connection.

Out-of-Home Placements

Except when complicating factors arise (such as severe risks of imminent harm or chronic out-of-control behaviors), hospitalization, residential treatment, and out-of-home placements are generally contraindicated in attachment-focused therapy. The reason for this is that the treatment goal is to foster an attachment between the child and the caregiver. Separation, therefore, may work against the formation of an attachment if the child perceives that the caregivers either do not want or are afraid of the child. When out-of-home placement is necessary, it should be done primarily because of safety issues. In such a case, it is very important for the caregiver to address the child's presumed distorted internal working model beliefs (e.g.,

"This may feel like we don't want you or don't love you, but we do. Our job is to keep you and everyone in the family safe. Right now we cannot keep you safe. We all need to learn how to better handle [specific behavioral problem] so that we can live safely together"). This explanation of the placement may need to be repeated many times, and in many ways, before the child can truly accept it. The caregiver then needs to be involved as much as possible in the child's treatment, while in the placement.

When children must be placed outside the home, for either short or longer-term placements, the attachment-focused therapy as described in this book must be modified. An adequate description of those modifications is beyond the scope of this book. Please refer to Appendix C for an abbreviated discussion of this topic. However, residential programs that use an attachment model will be the preferred placements for such children (Clark, Buckwalter, Robinson, Blackwell, & McGuill, 2011).

CHAPTER SEVEN

Special Considerations in Behavior Management

Children with a history of attachment-related trauma come to therapy with the knowledge that some adult failed to protect and care for them in the past. The impact of this experience creates the internal working models that become the road map to new relationships. The clinician and caregiver approach the therapy with intentions of helping the child heal. The child with a history of attachment-related trauma, however, is very likely to misperceive, at least initially, the intentions and actions of the adults. The caregivers, with their own attachment histories and experiences of being cared for, may respond in a variety of ways, some of which may not be helpful with this child. The child with a negative internal working model may believe that others are always hurtful, coercive, critical, and exploitive, and will abandon or reject the child, or that the child is bad, unlovable, unworthy, defective, and so on.

The process of treatment, whether therapy or therapeutic parenting, becomes a process of navigating through and around potential psychological land mines, in which efforts to connect with or help the child may be experienced by the child as threats of harm. It is important that the clinician and caregiver:

- Are explicit and transparent in their intentions.
- Accept and acknowledge that there will be ongoing instances where the child misperceives the intention and needs clarification.
- Constantly work to support a therapeutic environment that supports the child's perception of safety.

The roles of the clinician and caregiver are to:

- Protect the child.
- Listen and respond to the child in a manner that generates growth and development.
- Help the child learn safety, protection, problem-solving, and communication skills.

The role of the clinician vis-à-vis the caregiver is to:

- Provide support and acceptance regarding the caregiver's feelings and intentions.
- Provide help in understanding what is driving the child's behavior.
- Assist in understanding how past experiences of the caregiver may affect caring for this child and, when necessary, help the caregiver resolve those issues.
- Assist in developing and enhancing the caregiver's:
   Sensitivity
   Reflective function
   Commitment
   Insightfulness
- Provide guidance and advocacy so that necessary resources for the family are secured.

The clinician and caregiver will need to set appropriate limits and adhere to boundaries that protect the child, as well as the adults.

Many books on parenting techniques, as well as common advice from other parents and professionals, present behavioral techniques as efficient approaches to dealing with problematic behaviors in children. If behavioral techniques have worked successfully with a particular child, then they can be continued. However, for many children with histories of attachment-related trauma, their core beliefs are so negative and distorted that such common techniques as time-out or withholding of privileges may not only fail to work, but may also have unintended consequences. In the child's perception, the consequence reinforces the child's maladaptive internal working model.

Children with adequate experiences of security in their attachment relationships do not like experiences of discipline, but are usually able to endure them with minor and transient negative reactions. These children can do this because they have had adequate experiences of their caregivers being mostly benevolent individuals who protect and guide them. Moreover, these secure experiences with the caregiver have provided them with important modeling for interactive repair. Because this process has been reenacted many times as part of "good enough" parenting, these children are more likely to have internalized these experiences. Such children are better able to take the consequences, reflect on their misbehavior, and then take proactive steps to make amends.

In contrast, children with histories of attachment-related trauma have had relatively little experience with benevolence and active aid from caregivers. These children may misperceive the caregiver's actions as being punitive and may experience the caregiver's actions as fear inducing. The unintended result is that the imposed consequence can reinforce the child's distorted beliefs that the child is indeed bad and undeserving, and all caregivers are hurtful and untrustworthy.

Disciplinary interventions for these children can be especially challenging. Typically, it is more effective to use natural and logical consequences, coupled with empathy, as a way of addressing problematic behaviors. The child may still misperceive these efforts as punitive but can usually begin to challenge and modify these distorted perceptions over time, if the caregiver can consistently be both empathic and explicit in the intention.

As an example of disciplining a child, a caregiver might say something like this: "I know it must feel like I am just being mean, but my job as a good parent is to make sure that you learn from mistakes. When you break something that belongs to someone else you need to try to replace it or fix it. I'm sorry that means you can't go play right now, but as soon as this is fixed you can. Maybe next time you are angry with your brother you can come get me and we can figure out together what to do."

Protection and Limit Setting

Physical, emotional, and psychological safety for all parties is a prerequisite for trauma-focused therapy. The clinician and caregiver must explicitly, experientially, and consistently reassure the child that safety is the guiding principle. This is clear with respect to immediate protective responses to serious aggressive behaviors toward self or others.

However, the needs for protection and limit setting may be less clear with regard to other behaviors expressed in therapy. The clinician and caregiver will need to collaboratively define appropriate and inappropriate behavior within the therapeutic context for the child. Many children with attachment-disordered behaviors exhibit a range of very challenging behaviors. Some of them are symptoms of significant dysregulation (e.g., emotional reactivity, impulsivity, aggression) or of the child's profound fears of connection and vulnerability, which lead to powerful resistance to help or guidance from an adult. For both of these types of behaviors, profound shame is often the driving emotion. Children with profound, unresolved shame may behave in many ways. They may be easily triggered into automatic, conditioned responses of dysregulated fear, and act out behaviorally. These tension-reducing behaviors can be very challenging (e.g., drug abuse, self-mutilation). They may overtly attempt to push the adult away, and demean or undermine the adult's attempts to help. Conversely, they may also seek to punish themselves with self-injurious behaviors, or more indirect efforts at self-denigration, such as acting in a disgusting manner likely to elicit rejection from others. The overriding goal in the therapy is to demonstrate to the child that no feeling, behavior, or problem is so disturbing that it cannot be addressed. Similarly, the adults must demonstrate that nothing the child does will result in either abuse or rejection of the child by the adults.

This may be very difficult for caregivers who perceive the child's behavior as a purposeful rejection of or attempt to defy the caregiver. However, helping the caregiver learn to tolerate these expressions, while remaining curious about them, can lead the caregiver to increased empathy for how the child feels and what the child believes. Accepting the affect and perceptions that drive the behavior is different than accepting the behavior. Once a child feels understood and accepted, the child may better tolerate the consequences for unacceptable behavior. The current behaviors can then be better understood in the context of the child's traumatic history. When the clinician and caregiver can help the child feel felt by the adults and be supported in reflecting on what the behavior means in the context of the child's life, this in turn challenges the conclusions the child made in the past. Those conclusions are the basis for the child's negative internal working model beliefs. Those beliefs can be modified as new experiences challenge and disconfirm the beliefs, especially if new experiences create the possibility of new beliefs.

Examples of Child Behavior and Caregiver Response

A 10-year-old boy frequently wets his bed at night or urinates on the floor of his room. The parents encourage him to use the bathroom, leave the hall light on, and provide a night-light, yet the boy continues the behavior. The parents might believe he is purposefully defying their wishes and degrading their home.

To reframe in terms of the child's trauma history: It might be that when this boy was a small child in an orphanage, he was badly beaten if he left his bed at night. Consequently, when he awakens at night in need of the bathroom, it could trigger memories of the earlier abuse. His intense distress interferes with his ability to remember his new parents' reassurances and directions, leaving him with the compulsive need to somehow establish control.

As another example, a 12-year-old girl surreptitiously takes food from the kitchen and hordes it in her drawers and closet. The parents may react with frustration that the child will never ask for anything, but simply takes things. They may feel used and lied to about this.

A clinician could reframe it this way: If the girl experienced serious neglect as a younger child, she has known extreme hunger, and likely learned to survive by taking care of herself instead of relying on others.

Usually the clinician must take the lead in helping the caregiver reflect on the meaning of the child's behavior, in light of the history, and model empathic responses to the child. The caregivers may have empathy for the child, but often the seriousness of the behavior problems, and the lack of feeling connected to the child, render the caregivers hurt, frustrated, and defensive. The clinician can look for ways to begin to address this from the beginning of contact with the child. If the child exhibits behaviors in the session that might be considered inappropriate or even rude, the clinician can use those experiences to begin to reframe the behaviors. For example, "When Suzie hides her face like that as we talk, I wonder if it means that she is feeling embarrassed by our talking about this. This must seem really hard to talk about." Such an approach, contrasted against correcting Suzie and trying to make her sit up and converse, is likely to be more effective in redirecting the child's behavior and in increasing the caregiver's insightfulness and sensitivity.

If the child's behavior cannot be tolerated with patience and empathy, or cannot be safely redirected, then limits may be necessary during the session itself. Natural consequences, logical consequences, shortening the session so the child can behave appropriately for a short period of time, taking a "time-in" to relax, or stopping the session are all methods that can be used effectively with children. It is important to clarify the rules and discuss the consequences with the child so that the child understands the intention and purpose of the limits. This discussion should take place before the clinician imposes any consequence. It should also be made clear that the therapy will continue after any such break. This will reinforce that the misbehavior cannot be successful in undermining the therapy.

It is also important to find a way to reframe the child's behavior so that it is not simply viewed as misbehavior. An example might be for the adults to say, "It seems that you are having trouble using words right now, so showing us your feelings is the only way you can tell us what you feel. Maybe we should talk about something else now. What do you think?"

General Considerations

In general, the following concerns need to be considered in managing the behavior of children with histories of attachment-related trauma:

- Safety considerations include acknowledging the reality of seriously challenging behaviors, and the resulting need to develop effective strategies to keep everyone safe during the therapy.
- Special concerns for managing children with histories of trauma include the need to assess their needs and triggers. Common behavior management strategies such as ignoring misbehavior, using time-out, or withholding privileges may be perceived by children as confirming their distorted beliefs that others are abusive or neglectful instead of helpful, and that their important needs will never be met. This is in contrast to the relatively mild and transient resistance to limits expressed by children who are securely attached.
- For children who have experienced significant maltreatment and who have difficulty regulating their behavior and emotions, time-in will be more effective than time-out. The reason for this is that the child will only become able to regulate with the help of another. Time-in enables the

caregiver to regulate the child or help coregulate the child, so that the child can then, eventually, regulate self.

- Escalating behavior problems, coupled with caregivers' feelings of rejection and isolation, may lead to increased risk for child abuse.
- Punitive interventions are contraindicated and will probably retraumatize the child.
- Control battles tend to escalate children's resistance, rather than teaching increased self-regulation skills. Control battles create distance in the relationship. A primary aim of the caregiver is to maintain emotionally meaningful and therapeutic connections with the child (Becker-Weidman & Shell, 2010).
- Empathy should be used, along with natural and logical consequences, to help the child develop self-regulation and pro-social skills.
- Unresolved posttraumatic reactions and deficits in a "can't versus won't" framework must be examined. This means not assuming that all behaviors are intended as defiance, but rather that they may emanate from developmental delays in self-regulation, interactive repair, and other social skills. Children who are developmentally younger than their chronological age may not be able to act in an age-appropriate manner.
- Caregivers' attachment histories and experiences with their own caregivers strongly color how they will respond to the child.

While we certainly do not advocate ignoring or "rewarding" serious behavioral problems through lack of consequences, we do urge clinicians and caregivers to first try to identify, understand, and respond to the needs of the child expressed by the behaviors. First respond to the affect and perceptions driving the behavior, which can be accepted, before addressing the resulting behaviors, which may require some caregiver action. Using natural and logical consequences, combined with empathy, an appropriate response to the result of the child's behavior can then be determined.

Example 1

Incident
A 7-year-old adopted girl hits her mother during an aggressive tantrum. Mother develops a bruise on her face.

Behavioral Response
The mother might send the girl to her room for a long time-out, followed by taking away the girl's privilege of going over to her friend's house.

Therapeutic Response
Mother and daughter may separate briefly to calm down by being at opposite ends of the living room. In this way the mother does not abandon the child; this is a time-

in response. Mother then initiates the process of interactive repair. Once the child is reengaged with the mother and feels accepted and not shamed, they can together explore what happened and develop a new meaning. Only after the underlying affect is identified and explored and the misperceptions stemming from early negative relational experiences are uncovered can the behavior be addressed. Once the child feels felt, then exploring how the behavior could be different can occur and the child will also be able to repair her relationship with her mother. The mother can identify the skills and responses appropriate to handling the underlying feelings or needs. The mother can then discuss the implications of the child's actions (e.g., child was in a highly dysregulated state; mother is hurt; their relationship feels strained). To help repair the relationship, the mother could implement time-in and have the child help the mother make dinner instead of going over to the friend's house.

Note: The end result may look the same, yet there are important differences. In the first instance, taking away the planned play date with the friend does not logically connect with the aggression. This can feel to the child like the parent is punishing and withholding, which can reinforce the child's negative internal working model beliefs. In the therapeutic response, the mother ties the child's time-in directly to the aggressive episode itself. Further, she connects the subsequent consequence of time-in to the need to reinforce the relationship that was injured in the aggressive episode.

Example 2

Incident
A child breaks a sibling's prized possession.

Behavioral Response
The father might take away one of the child's own possessions and give it to the sibling, or ground the child for the week (e.g., no TV or video games).

Therapeutic Response
The father tries to help the child identify the underlying feelings or needs. The father provides empathy for the child's feelings and underlying perceptions. "He hates me, so I broke his toy." To this the father may explore how hard it must be to feel that the sibling hates the child. Once the child feels understood, then a discussion of ways of more appropriately getting those needs met may ensue. The father may then explain that the child needs to repair or replace his sibling's possession. This may require saving his allowance and buying a new one, or doing extra chores to reimburse the parent who replaced the possession.

Note: Again in this example, the parent is making an explicit connection between the child's actions and the consequence, but in a way that helps the child make reparations, instead of just feeling punished. Both of these examples become part of the therapeutic response of understanding what is driving the behavior, facilitating more appropriate responses by the child, and strengthening healthy development.

Collaboration With Schools and Others

Educating others about the child's needs includes:

- Previewing challenges associated with attachment disorders (e.g., splitting, confusion, traumatic reactions or triggers).
- Psychoeducation about the signs and symptoms associated with complex trauma and attachment-disordered behaviors.
- Enlisting support from others to communicate with caregiver and clinician as indicated.
- Contingency plans that provide support and collaboration so that consistent behavior management plans are developed for school, the bus, and the community.

Restrictive Behavior Management Techniques

Restrictive behavior management interventions are those that restrict, limit, or curtail a person's freedom of movement to prevent harm to self or others.

Restraints or therapeutic holds and similar physically restrictive behavior management interventions are safety techniques, not therapeutic techniques. Restraint can be necessary for safety if a child is at risk of harm to self or others. It should be used only when other less intrusive methods have been tried and have failed to protect, and when the person using these interventions has been properly trained. Anyone utilizing such a technique must be trained in it and only employ it when there is adequate safety for all involved. This technique should be discontinued as soon as the child has calmed sufficiently to no longer be a risk to self or others. However, the child may still be emotionally distressed. We encourage caregivers and clinicians utilizing this technique to explain its rationale to the child, and actively provide support to help the child regain control.

Children who exhibit attachment-disordered behaviors may not have developed the judgment or coping skills expected of other typical children at given chronological ages. Therefore, it is important that caregivers understand both the chronological and developmental age of the child, so that limits are appropriate for the child's specific needs. It may be appropriate to restrict certain freedoms and privileges for a given child based on developmental age, even when this would seem inappropriate based on the child's chronological age. For example, a typical 13-year-old may be allowed to go with peers, without a chaperone, to the mall. Yet, for example, a child aged 15 with attachment-disordered behaviors may not have developed adequate skills of judging the relative dangers of situations or strangers, problem solving with peers, impulse control, or knowing when to call the caregiver for assistance, to be safe at the mall. Similarly, a typical 8-year-old may be allowed to ride a bike alone around the block and back. Yet, a 10- or 12-year-old with attachment-disordered behaviors, who is impulsive and lacks good judgment, might not be safe doing this. Therefore, restrictions are imposed on these children to ensure their safety, and are neither punitive control efforts nor overprotection. They may represent a caregiver's best efforts at providing the level of protection the child actually needs.

Contraindicated Behavior Management Techniques

The following techniques are contraindicated and should never be used:

- Corporal punishment. Maltreated children are very likely to experience this as retraumatizing. Further, corporal punishment can reinforce the belief that those with power use it to hurt others, or the child may seek such punishment as a form of attention.
- Withholding nutrition or hydration or other techniques that might inflict physical or psychological pain, or discomfort.
- Use of demeaning, shaming, or degrading language or activities.
- Forced physical activity as a punishment. It is important to make two distinctions here. First, physical activity that is identified as helpful to the child in regaining composure and regulation (e.g., walking, playing basketball, jumping on trampoline) or that is prescribed by an occupational therapist for sensory integration, for example, may be therapeutic. Second, natural consequences that involve repairing property damaged by the child may also be therapeutic. These are distinguished from forced physical labor that is merely punitive and which is coercively and intrusively forced on the child.
- Punitive work assignments.
- Unwarranted use of invasive procedures for disciplinary purposes (e.g., crowding personal space, grabbing a child without the need for restraint for safety purposes). In contrast, limits and structure or supervision should be guided by the child's needs, should support the child's optimal functioning, and should provide supports for remediation of social and self-care skills.
- Chemical restraint. The administration of medication for the purpose of retraint.
- Manual restraint. A physical hands-on technique that restricts the movement or function of a person's body or a portion of their body.

The following techniques are not considered restraint:

- Holding a person without undue force to calm or comfort and with the person's consent and cooperation.
- Holding a person's hand to safely escort him or her from one area to another.
- Prompting or guiding a person who does not resist to assist in the activities of daily living.

CHAPTER EIGHT

Training, Consultation, & Competency

In this chapter, we will describe the importance of adequate training and consultation for the ethical practice of attachment-focused therapy. The practice of attachment-focused therapy with families of children who have trauma and attachment disorders requires specialized post-graduate training. In addition, adequate consultation or supervision is necessary. The families of children with trauma and attachment disorders present with a variety of complex difficulties that require a high level of competency.

Need for Specialized Training and Preparation

Specialized attachment-focused therapy is required to help families with children with complex clinical presentations and severely disordered behaviors, and families in significant crisis. Therefore, clinicians need to be adequately trained for the level of need presented by these families. Attachment theory and techniques derived from it may be acquired through reading or attendance at workshops, and then included in more general training in family or child therapy. However, clinical work with children and families who have experienced serious attachment-related traumas requires specialized training, ongoing consultation, or supervision before basic competency can be established. This approach to treatment cannot be safely learned through reading or attendance at educational workshops only. Supervised practice or consultation with an experienced and skilled clinician is essential for competency.

Attachment-focused therapy consists of a complex set of interventions directed toward helping caregivers create secure attachment experiences for the child as part of the process of trauma resolution. To support this process, the focus within and between sessions can shift from child to family to caregiver issues. Therefore clinicians need to have experience and expertise in child development, family therapy, and trauma treatment. If they have not had adequate experience in one of these areas, then additional training and consultation or supervision are essential.

The development of children who have experienced attachment-related traumas and disruptions has often been negatively impacted by these experiences. This is often most clear in the child's social and emotional functioning. It is important for the clinician to be knowledgeable about basic child development, to be able to recognize and assess developmental deviations, and to be able to conceptualize how treatment will attempt to remediate developmental deficits and delays to support the achievement of more normal developmental milestones.

Attachment-focused therapy is based on a relational model in which corrective experiences of attunement, intersubjectivity, reflective introspection, and collaborative meaning making guide the work. Therefore, it is essential that the clinician be able to develop strong therapeutic relationships with the caregivers and the child, so that the therapy itself is grounded in a sense of safety and security for all parties. This may not mean that the child is always happy to be engaged in treatment, but that the clinician and caregiver continually do their best to promote a positive relationship with the child. Additionally, it is important that the clinician actively promote interactive repair when there are disruptions in the therapeutic alliance. Interactive repair requires that the clinician monitor the degree of engagement, recognize disruptions in the level of engagement, and model effective repair through reflection and acceptance of the parent's or child's reaction, coupled with active support to reengage the parent or child. Within this model, working with the caregivers is essential and the maxim "Whatever the therapist wishes the parents to be able to do with their child, the therapist has to be able to do with the parents" is important to follow (Becker-Weidman, 2010b, p. 52).

Attachment-focused therapy may elicit strong feelings in clinicians given the often intense behavioral disturbances in the child and level of desperation in the caregivers. Work with clients who have experienced traumas can increase the risk of vicarious trauma or secondary traumatic stress, or compassion fatigue and burnout. Working with traumatized clients can increase the clinician's risk of strong countertransference. These are very real risks in this work. Therefore, it is essential that the attachment-focused clinician has good stress tolerance and coping resources, the ability to be affectively engaged and yet maintain adequate reflective capacity to be objective, and the ability to self-monitor in order to manage the therapist's own level of distress, while ensuring that the therapeutic focus remains on the child's and family's needs. Access to supervision or consultation is a necessary component of this work.

Supervision and Consultation

Attachment-focused therapy is not a technique-driven approach. The clinician may be directed by guidelines for phases of treatment or general approaches, but this is far from a manualized, step-by-step intervention. Therefore, it is essential that clinicians have adequate supervision or consultation so that the theory and concepts can be integrated and applied in individualized approaches, as indicated by the ongoing assessment of the child's and family's needs.

Clinical supervision is defined by Bernard and Goodyear (2009) as an intervention that occurs between a senior member of a helping profession with a junior member which is evaluative and hierarchical in nature and extends over time. Clinical supervision has the following purposes: enhancement of professional functioning for the junior member, monitoring of the quality of professional services, and gatekeeping for the profession.

Consultation is different than clinical supervision because it does not involve hierarchies or evaluations that can keep a member out of the professional helping field. New clinicians are required to obtain a certain amount of clinical supervision postdegree, but consultation beyond that is voluntary. Often consultation is between two peers.

Due to the nature of work involving attachment and trauma issues, we believe that clinicians in this field should voluntarily submit to ongoing and regular consultation. Many experts in the field of traumatology (Cerney, 1995; Perlman & Saakvitne, 1995; Stamm, 1999; Yassen, 1995) strongly endorse and recommend ongoing consultation for clinicians who work with traumatized individuals or families as a way to provide quality care to their clients and to prevent secondary traumatic stress to clinicians.

The following pages discuss in depth the importance and nature of clinical supervision and many although not all aspects of the presentation relate to clinical consultation as well.

The clinical supervisor should assess the developmental needs of the supervisee prior to beginning supervision. For example, the supervisor should consider the following:

- What are the supervisee's motivation and goals for supervision?
- To what extent is the supervisee seeking to validate an existing theoretical orientation versus being open to a more comprehensive formulation of clinical conceptualizations?
- To what extent is the supervisee willing to accept evaluation of technical weaknesses?
- What is the goodness of fit between the supervisee and supervisor? Clinical supervision is a relationship and is most effective when the relationship can provide what the supervisee perceives as a secure base (Bennett, 2008; Fitch, Pistole, & Gunn, 2010). In this way, the supervisor provides a

balance between support and assistance on one hand, with corresponding encouragement for exploration and self-discovery on the other hand. The balance between these two needs should be responsive to the supervisee's level of training, personal characteristics, and goals.

- Supervision should be guided by formal agreements that include the goals, expectations, and limitations of the relationship (Bernard & Goodyear, 2009; Cobia & Pipes, 2002; Desmond & Kindsvatter, 2010; Pearson, 2000). This agreement should be developed collaboratively between the supervisor and supervisee, and reviewed at designated intervals.

Supervision should provide supports that are relevant to the supervisee's stage of training. The integrated developmental model of supervision (Stoltenberg, McNeill, & Delworth, 1998) discusses the various needs of supervisees in relation to their professional development as clinicians.

Stage 1, beginning clinicians: The focus is on acquisition of basic skills, coupled with support and encouragement.

Stage 2, intermediate clinicians: The focus is more on developing alternative ways to formulate case conceptualizations and integrate interventions into a comprehensive treatment approach. Professional helpers in this stage of development also begin to have an increased awareness of transference and countertransference dynamics. They are no longer so focused on techniques but understand more fully how their personal attributes and the therapeutic relationship that they facilitate contribute to the healing process of their clients.

Stage 3, advanced clinicians: The focus includes more attention to personal dynamics influencing the effectiveness of the treatment and the development of supervisory skills. It is important for supervision and consultation in attachment-focused therapy to monitor and manage the following three specific areas of risk:

1. There are very real risks of vicarious trauma (also referred to as secondary trauma, stress reactions, compassion fatigue) (Figley, 1995; Stamm, 1999) and burnout in this area of practice (see Chapter 10).

2. Therapy for clients with histories of trauma or serious behavioral disturbances is typically provided at a greater intensity than more routine outpatient therapy. As a result, there is a corresponding need for more frequent monitoring to assess risk and progress, as well as developing contingency plans as needed.

3. Countertransference reactions by the clinician may emanate from the clinician's own attachment or trauma history (Figley, 1995; Stamm, 1999) in reaction to attachment issues emerging

in treatment. Some clinicians may be motivated to work in the trauma field due to their personal experiences with trauma. Such experiences can provide clinicians with potent empathy for clients and a driving passion to help others heal. However, these clinicians can be effective in this work only if they have resolved their own trauma histories. Such resolution is critical to being able to maintain objectivity and prevent reactivity, so as to be able to competently support the client with a trauma history in the process of healing.

Similarly, some clinicians drawn to this work may have had their own experiences of insecure attachment as children. These experiences may provide a foundation for empathy and understanding of clients' struggles. However, it is similarly necessary that clinicians have resolved these experiences to achieve security in their attachment style. Secure (also referred to as autonomous) attachment in adults means that they have been able to integrate both positive and negative feelings and emotions related to experiences with significant others to be able to feel a range of emotions, while not losing their own perspective of the present. This is critical in being able to provide support and guidance within a secure base to clients in the exploration of their attachment wounds.

Clinicians with unresolved histories of insecurity in attachment are less able to provide corrective experiences of a secure base. Those with dismissing styles of attachment may be prone to minimizing clients' emotional distress or may be easily distracted by various tasks instead of focusing on the difficult emotions, and work too quickly to make things feel better without real resolution of the underlying feelings. Those with preoccupied styles may become too focused on building and maintaining a positive interaction with the clients to be able to challenge the clients, as needed, or may be too vulnerable to personalizing the clients' negative reactions in therapy. Those with disorganized or unresolved attachment styles may likely be suffering too acutely from their own fears and dysregulation to be able to provide attunement to a struggling client.

Supervision and consultation, at all levels of competency (e.g., beginning, intermediate, advanced), are important resources in helping the clinician maintain therapeutic objectivity and maximize effectiveness.

Competency

Competency in the provision of attachment-focused therapy is supported by good professional preparation across the following areas:

- Graduate education with course work in child development, developmental psychopathology, attachment theory and research, trauma theory and research, basic counseling skills, assessment skills, family systems theory, and related areas.

- Specialized training in applications of attachment and trauma theories and research in clinical work with children and youth exhibiting attachment-disordered behaviors.
- Supervised practice in the application of the above training in individual cases so that skills in assessment, treatment planning, intervention, crisis management, and evaluation can be developed and integrated into individual cases. Technical competency cannot be assessed except through assessment of actual practice. Therefore, audio and video taping of therapy sessions, or direct observation, are important supervisory tools in determining the competency of a clinician.
- Monitoring of the clinician's own mental health and stable functioning. This is sometimes called concern for the "person of the therapist" (Aponte & Carlsen, 2009). Trauma work can be especially challenging and requires a strong ability to set and maintain professional boundaries, as well as attend to self-care needs. A clinician whose own mental health and functioning are compromised faces significant risk that clinical competency will be compromised as well, regardless of the level of training or experience.

Although we support more training and experience in working with trauma and attachment difficulties in graduate school programs, we feel that junior members of the field should not work alone with clients and families struggling with major attachment challenges or complex trauma. Prelicensed and Stage 1 clinicians are understandably focused on perfecting techniques and intervention strategies and so much of the work with attachment and trauma issues involves the advanced abilities of establishing and facilitating the attunement and relationship process.

Monitoring the Field of Attachment Therapy

All clinicians providing therapy services to individuals and families with attachment challenges should be fully trained and licensed professionals (or should have authority to practice in their jurisdiction). They should have a full understanding of their professional code of ethics. Beyond the boundaries and standards identified by licensure, certification, and professional organizations, there are other organizations that attempt to regulate or promote ethical and careful attachment therapy protocols, such as the Association for Treatment and Training in the Attachment of Children (ATTACh) and the American Professional Society on the Abuse of Children (APSAC). ATTACh has a registration process for practicing therapists who agree to abide by ATTACh's principles of noncoercive and ethical treatment and who have approved educational and training experiences.

CHAPTER NINE

Ethical Considerations

The purpose of this chapter is to articulate the understanding that clinical work with clients enhances their well-being, while respecting their dignity and integrity. Clinicians need to be aware of the influential position they occupy with clients and therefore honor this trust by ensuring quality care and accuracy in representing the nature of the services provided, and protecting the client from potential harm or exploitation.

We seek to encourage and inspire high standards of ethical practice in the delivery of interventions that are focused on enhancing attachment and trauma resolution. The multidisciplinary membership of attachment therapy providers represents professionals from psychology, social work, mental health counseling, marriage and family therapists, nursing, and related human service professions. Therefore this section provides common themes across various professional codes of ethics (e.g., see National Association of Social Workers, American Psychological Association, American Counseling Association, and American Mental Health Counselors Association codes of ethics). This section is not intended to replace any member's professional code. Indeed, every clinician providing trauma and attachment treatment is expected to be familiar with, and adhere to, their respective professional association ethical code, applicable laws, and regulations of their jurisdiction, as these are the primary legal and ethical authority for any professional.

Competence

Clinicians are expected to provide services only within the boundaries of their competence, which is based on education, training, supervised experience, consultation, study, or other professional activity. Given the complexity of the work involved in providing attachment and trauma treatment to children and youths who are often severely disturbed, specialized training and supervision or consultation is required. Such training should include the following, at a minimum:

- Solid grounding in child development
- Attachment theory and research
- Trauma theory and research
- Differential diagnosis including psychiatric and developmental disorders
- Child and family therapies
- Best practices in trauma-informed care
- "Ethics Guidelines for Clinicians" (see Appendix A)
- Issues that affect the clinician (e.g., vicarious trauma, countertransference)

There are many approaches to attachment-focused treatment. We do not advocate or require adherence to any one model. Instead, we support integrated, multimodal approaches to treatment that begin with a comprehensive assessment, are appropriate to meet the comprehensive needs of the individual child and family, and are congruent with "Ethics Guidelines for Clinicians" (Appendix A). Further, we strongly believe that the greater the clinician's base in theory and practice, the more competent the clinician will be in choosing, adapting, monitoring, and modifying approaches to meet the needs of individual clients. Attachment-focused treatment is not a one-size-fits-all approach that can be learned and implemented by rote adherence to a set of interventions. We recognize that to become proficient in the use of promising attachment-focused approaches, clinicians require expanded initial training, supervised experience, consultation, and continuing education. We do not believe that independent study or attendance at a workshop alone are sufficient to establish proficiency in the delivery of these models.

We recognize that the field of attachment-focused therapy is relatively new and there are limited resources around the country to meet the needs of children. If a clinician accepts a case of this nature, or discovers these issues in the midst of ongoing therapy, and no appropriate referral sources are accessible to the client, the clinician assumes the responsibility of making reasonable efforts to develop competence in this area. This would require seeking additional training, supervision, or consultation, and providing informed consent to the family about both the limits of competency and the plans in place to support increased competency.

We also recognize that competency in this area of treatment is dependent on an ever-expanding body of professional knowledge derived from research in various areas (e.g., academic research, developmental psychopathology, trauma, neuroscience, clinical best practices, and practice guidelines). Therefore, all clinicians who practice attachment-focused treatments are expected to maintain competence through continued education, training, consultation, and additional supervision, as necessary.

The demanding nature of this work also means that competency is based on the clinician's stable and healthy functioning. We expect that clinicians will be aware of the risks of vicarious trauma and burnout, maintain healthy interpersonal relationships, monitor their own functioning, and set limits for themselves to ensure their own adequate functioning.

We expect that any clinician who assumes responsibility for consultation, supervision, or training has the necessary knowledge, skills, and experience to ensure that the service is within the clinician's scope of competency.

Informed Consent

The clinician has a duty to provide information to both the child and family in clear and understandable language, including the following:

- The purpose of services
- Approaches to be used
- Limits of proposed services
- Risks and benefits of approaches
- Reasonable alternatives
- Time frames
- Costs
- The voluntary nature of the agreement (i.e., right to refuse treatment and withdraw from treatment)
- Limits of confidentiality

The provision of informed consent is not a one-time event; rather, it is an ongoing process in which the clinician seeks to ensure, at every step of treatment, that the client understands and accepts the terms, conditions, and expectations of the service. Throughout the process of informed consent, the child and caregivers must be provided sufficient opportunity to ask questions and get answers regarding their treatment. Good informed consent is present in therapeutic relationships, in which the clients trust the clinician enough to voice questions and concerns, and the clinician is sensitive to the client's verbal and nonverbal cues.

Informed consent must be documented in writing. The written consent form should include a clear time frame and the elements outlined above. While caregivers have the legal right to consent to treatment for their minor children, the clinician should be apprised of relevant state laws that determine the age of consent for minor children within the respective jurisdiction.

Obtaining informed consent from children in this form of treatment is especially challenging. Often these children present with serious behavior problems that pose significant, if not imminent, risk to self and others. In circumstances such as these, the initial focus of treatment may be ensuring safety for all. Obtaining informed consent from the child may not be fully possible, as the child may initially require more directive approaches to interventions that ensure safety. For example, containment, hospitalization, or other highly structured interventions may be necessary.

We assert that while ensuring safety may be therapeutic, this process is not the same as the treatment addressed in this book. Clinicians' and caregivers' continuing focus on the child's compliance, beyond immediate serious safety concerns, poses very real risk of undermining the development of a secure attachment base. Effective attachment-focused treatment seeks to create safety to help the child access underlying fears and distorted beliefs about self and others, so that they can be resolved in the context of nurturing support in the present.

We recommend, even as safety measures are implemented, that the clinician and caregivers explain the intentions of, and the criteria for, the measures being employed. They could say, for example, "We will not let you hurt us or yourself. Our job is to keep everyone safe. It is okay to be mad, but it is not okay to hit others when you are. You seem to be unable to control that right now, so we are going to hold you until you calm down. When we feel the tension in your arms relax, we will let go. We will let you up when we see that you can move without hitting or kicking anyone." This is different from methods of imposing safety measures, such as restraint, without explaining the intent of the measures. To handle it in that way is to risk reinforcing for the child that the adult is simply trying to control or, worse, hurt the child.

One of the special challenges in providing attachment-focused treatment is that children with attachment difficulties present with profound resistance and seeming inability to form trusting relationships. These relational difficulties at the core of the disturbed functioning derive from defensive responses the child developed to survive and cope with traumatic experiences. Therefore, the establishment of a therapeutic relationship becomes more of a treatment goal than an early prerequisite for treatment. This challenge does not negate the need for informed consent from the child. Indeed, treatment that does not sensitively attend to the child's fears and conditioned emotional responses, while making ongoing attempts to build a therapeutic alliance, may impede the development of the secure attachment base or, worse, risk retraumatizing the child. It is important to provide a developmentally appropriate rationale of treatment for the child, develop specific goals for all parties (caregivers and child), and provide clear explanations of the components of treatment.

There are a number of ways to engage the family and child in developing a treatment contract and informed consent. Again, the clinician's own approach and style, as well as the unique needs of the child and family, will determine the most appropriate way to develop informed consent.

Sometimes simple approaches, such as using the Sentence Completion Form during assessment, can help generate a discussion of issues related to the need for treatment. In the following example, the child completes the sentence and the caregivers and clinician review the answers with the child, discussing how treatment can help. For instance, a child may write such things as:

- Mother and I always fight about_____.
- My father thinks I _____.
- Most kids don't like me because _____.
- The thing that most scares me is _____.
- Teachers are mean to me when _____.

The ensuing family discussion may lead the child to want these things to be different, and to agree to work toward that end. The family and clinician can discuss how treatment may be helpful, and in so doing may begin to secure the child's informed consent and cooperation.

Other clinicians may see the development of informed consent as an opportunity to also provide some important psychoeducation about the process. In this case, a more detailed description of the treatment would be provided by the clinician. The following is sample script of a rationale for a younger child. (Note: This is an example only. It is not prescriptive of what should be said. Every clinician will make adaptations based on their own approach and style, as well as the developmental age and individual needs of the child and family).

Many kids think when they come to counseling that it is because they are bad or that their parents are just mad. We know that parents come to counseling with their kids when they want to make their families happier, when they want their children's hearts to be able to feel good things. We think that when [refer to trauma at the level of detail that fits the child's capacity to manage the material] happened to you when you were little, you were probably feeling very scared and alone. You might have thought that it was your fault or maybe even that no one loved you.

Now you are with this mom and dad and they love you very much. But they can see that it is hard for you to let the love inside. It looks like your heart is still full of hurt and scared and mad. When those feelings are big and strong, they can push the good feelings of love and happiness away. Sometimes when those feelings are big and strong they come out in "behaviors." Your parents feels sad then, because they know you are a good kid and they want you to know you are loved, good, and safe. I want to help you learn to let those good feelings in and let those feelings that hurt go away.

I want to help you and your mom and dad to learn to love each other and help each other. That will mean learning about how both of you feel and why, practicing ways to feel safe together, and learning new ways to handle feelings. And your parents also have things to learn to do differently. They want to be better parents to you. Lots of things will be fun. Some things might be harder, but we will help you when it is hard. Like when kids fall down and scrape their knees. Good parents help clean the hurt up so it can heal. Sometimes it hurts a little when Mom or Dad puts medicine on it or washes it. But the hurt doesn't last long and it helps the knee heal faster. Good moms and dads help their kids feel better so the kid knows he isn't alone.

A rationale for an older child might be something like this:

Lots of kids think when their parents bring them to counseling that they are bad or their parents are just mad. I don't think that. I know that parents who come to this kind of counseling want their kid's heart to heal from the hurts that happened. I know that they want to become better parents. I have helped lots of families and kids who have had hard things happen to them, like when [describe relevant trauma example] happened to you. Most kids, when they come here, don't want to be here. They have a hard time trusting other people, and why shouldn't they? They have been hurt before.

I understand you might not feel like you can trust me. I would like to earn your trust, but I know that will take time. Most of all, I want you to learn to be able to trust your parents, so we may work on why things like [examples of presenting behaviors] are happening. And your parents know that they also need to work on things like [examples of what they want to do differently, such as not yell]. I know from other kids that sometimes the hurt, anger, fear, and sadness come out in behaviors. I also know from other kids that sometimes kids think they are bad or not worthy of love, based on what happened to them in the past. Many times, those things are really not true after all, but until a kid can figure that out, he will still act as if they are. I would like to help you figure out how to identify and make sense of your feelings about the past, and learn safer ways to handle them. Lots of times when kids have gone through really hard things, their bodies, and even their minds, can keep reacting like the old stuff is still happening. They have forgotten they actually survived. This can feel kind of scary and even crazy sometimes, but it isn't crazy at all. The way your body learned to react allowed you to survive, and that's a good thing. It is only a bad thing when it keeps you from being able to really live in the present, open to new things and new relationships.

I also want to help you and your parents figure out how to live together, help each other, and trust each other more. No matter how old we get, or where we go in our lives, we all need to know we belong, and that there is someone who will always be there for us.

Here is a short description of how I work to help people with these things. [Give description.] We will probably start with [first item]. As we go along I will try to let you know why I am doing certain things, and I hope you will get to where you can trust me enough to ask questions or share what you really think and feel. Sometimes what we do together will seem easy. Sometimes it may be hard for you, and sometimes hard for your parents. My job is to make sure that it isn't ever too hard for any of you, so I will be paying close attention to trying to figure out how you feel, and how your parents feel about things as we go along. If you can't tell me that in words, then I have to try to figure it out by how your face and/or body look, or how you act when someone asks you something. That is harder to do, and I might get it wrong sometimes. If I do, I'll notice that and apologize, and try to figure out how to help you and your parents talk about the problem.

My job is kind of like a coach. I know some things that help people deal better with feelings and behaviors, but I can't do the work for the person. I will try to show or explain, then help you practice, so you can do it better in real life. Sometimes children don't want to practice, or think it is too hard, or feel like they will be laughed at if they try. A good coach will push a little bit, but only when the coach believes the player can do it, and that it will help the player become even better. A good coach doesn't push too hard, or push before people are really ready.

It took a long time for your feelings, thoughts, and behaviors to develop, so it will take some time for us to help them change. It has also taken a long time for your parents to develop how they feel, think, and act. Sometimes kids worry that they will have to go to counseling forever, but that isn't how it works. We will work on improving how you all communicate and solve problems together. You and your parents will learn some new skills that will hopefully make your life together better for all of you. It will take us working together to be able to understand what really needs to change. Therapy isn't just about stopping certain behaviors. Real change comes when kids feel better about themselves and can really trust their parents to help them no matter what. That's when we will know therapy is done. It will probably take us at least [time estimate], but it could be longer or shorter depending on how well we work together.

The examples above would not be provided all at one time, but rather offered in segments over time as appropriate. Again, this is provided for illustrative purposes only and would be adapted to the clinician's approach and style, as well as the individual needs of the child and family.

Assessment and Professional Opinions

The complexity inherent in the presentation of children and families with attachment disturbances necessitates a comprehensive assessment (see Chapter 5). Assessment tools and processes should be based on best practice standards. Assessment instruments should have established validity and reliability for use with the client population being assessed. Symptom checklists are appropriate only as an initial screening tool and should not be the basis of a diagnosis.

It is important for the clinician to understand the special requirements of providing service within an emerging field of practice. Clinicians are often called upon to provide professional opinions about assessment, prognosis, and treatment recommendations for clients. While all clinicians need to take into full account the limits and uncertainties of present clinical knowledge and techniques, in making public statements or rendering professional opinions, this is especially true for clinicians who provide attachment-focused treatment.

Privacy and Confidentiality

Ensuring the protection of clients' privacy is a primary responsibility of all clinicians. The right to privacy belongs to both the child and family, and therefore they must be informed of both the right to confidentiality and the limits of such a right. Disclosures of confidential information must be based on appropriately executed consents by the child and/or legal guardian.

Limitations to privacy and confidentiality include the clinician's mandated legal responsibility to report child abuse and, in some jurisdictions, requirements to disclose information to authorities concerning parties involved in a formal investigation of child abuse. Clinicians should be familiar and comply with the laws and regulations of their respective jurisdictions and regulations governing other reporting responsibilities arising from the duty to warn or protect. Other limitations to privacy and confidentiality involve the rights of insurance providers to review records of services paid for by the insurance carrier. Clinicians should include any limitation to privacy and confidentiality in the written consent to treatment, or client's rights and responsibilities form.

When families are involved in treatment, the clinician must, from the onset of treatment, clarify expectations regarding each individual's rights to privacy. Clinicians should know their jurisdiction's laws and regulations regarding the age at which children can independently access mental health treatment and ensure that reasonable steps are taken to conform to them when obtaining informed consent. Clinicians should also be aware of how their jurisdiction handles parental access to records concerning minor children, especially in cases of divorce, separation, disputed custody, termination of parental rights proceedings, and other situations in which custody and right to consent are at issue.

Clinicians must ensure that they do not disclose identifying information during consultations, training, or teaching, unless they have obtained specific consent for use of client information in that format. Clinicians must obtain specific consent for the audio or video taping of sessions with clients, and additional consent if those recordings are to be used for training or teaching purposes. The handling, storage, and destruction of audio and video tapes must also be explained.

Conflicts of Interest and Dual or Multiple Relationships

Conflicts of interest occur when the clinician and client have dual relationships (e.g., counseling and another relationship such as business or social), or in situations in which the client's needs may be at odds with those of the clinician (e.g., the client giving a story to the media about progress in treatment might help the clinician's practice or communicate important information about treatment, but at the expense of the client revealing personal information that the client might later regret becoming public knowledge). It is the clinician's duty to protect the client. Any situation or relationship that interferes with the clinician's exercise of objective professional judgment is a conflict of interest. The client's needs should prevail in such situations.

Dual or multiple relationships represent a special type of conflict of interest. These relationships should be avoided, if at all possible, so that the clinician is able to maintain clear professional boundaries with, and objective decision making about, the child and family. In smaller communities it may be impossible to avoid dual or multiple relationships when there are fewer clinicians and more chances to come in contact with others. In these cases, it is important that the clinician assume the responsibility of obtaining informed consent from the child and caregivers, seeking consultation, and documenting efforts to delineate clear boundaries and expectations.

The risk of dual relationships is particularly common when working with trauma and attachment challenges because caregivers and clinicians touched by these issues may attend some of the same conferences. Moreover, the limited support network that may exist in many communities, coupled with criticism from other potential supports in the community, may result in clinicians and caregivers feeling alienated from others who do not understand or support their efforts. While collaboration and alignment of the caregiver and clinician within the therapeutic relationship is a benefit to the treatment, the clinician must remain on guard against a breakdown in healthy professional boundaries, which can compromise the clinician's judgment or effectiveness.

Physical Contact With Clients

Attachment-focused interventions may involve the use of touch. Clinicians are encouraged to follow the advice provided in the National Association of Social Workers (1999) Code of Ethics or the appropriate section of their professional association's code of ethics, and "not engage in physical contact when there is a possibility of psychological harm to the client as a result of the contact (such as cradling or caressing clients). Social workers who engage in appropriate physical contact with clients are responsible for setting clear, appropriate, and culturally sensitive boundaries that govern such physical contact" (NASW, 1999, Section 1.10, Physical Contact).

The use of physical contact within attachment-focused treatment may be important for purposes of resolving conditioned fear reactions to emotional or physical closeness, as well as for providing comfort and soothing to a child. Appropriate (i.e., sensitive and nonabusive) physical contact may be used in treatment but is not required in attachment-focused therapy. Such contact, if used, must be carefully dosed so that the child has the opportunity to gradually access and overcome fears of contact in a manner that is developmentally appropriate. Requiring physical contact on the adult's terms, except in circumstances of danger (e.g., utilizing restraint on a child who is out of control), is countertherapeutic and may risk retraumatizing the child.

Documentation and Access to Records

All services provided should be documented in a timely and accurate manner, and the records maintained in a confidential location. The client or guardian should be granted reasonable right to review the records and obtain copies of them as allowed by law.

The documentation should reflect the services provided, rationale for services, and specific recommendations. This will facilitate the delivery of services as well as ensuring continuity of service should the case be referred to another provider. Given the controversy that often surrounds attachment-focused treatment, and highly publicized cases of child abuse involving adopted or foster children, where the caregiver is alleged to be following "attachment therapy" practices, the clinician is encouraged to be clear when documenting the rationale for interventions, the training or advice given to caregivers, and the ongoing assessment of safety concerns.

Referrals

The clinician assumes responsibility to provide information and assistance to the client when other professionals have specialized knowledge or expertise that is needed by the client. Should the clinician determine that the treatment being provided is not effective, or the client is not making progress, referral to another clinician may be prudent.

We strongly recommend that referrals be made only to clinicians who are known to use practice protocols that are safe and ethical and who have credentials and training that meet the guidelines in this book. If there is no qualified clinician in the local area, then the treating clinician should make a reasonable effort to ensure that referrals are made in a manner that helps the client have multiple resources from which to choose, evaluate the potential referral sources, and seek consultation as needed.

Termination

The clinician shall periodically collaborate with the client and family to assess progress toward treatment goals and termination criteria. If the clinician and family agree on readiness for termination, then a planned termination and aftercare plan can be mutually developed. However, if the clinician and family disagree about the child and family's readiness for termination, the clinician should document these concerns and inform the family in writing of the basis for the decision, and any recommendations for postdischarge follow-up.

The clinician should ensure that a plan is in place to refer a child and family if treatment is ineffective, the child is not making progress, or the needs of the child or family exceed the scope of competency of the clinician. Given the complexity of many cases involving attachment-related trauma, it is especially important that the clinician not abandon the family, but rather provide active support, assistance, and advocacy in helping the family secure the appropriate level of care or other resource for treatment.

Advertising, Endorsements, and Public Statements

Clinicians who serve families of children with histories of attachment-related trauma are likely to encounter desperate caregivers who are vulnerable to undue influence and promises (implied or otherwise), due to the extreme crises in which the families often find themselves. Therefore, it is important that clinicians exercise a high degree of professional discretion in how they promote their work, so that caregivers encounter compassionate, helpful, and optimistic, but ultimately objective, resources in the decision-making process concerning treatment for their children.

Clinicians should not solicit testimonial endorsements from current clients (including requesting to use a prior statement as a testimonial endorsement) or from any past clients who, because of their particular circumstances, are vulnerable to undue influence and may be unable to give true informed consent to the use of such testimonials. Clinicians are expected to ensure that advertisements and public statements about their practice, credentials, education, experience, and so on are accurate. It is considered unethical in most professional codes of ethics to offer guarantees of treatment effectiveness.

Clinicians serve an important role in public education and advocacy concerning the needs of children with attachment-related trauma. It is important that clinicians ensure that their statements are:

- Based on professional knowledge, training, and experience
- In accordance with current scientific research and theory
- Otherwise consistent with professional ethical obligations

Impaired Professionals

Clinicians have a duty to monitor themselves as they work in this area. Vicarious trauma, secondary traumatic stress, compassion fatigue, and burnout are all occupational hazards. Countertransference (e.g., negative feelings toward angry caregivers, child welfare systems and personnel, community members who blame caregivers, and the child who may actively reject efforts of help) is another occupational hazard that requires recognition, attention, prevention, and intervention, as necessary. It is important that clinicians maintain networks for consultation or supervision so that assistance can be obtained, as needed, in processing feelings, developing intervention plans, and monitoring functioning. Clinicians whose objectivity or capacity to provide corrective experiences of sensitive and attuned support is affected in a particular case should seek an appropriate referral for the client.

If a clinician has reason to suspect that another clinician's ability to function effectively is impaired, that clinician should first reach out to the colleague to see if an informal discussion can guide the colleague toward resolving issues that may be negatively impacting that clinician's ability to practice. If such informal efforts are not successful, and ongoing concerns about potential client harm exist, then further steps should be taken as governed by the clinician's professional association and licensing body.

CHAPTER TEN

Vicarious Trauma & Clinician Self-Care

A willingness to entertain the possibility that bad or harmful and even horrible and horrific experiences can happen to children is essential for the clinician to be able to attend to the indicators of abuse and neglect. The courage to confront these realities and work toward resolution is necessary for attachment-focused therapy to be effective. The clinician's ability and willingness to ask about abuse and neglect gives children permission to talk about the abuse. The clinician's ability to explore experiences related to abuse and neglect, including any pleasurable feelings associated with sexual abuse, for example, allows children to evaluate and correct any distortions and inaccurate perceptions they may have about acceptable or unacceptable behavior. Through this exploration, children also learn to manage their fear, anxiety, sense of powerlessness, and anger (U.S. DHHS, 1994).

To be effective, therapists must possess certain traits or characteristics. The capacity to tolerate strong affect without becoming dysregulated is essential. Therapists must be comfortable with ambiguity. To be able to be curious and explore various meanings, therapists must not rush to judgment and assume that their understanding of a situation is a fact. Therapists must have a reasonably well-developed reflective function, be insightful, and have some understanding of their own patterns of attachment.

While openness and willingness to explore traumatic material with multiple clients in repeated sessions are necessary for this work, they also pose a very real risk of secondary traumatic stress reactions in the clinician. Understanding and being able to better proactively manage this reaction are important to the clinician's well-being, functioning, and retention in the field.

It is also important to recognize that caregivers are vulnerable to feelings of secondary traumatic stress, vicarious trauma, or compassion fatigue as they attempt to create attuned connections with a traumatized child. Consequently, clinicians must simultaneously monitor their own reactions while sensitively trying to gauge those of caregivers. In this way, clinicians can better ensure that adults are able to reliably provide sensitive and attuned responses to the child. If caregiver needs in this respect are significant, then they should be addressed before proceeding with additional attachment-focused therapy with the child. The following sections should be considered to apply to both clinicians and caregivers. Where clinicians might be recommended to seek supervision or consultation, caregivers might be recommended to explore difficulties with the therapist to address these issues.

Occupational Hazards

Vicarious trauma, secondary traumatic stress, and *compassion fatigue* are terms that are often used interchangeably to describe the impact of acute responses to bearing witness to stories of maltreatment, loss, and other trauma. These reactions can come on suddenly if the exposure to traumatic content is significant.

Vicarious trauma has been called the transformation of the clinician's inner experience as a result of empathic engagement with survivors of trauma and the specific traumatic material they share (Figley, 1999; Phillips, 2004). This is contrasted to burnout, which is the response that tends to develop over time in response to the external factors associated with conditions of one's job (e.g., lack of supervision or support, heavy caseloads, unsafe work environment, productivity pressures).

Signs and symptoms of secondary traumatic stress are nearly identical to those of PTSD. In addition, these symptoms can have a pervasive impact on clinicians' views of themselves and the world, and their belief systems, interpersonal relationships, and functioning in various areas. The result can be a serious disruption of clinicians' sense of emotional vitality, trust, and hope.

The clinician might respond with a myriad of possible reactions (see next section). In addition, the clinician might experience intense emotions of helplessness, anger, and shame. The shame may derive from what has been termed "witness guilt" (Herman, 1992). Without an understanding of these reactions, clinicians will likely be caught off-guard and may personalize the feelings (e.g., "What is wrong with me?" "I must not be a competent clinician"). However, by understanding these reactions, the clinician can be alert to signs of such responses and be better prepared to manage them appropriately.

The goal is to recognize the need for, and seek, appropriate self-care strategies instead of pathologizing this inevitable reaction to empathic attunement (McCann & Pearlman, 1990). The clinician's reactions are not in and of themselves either positive or negative; rather they can offer windows of opportunity for insight and compassion (Ziegler & McEvoy, 2000).

Signs and Symptoms of Distress

The following factors may indicate distress in clinicians or caregivers:

- Physiological (e.g., hyperarousal, sleep disturbance)
- Somatic (e.g., physical complaints, increased illness)
- Emotional (e.g., anxiety, depression, irritability, anger)
- Behavioral (e.g., overworking, changes in eating, impaired judgment, preoccupation)
- Interpersonal (e.g., withdrawal, isolation, displaced anger)
- Spiritual (e.g., loss of faith, generalized anger, loss of sense of purpose)

Self-Assessment of Countertransference Reactions

Attunement and reflective capacity require the clinician to be emotionally and psychologically present and to bear witness to often severe emotional suffering in clients. This engagement requires the clinician to enter into the intersubjective sharing of experience and affect.

Posttraumatic responses in the clinician can hamper the ability to provide attuned responses to the child and caregiver, as well as impede the development of a "holding environment," in which there is safety and support necessary for resolution of the traumatic memories and conditioned reactions.

The clinician must be attentive to managing countertransference reactions. Countertransference reactions include the clinician's conscious and unconscious responses and feelings, as well as verbal and nonverbal reactions to interactions with the child and family that are grounded in the clinician's past and that are not a direct response to the present. These various reactions can be based on the clinician's theoretical perspective, training, and experience, as well as the clinician's own person (e.g., age, gender, marital status, race, culture), personality, history, and needs.

The clinician has a duty to monitor self-functioning and attend to self-care needs. The following are steps toward monitoring one's professional and personal functioning:

- Supervision or consultation
- Boundary maintenance and personal limit setting
- Managing cases within scope of competency
- Referral of cases when unable to maintain objectivity

Assessment of countertransference reactions (Phillips, 2004, pp. 213–215) can include the following considerations of one's personal responses:

- What are the conscious feelings elicited by work with this client?
- What are the associations made during sessions?
- Are these thoughts and feelings familiar, unusual, more extreme than usual, appropriate to the situation, persistent, or anxiety producing?

- Are these feelings and thoughts outside of awareness, appearing instead in dreams, fantasies, bodily sensations, or behavior?
- Are the reactions to the traumatic material itself, the client's response to symptoms, family dynamics, or clinician factors (e.g., history, coping, current stressors)?
- Are there indications of defensive responses (e.g., distractibility, overdistancing, rigid neutrality, avoidance, intellectual response to the events but not the person, verbalizing concrete reassurances without emotion)?

Supervision and Consultation

There are significant differences between supervision and consultation. In supervision, the supervisor has more power than the supervisee and can direct the supervisee's practice. In consultation, the consultant and consultee are more equal. The consultee can accept or reject the consultant's suggestions. The supervisee has some obligation to accept the supervisor's suggestions.

Supervision and consultation are important in providing assistance to the clinician in exploration of countertransference responses and reactions. Supervision and consultation provide support from a professional resource, who may have greater objectivity and perhaps greater experience and training. Supervision and consultation can be helpful in the following:

- Identifying and clarifying which reactions and dynamics originate in the client versus the clinician
- Reconsidering the conceptualization of the case to be able to integrate new perspectives
- Identifying alternative treatment approaches or reinforcing existing ones
- Evaluating the progress in therapy to develop appropriate plans

Treating attachment disorders and trauma can be triggering to clinicians if they do not have a clear understanding and acceptance of their particular attachment patterns. The use of supervision or consultation to complete an attachment history will increase awareness and clinicians' ability to reflect and respond therapeutically to their clients.

The process of supervision and consultation may also provide helpful perspectives for the clinician to identify, reflect on, and understand what is happening in the therapy itself. This can be especially true if the clinician's countertransference has roots in the client's unconscious reactions or traumatic memories that cannot be verbally processed. When these circumstances arise in therapy, the client may utilize an unconscious defense of projective identification. Simply put, this is a process of evoking in others experiences that the person is unable to claim (Wallin, 2007). This can give rise to what is called a "parallel process" (McNeill & Worthen,

1989) in which the dynamics within the supervisory relationship between the clinician and supervisor can begin to mirror the dynamics between the client and clinician in the therapy itself. Identification of this process can be very helpful in enhancing the clinician's empathy for what the client may be feeling and may be unable to identify and express.

Other Supports for Maintaining Balance

The clinician may need to pay attention to healthy lifestyle patterns (sleep, rest, relaxation, diet) since the clinician's physical health is important in managing stress effectively. Trauma work can be stressful and draining for both the client and clinician. The clinician needs to model this area of self-care for the client. It is important for the clinician to maintain a healthy balance between work and personal life spaces.

Trauma therapy can be extremely draining as well as rewarding. Clinicians faced with families in desperate situations are vulnerable to becoming overinvolved in trying to help. Trauma clinicians need to pay close attention to issues of balance in their lives. It is a truism of life that it is very difficult to give what one does not have. But it is equally important to remember that security in attachment is also fostered through the mutual sharing and intensification of positive affect between the child and caregiver (Schore, 1994). It can be difficult, if not impossible, to support families in finding joy, excitement, pride, and so on, if the clinician cannot model and attune to these positive emotions. Similarly, families struggling with serious behavior problems in the child need to learn to celebrate small steps and find pleasure in life. Attunement is a two-way street and emotions can be contagious. The clinician can feel with the client, and the client can feel with the clinician. Clinicians who maintain balance in their personal lives are better able to provide supports for a range of emotional experience within the therapy itself.

Balancing caseloads is another way clinicians can take care of themselves. The emotional and psychological demands of providing constant attunement to wounded and seriously disturbed children and their desperate caregivers can be overwhelming. Clinicians who balance their caseloads in terms of level of severity, types of presenting issues, and so on, may find these limits provide a more manageable self-protective structure for their clinical work and prevent or lessen the risk of burnout and other forms of traumatic stress.

Clinicians may also benefit from limiting exposure to traumatic or violent material (e.g., news, movies, TV). Modern media is full of graphic traumatic material, material that is traumatic. The risk to the clinician is in either being overwhelmed or becoming desensitized to traumatic material. Either response will interfere with effective attunement with a traumatized client. Therefore, many clinicians find that limiting such exposure, especially when feeling vulnerable to traumatic stress, burnout, or stress, is a helpful prevention method.

In a parallel to the work of therapy, specific attention to trying to make sense of experience can also be helpful in resolving traumatic feelings and reactions. Clinicians, just like the traumatized client, need to find ways to make sense of experience constructively. Saakvitne and Pearlman (1995) identified five need areas as particularly susceptible to the effects of psychological trauma: safety, trust, esteem, intimacy, and control. They are relevant areas of vulnerability for trauma clinicians as well as for survivors. These needs, coupled with the associated beliefs within each area, influence all relationships, including the therapeutic relationship. Therefore, clinicians' own vulnerabilities can have a major impact upon both personal and professional relationships.

Self-care strategies aimed at restoring a sense of connection with others help to counter the isolation that can mark secondary traumatic stress. Moreover, these strategies can provide a testing ground for schemas that have been disrupted through the trauma work. The importance of professional and personal connection is illustrated by the trauma clinician sample: over two thirds found it helpful to attend workshops, talk with colleagues between sessions, and discuss cases informally; and in the personal realm, to socialize and spend time with family and close friends.

Similarly, the process of transforming victim to survivor through action and advocacy can be helpful to clinicians as well. Many clinicians working with trauma find help in managing their reactions to clients' trauma by becoming involved in advocacy issues such as the prevention of child abuse or domestic violence. Others work to support foster parents or become mentors for at-risk children. Others become involved in humanitarian efforts to support orphanages or social justice causes. In this way, they transform their concern for child victims into efforts to protect other children and prevent future trauma. This can be another powerful way to make meaning of the trauma by turning awareness into action.

Ethics Guidelines for Clinicians

Here we'd like to set guidelines and standards for ethically and clinically appropriate treatment for children with attachment problems. This document is intended to provide guidance to parents and therapists so that they avoid the use of coercive techniques. We believe that a central focus of treatment for children with attachment problems is to create an environment in which the family can safely work to integrate previously unmanageable information and emotions related to early traumatic experiences with caregivers.* Those posttraumatic emotional reactions interfere with the development of healthy relationships and may have serious negative effects on a child's overall development.

In recent years, several organizations have issued statements regarding treatment for children with attachment disorders. We concur with the American Psychiatric Association's position statement on reactive attachment disorder that "there is a strong clinical consensus that coercive therapies are contraindicated in this disorder" (2002, p. 1). We also concur with the American Academy of Child and Adolescent Psychiatry (2003), "Practice Parameter for the Assessment and Treatment of Children and Adolescents with Reactive Attachment Disorder of Infancy and Early Childhood." In addition, we support the recommendations in the "Report of the APSAC Task Force on Attachment Therapy, Reactive Attachment Disorder, and Attachment Problems" (Chaffin et al., 2006).

A child with a serious infection may need an injection to promote healing. Young children react to shots with predictable resistance and emotional distress.

*In this document, *treatment* refers to both psychotherapy and parenting.

Nonetheless, parents persist due to the overriding concern for the child's long-term health. Nurturing parents use this as an opportunity to provide comfort and to make meaning of the experience.

Decision-Making Process: Is It Coercive?

Where does appropriate therapeutic confrontation end and coercion begin? In beginning to answer this question, we believe that lists of dos and don'ts, while useful, are inadequate. Too many unique situations are encountered in a therapeutic setting, and no list can ever be complete or sufficient. Rather, we think it useful to provide therapists and caretakers with principles and guidelines.

It is our thinking that the field of child treatment in general, and practitioners of attachment-based treatments, specifically, would benefit from a greater understanding of what interventions and techniques constitute coercion and how this differs from the use of appropriate therapeutic confrontation or direction. It is one thing to oppose the use of coercion in treatment; it is quite another to more specifically articulate its definition.

In many instances, the distinction between appropriate therapeutic confrontation and coercion is clear. One can also draw clear guidance from legal standards that define child abuse and neglect or ethical standards that seek to ensure the safety of the client. In addition, various professional codes of ethics, such as those of the National Association of Social Workers and the American Psychological Association, provide guidance and standards. Where such "bright white line" distinctions end, one enters the gray area of potential harm where there are no clear guides for actions. In these cases, a framework for ethical decision making should be the guide. Without clear standards of appropriate behavior or intervention, one must look to how research or other accepted standards can be applied to the situation. There are three important principles to consider:

1. Is the approach principled; is it grounded in ethical values?
2. Is the approach reasoned; is it based on valid rationales? Is the approach grounded in relevant research and theory?
3. Is the approach generalizable; can it be applied to other situations (instead of being immediately expedient for this individual circumstance)?

These principles need to guide the consideration of what is and is not coercion in any situation that falls into a gray area. Ethical decision making in gray areas is an ongoing process of thoughtful consideration, development of a plan, and continuing review and modification of the plan as needed.

For example, some have suggested that touch has no place in therapy, but we believe that affectionate, voluntary touch can offer support, encouragement, and safety for a child. To determine the appropriate parameters for the use of touch we would consider whether:

1. It is grounded in ethical values and carried out in a way that is respectful of the child's development and history.
2. It is grounded in valid rationales in that there is significant research indicating the value of nurturing touch in physiological regulation and neurological development (Hofer, 1984; Field, Healy, & Goldstein, 1990; Schore, 2001).
3. It is a practice widely used by adults with children.

In contrast, we do not believe that it is appropriate for parents or therapists to hold a child forcibly, while insisting on emotional engagement on the adult's terms. For example, forcibly holding the child and demanding eye contact or emotional sharing is premised on the adult's expectations and is not responsive to the child's state (e.g., shame, terror). This technique is not supported because:

1. It is a violation of the child's dignity and autonomy.
2. It intentionally causes dysregulation and may retraumatize the child. Nor is there any generally accepted theory that would support such an intervention.
3. It is not a practice generally used with children.

In such complex situations it is helpful to consider the interaction of other principles that may guide decision making. These would include the consideration of the interplay among the parent's or therapist's behavior and intentions; the child's perceptions and experience; power differentials in the relationship; and the nature and quality of the relationship between the persons involved. This approach leads to a focus on the effects of the parent's or therapist's actions on the child and on the child's experience of the action. In effect, we are suggesting that consideration of the intersubjective experience is of primary concern (Becker-Weidman, 2010b).

Critical Concepts

Decision making in complex treatment situations with the population of children damaged by chronic, early maltreatment within a caregiving relationship involves the consideration of a number of critical concepts and how the concepts apply to specific individuals and situations. Practitioners and parents would do well to have a working knowledge of these critical concepts, which are described in the following sections.

Regulation and Dysregulation

An important concept is regulation versus dysregulation of emotions, impulses, behavior, and physical states. Security provides children with opportunities to develop the capacity for regulation. Lack of sustained regulation of the developing child by an attuned caregiver puts the child at risk of inadequate development of the capacity to regulate physical, psychological, cognitive, and emotional states (Cook et al., 2003). Research has shown that children learn best during times when they are emotionally, physically, and psychologically regulated (e.g., when the child is in a calm, receptive state; Schore, 2001). It is important to support and promote children's regulation during interventions. If a child becomes dysregulated, attempts should be made immediately and directly to restore regulation as soon as possible (e.g., a parent might actively assist the child in regaining a calm, receptive state by soothing the child and making sense of the experience).

Dysregulation occurs when the developing child's capacities for managing physiological, emotional, cognitive, sensory, behavioral, or interpersonal functioning are overwhelmed by distress to the extent that the child is unable to regain equilibrium independently. Dysregulation should never be a goal of an intervention; indeed, it may undermine other progress by reinforcing the child's internal working model that others are hurtful, untrustworthy, and neglectful. Sometimes children with disorders of attachment and histories of trauma become dysregulated and respond with angry or aggressive behaviors that require safety interventions that are perceived as more forceful than empathic. In situations where safety is threatened and less intrusive approaches have been tried and failed, it may become necessary to use restraint including physical holding to maintain safety. In these special situations, the use of force should be terminated as soon as possible, and efforts made to repair the break in the relationship that results from its use. In these instances, it is important to note, the restraint is not a therapeutic intervention. The restraint is performed solely to protect persons or property from significant damage. Given that children with histories of trauma may misperceive the actions of others as intentionally hurtful, it is critically important that the adults help the child make meaning of such experiences (e.g., "We are keeping you safe when you are out of control and trying to hurt yourself or others" to counter the child's likely perception, "They will hurt me or I am bad").

When dysregulation does occur during treatment, interventions must be incorporated that will assist the child in regaining regulation and managing the distress. This concept is also called *interactive repair* (Tronick & Gianino, 1986). When the child responds with discomfort and distress, the therapist or parent uses empathy and emotional support to help regulate the child's affect so that the child does not move into dysregulation. While experiencing discomfort and distress, the child maintains regulation of affect, cognition, and behavior. However, when a child shows terror, rage, or dissociative features, indicating movement into dysregulation, the child requires help to regain a calm receptive state. So, for example, in a therapeutic situation a child may willingly discuss an event that is upsetting and increases the child's discomfort and distress. However, if the child then indicates a desire to stop, yet this signal is ignored by the therapist or parent, so that the child is forced to continue, this is coercive. This does not mean that the therapist or parent join with the child in avoidance of this painful material. Instead it means that they stay attuned to the child's needs and work to "dose" the exposure to this material in a way that supports the child's ability to process and integrate the information. For example, they may say something like, "Okay, sure, we can stop now and come back to this later." This gradual consolidation of the material within the context of a helpful, sensitive relationship promotes a greater sense of security in the child, which in turn facilitates greater security in attachment. As the child comes to experience the helpful and healing aspects of exploring a painful past (as integration is achieved), the child will become more willing and able to deepen the exploration in the future (Becker-Weidman, 2010b). The child will recognize that they are discussing disturbing and painful experiences because it is helpful. As the child experiences the positive intentions of the caregiver and therapist, the child's negative internal working model of self, other, and relationships begins to change. This is very different from earlier approaches in which continued confrontation and exposure to painful material was maintained or increased until the child was exhausted or had a "breakthrough." Such an approach is coercive and indeed countertherapeutic due to the risk of retraumatizing the child. In addition, treatment is coercive if a child becomes dysregulated, even through an unintended triggered reaction, and the therapist or parent does not attempt to decrease the child's dysregulation and repair the relationship break. Power struggles and control battles may only serve to increase dysregulation and are not recommended. In summary, this framework leads to the conclusion that it is the therapist's and caregiver's responsibility to maintain regulation and that these adults should accept responsibility when dysregulation occurs. While the resulting dysregulation may be by accident and unintended, the caring adult in the relationship is the one who must provide regulation and initiate interactive repair.

Helping the client to explore traumatic memories or conditioned emotional reactions in order to promote integration is an appropriate goal of treatment. It is the process of exploration and how it must be handled that is the focus of this appendix.

Research on maltreated children has shown that a significant percentage experience chronic dysregulation (Teicher, 2002). Extreme cases may result in chronic defensive manifestations (e.g., hypervigilance, compulsive self-reliance, dissociation). These children may be highly reactive and very difficult to assist in reregulation. Their defensive reactions are rooted in anxiety and profound fear from their traumatic experiences. It is important to recognize that even gentle and sensitive interventions may be perceived by these children in a threatening way and may push them into a dysregulated state. For this reason the therapist or caregiver must be very cautious, and the adult's sensitivity, responsiveness, reflective function, attunement, and insightfulness become particularly important. The therapist or parent may still provide such interventions even knowing that the child may be triggered into a dysregulated state, but must take care to appropriately "dose" the intervention so that the child is not overwhelmed and is still able to perceive the adult as actively working to assist the child in handling the difficult emotions that arise. The intention is to provide the corrective emotional experiences of concordant intersubjectivity that will help the child resolve maladaptive reactions.

Therapeutic Window

The concept of a therapeutic window is related to the concept of dysregulation and is helpful in understanding effective treatment for victims of childhood maltreatment (Briere, 2002). A therapeutic window is the psychological space in which a client is able to learn and change because the experience neither overwhelms the individual's defenses nor allows the client to move to the relatively easy (and often preferred) avoidance of the traumatic material. In other words, the client is engaged to experience affect, but not so much as to become dysregulated nor so little that the intersubjective experience is merely a cognitive dialogue. The challenge is to activate conditioned emotional reactions (i.e., triggers) to access avoided emotional content, but to do so only in a way that does not overwhelm the individual's coping resources. If such resources are overwhelmed, then the individual may be flooded by intrusive stimuli and retraumatized.

In *The Developing Mind*, Daniel Siegel describes dysregulation:

> Each of us has a "window of tolerance" in which various intensities of emotional arousal can be processed without disrupting the functioning of the system. . . . One's thinking or behavior can become disrupted as arousal moves beyond the boundaries of the window of tolerance. . . .The width of the window of tolerance within a given individual may vary, depending upon the state of mind at a given time, the particular emotional valence, and the social context in which the emotion is being generated. For example, we may be more able to tolerate stressful situations when surrounded by loved ones with whom we feel secure and understood. Within the boundaries of the window, the mind continues to function well. Outside these boundaries, function becomes impaired . . . under these conditions, the "higher" cognitive functions of abstract thinking and self-reflection are shut down. . . . The mind has entered a suboptimal organizational flow that may reinforce its own maladaptive pattern. This is now a state of emotion dysregulation. (1999, pp. 253–255)

Informed Consent

Another issue is the child's informed consent. Psychotherapy with children involves special considerations. Children generally do not present themselves for therapy; their parents or other caregivers do. Children cannot fully comprehend and assent to treatment in the way an adult can. Children's reactions range from cooperation to acquiescence to resistance. One important situation that highlights issues regarding coercion is when the child's reactions move toward resistance. A potential danger occurs when caregivers or therapists perceive the child's severely disruptive behaviors as requiring an escalating response to confront and control the behavior without a simultaneous focus on the distorted perceptions and beliefs that may be driving these behaviors. One technique would be to avoid control battles in which the child is given only one option of responding. Choices that are within the adult's accepted limits of safety and appropriateness may help the child feel less controlled and therefore less threatened. Assuredly, many children who come for therapy have high control needs. However, it is our experience that addressing the internal beliefs, perceptions, and emotions that drive these needs is the proper stance for an attachment-focused therapist. Engaging in power struggles is contraindicated and counterproductive.

The autonomy of the child is an important consideration and one that must be considered within the overall context of the child's developmental age and functioning. In the course of healthy development, increasing autonomy and responsibility are granted as a result of demonstrated accomplishment and competence. For example, the 12-year-old with years of evident responsible behavior may be allowed to go to the mall with friends, while a 16-year-old with a disorder of attachment and years of dangerous behaviors, impulsivity, and poor choices may not be allowed to go to the mall except with an adult. Similarly, the parent of a child with only mild social anxiety may deem that the child's negative feelings toward therapy might outweigh any skill training to be learned and decide not to push the child at that time. Yet a parent of a child with a much more disabling trauma-based attachment disorder might well perceive that any negative feelings engendered in the short run are well worth the long-term benefits of improved family functioning and supported developmental functioning. The parent and therapist realize that the child's negative reaction must still be handled sensitively and with constructive assistance to help move the child toward greater regulation within the context of the therapy. This is done by helping the child make meaning of the situation so as to begin to perceive the positive intentions of the adult while receiving active assistance to manage and cope with the feelings engendered. These efforts help the child stay within the therapeutic window and maximize the chance for successful resolution of posttraumatic responses. Similarly, there are times during normal discipline when parents will knowingly increase the child's discomfort by normal disciplinary practices such as saying no or enforcing limits (e.g., enforcing a reasonable bedtime). At these times, children need to be assisted to maintain or regain regulation without the parent giving up on the reasonable disciplinary point.

Shame

The role of shame is important to consider in this context. Children who have experienced chronic early maltreatment within a caregiving relationship or who have had other adverse experiences have experienced pervasive shame without interactive repair as a normal state of being. They bring this shame into new relationships and tend not to trust when a parent or therapist attempts to provide interactive repair. They frequently misperceive the intentions of others, based on their past negative experiences with caregivers. As a result, parents and therapists have a particular obligation to avoid any intervention that might increase the child's shame. Moreover, if a child is seen as experiencing shame as the result of an adult's behavior, the adult should immediately reach out to the child in interactive repair. Similarly, helping the child understand that the adults do not see the child as bad even when they discuss inappropriate behaviors is a primary goal of treatment. Without this understanding, the child will not be able to learn to trust and work cooperatively.

Developmental Level of Functioning

> Giving a child a choice to play "momma bird/baby bird" and feeding the child by hand may be a delightful and relationship-enhancing experience for parent and child.
>
> Telling a 13-year-old that she cannot go to the mall unsupervised or with peers because of her socially indiscriminate behavior is not coercive if the child lacks the ability to do what age peers do. Indeed, she would be at risk in that situation.

Another critical issue to consider is the child's developmental age and functioning. Trauma tends to distort emotional and social development, and the level of functioning may also fluctuate dramatically from one day to another depending on the degree to which traumatic triggers are affecting the child (van der Kolk, 2005). One generally accepted psychometric instrument for assessing the level of developmental functioning is the Vineland Scales of Adaptive Behavior II (Sparrow, Balla, & Cicchetti, 1984). One study (Becker-Weidman, 2009) found that children who met the *DSM-IV* criteria for reactive attachment disorder and the clinical criteria for complex trauma were significantly (statistically and clinically) developmentally younger than their chronological age in the domains of communication, daily living skills, socialization, and, for younger children, motor skills. Proper assessment of social and emotional functioning can help guide selection of developmentally appropriate interventions. Activities that appear regressive given the child's chronological age may be considered by some to be coercive; however, when an intervention is developmentally appropriate and provided in a sensitive and attuned way, it is not coercive. How one interacts with a child is best based on the child's developmental age, not the chronological age.

For example, a 12-year-old child whose social and emotional functioning is at the 4- or 5-year-old level may benefit from activities that younger children usually enjoy if these activities are conducted in a voluntary and well-attuned manner. Such activities are not inappropriately regressive but are developmentally appropriate and provide an emotional experience of attunement the child missed in early development.

Continuing this example, if the parent and child are involved in a nurturing activity and the parent is comfortable with offering a sippy cup or bottle and the child willingly accepts it and does not become dysregulated, it is not coercive. If the activity comforts the child, then it is not coercive. In fact it may be quite comforting and helpful for the child to experience an activity that the caregiver would have provided if the caregiver had the child at a younger age, and that the child missed. On the other hand, if the child has a tantrum like a 2-year-old, and the parent or therapist forces the child to drink from the sippy cup because the child is "acting like a 2-year-old," this would be coercive because it would intentionally increase the child's shame, leading to further dysregulation.

It is important that the parent and therapist are acutely sensitive to the child's experience of such an activity. The power differential in the adult-child relationship makes it critical that the adults ensure that such an activity is truly voluntary on the part of the child. Due to the power differential, the child may comply with such a request, and it might be interpreted as voluntary. Such compliance may be internally dysregulating to the child, and the intervention would be countertherapeutic. It may be difficult for the child to freely disagree to engage in the activity. Therefore the therapist and parent must pay careful ongoing attention to the child's cues, both verbal and nonverbal.

Meaning of Behavior

A final consideration in determining whether an intervention is coercive is to focus on the deeper rather than the surface meaning of behavior. It is important to consider intention, effect, and process, and to focus on the effects of the behavior on the client. If one must force the child to engage in the activity despite the child's protests, then the action is coercive.

Is asking a child to sit and think for a few minutes coercive and abusive or therapeutic? It is not the action that determines whether this request is coercive or supportive, but the intention, effect, and process. How the child is asked to sit quietly for a few minutes to contemplate some interaction, exchange, or choice is one factor. Is the action implemented to punish or dominate and is the action intended to enforce compliance for the sake of compliance? These would be factors that make the action coercive and not therapeutic. If the action is implemented to provide the child with a brief time-in or time-out to gather thoughts, and the child is capable of self-regulating, then this action is therapeutic. Demanding rigid compliance and turning the interaction into a power struggle that must be won by the parent or therapist by having the child sit exactly as instructed turns a potentially therapeutic activity into a coercive power battle for compliance by domination. It is not appropriate to demand that a child sit "your way" as long as the child is sitting quietly. Similarly, forcing engagement on the adult's terms is countertherapeutic. Of course, at times appropriate limits need to be set and enforced in the course of normal parenting (e.g., brushing teeth, going to bed, table manners) or in any situation where safety concerns exist.

For any activity to be therapeutic, it must be implemented in a developmentally appropriate manner, based on the child's level of developmental functioning (Perry et al., 1995). For example, while it may be appropriate to ask a 12-year-old child to sit and take a break in order to regulate behavior, it would not be appropriate to expect a child who is developmentally functioning as a 5-year-old to sit quietly for 20 minutes.

Summary

In summary, we recognize that children with disorders of attachment and complex trauma present with very challenging behaviors that are defensive reactions to profound fear and shame. It is our position that there is never a basis for the use of coercive interventions in parenting or psychotherapy. Instead these children need corrective experiences of attunement, security, and regulation to heal their post-traumatic reactions; they require positive concordant intersubjective experiences. We believe that addressing the internal beliefs, perceptions, and emotions that drive these behaviors is the proper stance for attachment-focused treatment. Engaging in power struggles and control battles is contraindicated and counterproductive. The concept of a therapeutic window is helpful to understanding effective therapy for victims of childhood maltreatment. The challenge is to activate conditioned emotional reactions (triggers) to access avoided emotional content, but to do so only in a way that does not overwhelm the individual's coping resources and promotes a sense that the adult is an active source of support and assistance. In addition, all interventions should take into account the child's social, emotional, and developmental level of functioning so that the approach is congruent with the child's developmental needs and age, and provides corrective emotional experiences for reparation of the early experiences of maltreatment, insecurity, mistrust, and fear.

We believe that ongoing research in the fields of trauma, attachment, and neuroscience will and should continue to inform the practices of attachment-focused therapy. Best practice should always be dictated by state-of-the-art knowledge. Given the many challenges of attachment therapy and the relative newness of the field, therapists who practice attachment therapy have a special duty to stay current with developments that affect the evolution of this field.

Screening & Assessment Resources

Antisocial Process Screening Device: www.hare.org/scales/apsd.html

Beck Anxiety Inventory: Pearson Education, http://www.pearsonassessments.com/HAIWEB/Cultures/en-us/Productdetail.htm?Pid=015-8018-400

Beck Depression Inventory–II: Pearson Education, http://www.pearsonassessments.com/HAIWEB/Cultures/en-us/Productdetail.htm?Pid=015-8018-370

Beery-Buktenica Developmental Test of Visual-Motor Integration: Pearson Education, http://www.pearsonassessments.com/HAIWEB/Cultures/en-us/Productdetail.htm?Pid=PAg105&Mode=summary

Behavior Assessment System for Children: Pearson Education, http://www.pearsonassessments.com/HAIWEB/Cultures/en-us/Productdetail.htm?Pid=PAa30000

Behavior Rating Inventory of Executive Function; parent, teacher, and pre-school versions: PAR, 800-331-8378, http://www3.parinc.com

Child Apperception Test: CPS Inc., PO Box 83, Larchmont NY 10538

Child Behavior Checklist, Teacher Report Form, Youth Self-Report, ages 1½–5, 6–18: ASEBA, http://www.ASEBA.org

Conners Rating Scales–Revised: Pearson Assessments, http://psychcorp.pearsonassessments.com/HAIWEB/Cultures/en-us/Productdetail.htm?Pid=PAg116

House-Tree-Person: Western Psychological Services,
    http://portal.wpspublish.com/portal/page?_pageid=53,70613&_
    dad=portal&_schema=PORTAL
Parenting Stress Index: PAR, 800-331-8378, http://www3.parinc.com
Sensory Integration Inventory Revised for Individuals With Developmental
    Disabilities: http://www.therapro.com
Sensory-Integration Screener: Center for Family Development,
    http://www.Center4FamilyDevelop.com
Stress Index for Parents of Adolescents: PAR, 800-331-8378,
    http://www4.parinc.com/Products/Product.aspx?ProductID=SIPA
Trauma Symptom Checklist: PAR, 800-331-8378, http://www4.parinc.com/
    Products/Product.aspx?ProductID=TSCC
Trauma Symptom Checklist for Children: PAR, 800-331-8378,
    http://www3.parinc.com
Trauma Symptom Checklist for Young Children: PAR, 800-331-8378,
    http://www4.parinc.com/Products/Product.aspx?ProductID=TSCYC
Vineland Adaptive Behavior Scales–II: Pearson Education,
    http://psychcorp.pearsonassessments.com/HAIWEB/Cultures/en-us/
    Productdetail.htm?Pid=Vineland-II

Out-Of-Home Placements

This book was written primarily for therapists doing attachment-focused family interventions. At the core of such therapy is the strengthening of attachment between the child and the parent or primary caregiver.

In attachment-focused therapy, the therapist serves as a resource to guide the caregiver-child dyad toward greater security in their attachment relationship. The therapist is very much in a role of consultant, guide, and coach to the caregiver and child in modeling and supporting a secure base for both. Yet it is mainly the caregiver's interactions with the child that are considered the primary curative element in the resolution of the child's history of relational trauma. When the child is living in an out-of-home placement such as a residential treatment center, then an attachment model of treatment (Clark et al., 2011) is necessary. In these situations, one or two care staff in the out-of-home placement act as primary caregivers, participating in treatment and being emotionally available to the child in concert with the parents.

Except when complicating factors arise (such as severe risks of imminent harm or chronic out-of-control behaviors), hospitalization and out-of-home placements are generally contraindicated in attachment-focused therapy. Since the treatment goal is to foster an attachment between child and caregiver, separations such as these may work against the formation of an attachment. Therefore, when children must be placed outside the home, for either short or longer periods, the attachment-focused therapy described in this book must be modified. An adequate description of those modifications is beyond the scope of this book. However, the following discussion provides some overview of key considerations.

Acute Psychiatric Hospitalizations

Acute psychiatric hospitalizations may be necessary when there is an imminent risk of serious harm from the child's attempts to harm self or others. While such a placement may be necessary to assess and stabilize the child, it is not without its risk of unintended consequences. A child with a history of attachment-related trauma and the resulting distorted internal beliefs (e.g., "others don't care about me or want to get rid of me"; "I am a bad, unlovable person") may be especially vulnerable to the triggers involved in the process of such a hospitalization.

Indeed, the child may not understand the true purpose of the hospitalization, and may instead perceive that the caregivers do not want or are afraid of the child Therefore, when children with this history require out-of-home placement, it is important for caregivers to address their child's presumed distorted internal working model beliefs.

This explanation of the placement will need to be repeated many times and in many ways before the child can truly accept this. These are important opportunities to acknowledge the child's feelings and fears, while countering negative and distorted beliefs.

Examples of Explanations

- This may feel like we don't want you or don't love you. But we do. Our job is to keep you and everyone in the family safe. Right now we cannot keep you safe. They can better keep you safe until we can all learn how to better handle [specific behavioral problem] so that we can live safely together.
- This may feel like we are punishing you for being bad, but that is not what we are doing. Instead, it seems to us that your feelings are so big and frightening that they are hard for you to control. When people have feelings this big and scary they can come out in [specific behaviors]. This means that the person needs special help to be safe and to figure out how to handle those feelings. That is what they do here.
- Just like I would put a Band-Aid on your cut, but would need to bring you to the urgent care center if the wound were beyond what I could safely help with, I am bringing you here so that you can get home soon.

Additionally, the parent or caregiver needs to explicitly reassure the child to the degree possible, for example:

- This is probably going to last for [predict length of stay]. When we have better figured out what is going on and how to help you stay safe at home, you will come back home [unless the parent anticipates that this might instead be a step toward longer-term residential placement]. I will see you [specify visiting times and policies].

In spite of the caregiver's clear explanations, the child may still feel powerfully triggered by earlier experiences of fear, shame, or abandonment. The child may then act in ways that are congruent with those core negative beliefs (e.g., "I don't matter to them"; "they will leave me anyway"). The child may resist or refuse contact or visits with the caregiver. The caregiver, worn down by the child's difficulties and feeling hopeless, may respond with defensiveness and blame. Hospital staff often misinterpret this reaction as a lack of attachment or an indication of problems in the home. Community therapists who have been working with the family need to play an active advocacy role in helping the hospital staff understand the child's history and the context of the current crisis.

The caregiver needs to be involved, as much as possible, in the child's treatment while in placement. Acute care hospitals, with shorter and shorter lengths of stay, may be more singularly focused on stabilization and discharge than in-depth therapy. This can create real frustration for the desperate caregiver who wants to make optimal use of this respite. The community therapist may be a resource to both the hospital staff and the caregiver in negotiating an acceptable discharge plan.

Children may have very different reactions to such a placement. Some may cooperate with the hospital staff and then be glad to be home, having an increased awareness that there are very real consequences to their dangerous actions. Some children may improve because this may have been the first time that they were removed from a placement and then returned home. This experience may reinforce and affirm the parents' commitment to the child and the experience of being part of a family. Some children may seem unchanged by the experience. That is, there is no appreciable difference in behavior before or after the placement. This can be very frustrating to caregivers. Therapists can help reinforce that such placements are not treatment options but are more focused on crisis stabilization. Real treatment success is more typically achieved in the slower process of outpatient therapy. Others may return home in a condition that seems worse. Often in such cases, the child remains frightened by the separation and is angry at the caregiver for allowing it to occur. In this case, it is important to realize that underneath this behavioral reaction is actually the burgeoning awareness in the child that there is security in the relationship with the caregiver. Protest is actually a normal response to separation from an attachment figure. Yet the caregiver may have a very difficult time understanding this and may interpret this reaction negatively. This can be a very potent opportunity to help the caregiver reframe the intention of the child's behavior and foster an opening for greater connection.

On the other hand, it is not unusual for children who have experienced multiple foster placements and other disruptions to experience the placement and return home as a positive and settling experience. For many children it may be the first time that they have been placed out of a home and then returned to the same home. This experience may reinforce the parents' message: "This is your home and we are your family and we will take care of you and when we cannot we will find those who can; but this will always be your home and family."

Residential Treatment

Placements in residential treatment facilities are typically longer stays of months. Such a placement usually occurs only after a child has had several other levels of care that have not been successful. Residential treatment facilities can differ as to target populations served, treatment models used, and general philosophy about caregiver involvement.

While some residential treatment facilities have adopted an attachment-focused and trauma-focused approach to treatment (Clark et al., 2011), most still focus on behavior management, behavior modification, and behaviorally focused approaches. Typically, attachment- or trauma-focused centers tend to involve parents and caregivers more actively and meaningfully in treatment and they, along with the primary care worker in the center, form the core treatment team, using attachment-focused methods (Clark et al., 2011). Other, more behavioral, centers may involve caregivers typically in parent conferences and family therapy that is focused more on behavioral issues than on relational skills. While it can be possible for a therapist working in a residential treatment facility to incorporate attachment-focused interventions, there are a number of challenges to doing so. Those challenges increase to the extent that the therapist is working in isolation, versus being part of a treatment system with a congruent philosophy and approach.

The caveats provided above about how these children are likely to perceive an out-of-home placement are also true for residential placements, perhaps even more so given the extended length of such placement. Therefore, it is necessary to help the caregiver find ways to explain the placement that are sensitive to the child's likely distorted internal beliefs. The parent or caregiver will also need to clarify and reinforce expectations about contact, visits, and so on during the placement. Here are two possible examples of what caregivers might say:

> This makes me really sad. I had hoped by now that we would find a way to help you manage all these really big feelings so that we could be safe. Some things have gotten better [give examples], and yet there are still some things that can be really hard for us to handle sometimes. I worry that you feel like this means you are bad or that we don't love you. That isn't true. What it really means is that there is still so much hurt inside that it is bigger than you can handle or than we can handle safely together. So we need to get some special help from people who know how to help children heal from these kinds of really big hurts, and who help parents know how to help kids better. It means we will have to live apart from each other for a while. But this is to make it possible for us to be able to live together again safely and in a good way. That is what I want for us.
>
> Sometimes even when people love each other and are in a family they have to live in different places for a while. You will still be our child. We will still be

your parents. We will still be a family. Only for a while we will live in different places. The place where you will be is a place for kids that have been hurt too, a special kind of place where people are trained to know how to help kids heal the hurt inside. It isn't for bad kids; it is for kids with a lot of hurt. I wish we could have made these hurts better ourselves, but even though we tried, we haven't been able to do that enough for you to really feel good about yourself or us. We have some things we need to work on and you have some things you need to work on. Hopefully we can do that in a better way when we aren't fighting with each other all the time. I feel sad about this, but I still believe it is possible for us to learn to live together in a good way.

Adapting the Approach

Therapists working in residential treatment facilities can utilize many of the concepts in this book in their own clinical work. The attachment-focused therapy approach we are advocating includes key focus areas such as the following:

- Helping the child achieve greater self-regulation skills
- Helping the therapist and caregiver appreciate that beneath the expression of problematic behaviors are a potential host of issues including unmet needs, traumatic triggers, and distorted beliefs
- Providing the child and adults with safe and supportive ways to explore and resolve the child's triggers and negative beliefs
- Remediating deficits in areas of social and emotional functioning to improve the child's capacity for improved, developmentally appropriate functioning

All of these are possible in residential treatment facilities.

In programs using an attachment model of treatment, the care staff are central to treatment. A primary worker would be assigned to be the child's primary contact, acting as a parent surrogate and working in close concert with the parents. The parents and primary worker would then be involved in therapy with the child. Such an approach can be effective if the overarching goals are focused more on developing relationship skills than on simply resolving behavioral problems.

It is important that the facility find ways to engage parents and caregivers in meaningful ways in their children's treatment. The creative use of technology, such as Internet video conferencing, Skype, and VoIP, can allow for weekly therapy sessions and frequent or even daily contact. This may occur through frequent and regular discussions between the therapist and caregiver to nurture a collaborative partnership, extended visits between the caregiver and child, and family therapy sessions.

Challenges for Therapists

There are many significant challenges for the therapist working in a residential treatment facility with youths who have disturbances or disorders of attachment.

First, the facility may not recognize attachment-related difficulties or complex trauma as conditions requiring a different treatment approach. If such a clinical formulation is not permitted or supported in the facility, the therapist might still include a focus on attachment through specifying attachment-related trauma on Axis IV of the multiaxial diagnosis as the primary stressor. Second, the therapist may be frustrated that program and milieu practices conflict with an attachment-focused approach. For example, consequences and privileges may be tied to point systems based simply on behaviors rather than on the nature and quality of relationships with primary staff and parents. The therapist might see the value in not imposing a negative consequence when the child is processing difficult feelings, yet be expected to do so by program standards, or consequences may be punitive rather than focused on relationship repair. Third, the potential for splitting and other unhelpful defensive reactions can become a reality when the child interacts with many different staff persons over different shifts. These are but some of the challenges likely to be faced.

Therapists who attempt to work from an attachment- or trauma-focused approach within a residential facility will need to be well-informed on current research and theory, so that through preparation, they may become strong advocates for this approach. Therapists should continue to advocate for policies and procedures that are congruent with such research. They should also look for outside consultation or supervision from someone with expertise in this approach. In addition, the use of consultation and an offer of training for the program's clinical director, senior management, and supervisory staff may be helpful in allowing for an adjustment in the treatment model for a particular child.

Special Considerations

Many children with significant attachment difficulties actually can seem to function quite well in an institutional setting, particularly children with an avoidant pattern of attachment and those who have extensive histories of residential or orphanage care. These children may experience the institutional setting as familiar and comfortable. The lack of emotional intimacy and authenticity can also feel familiar and comfortable. This can create the false impression that the real problem must be the parents or family. It is important to remember that institutional settings differ from family settings in significant ways that have a direct bearing on how the child functions in each. Most families expect and require some degree of emotional closeness, shared values, and acceptance of parental authority. Privileges may be tied to objective standards (e.g., good grades earn a specific reward) but are usually earned through real experiences of reciprocity and shared interests (e.g., where special times may more likely be shared activities).

Many children with attachment-related difficulties have significant challenges with these expectations. For these children, the relatively impersonal nature of an institutional setting is easier to navigate. The expectations tend to be based more on objective standards (e.g., doing chores, not fighting) and less on the quality of the interactions. Consequently, these children may master the behavior-based point system with relative ease. The reality that they interact with a number of different staff each day may help provide a buffer against any intensely personal interactions that may trigger unresolved trauma. Moreover, the high degree of structure reinforced by a whole staff can help provide an effective environmental container for even the most easily dysregulated child. Therefore, they can seem to be making progress or doing well, when in reality the core of their difficulties (e.g., distrust of others, fears of emotional closeness) remain relatively unrecognized and unresolved. These children may be particularly vulnerable to problems when they return home, where the expectations, quality of relationships, and structure are very different.

On the other hand, it is more common for children with disorders of attachment to do poorly in behaviorally based residential treatment programs. Point systems to earn privileges typically work because the points (e.g., stars, levels, stickers) are surrogates for the approval of parents or staff. If the child does not value relationship or is fearful of intimacy, then the points will have no value and the child may remain on the lowest level.

Another important consideration is that often children with attachment-related difficulties may respond to the out-of-home placement with little overt distress, or may even act indifferently toward, or refuse contact with, the caregiver. This may be interpreted as evidence of a lack of attachment or problems at home. This may be due in part to the very real relief that the child might feel initially at being removed from the struggle with the caregiver or family. It may also be due to a well-learned, self-protective defensive response (e.g., "I will reject them before they reject me for good"). Whatever the source of the child's resistance to contact, it is imperative to realize this is most likely a defensive response, and not an accurate reflection of the true meaning or potential for the relationship. Allowing time and space for such a child to adjust or adapt to the institutional placement, instead of having contact, may actually backfire and reinforce the child's underlying fears that the real intention of the caregiver is to abandon the child. During this period, it is critically important to attempt to make the child's fears explicit so that they can be evaluated more objectively and countered.

Some examples of what therapists might say in such a situation:

- It is hard to be in a new place like this. Lots of times kids worry that their parents don't really want them anymore or maybe are glad they are gone. Then it can make sense that a kid might not want to talk to the parents or visit with them, because it hurts too much. But here is what makes me think that your parent does care about you: [give specifics]. I wonder how much you believe that. Some, or not so much?
- Sometimes when families have had lots of fights before a kid comes here,

the kid can think that the parents are so mad at him that they don't want him back. I know you and your parents had a lot of conflicts before you came here. Sometimes your mom still gets mad when you talk. Do you ever worry that maybe she will stay mad and you won't go home? Sometimes the mad feelings are really just hurt feelings. Maybe she feels hurt that she couldn't find a way to make things better for you so you could stay there instead of coming here. Maybe her mad is frustration that it is taking so long for things to be better with you both. Could we talk with her about these feelings instead of keeping them inside you?

Another important consideration, discussed in the chapter on assessing children with attachment issues (Chapter 5) in this book, is that children with histories of attachment-related trauma may have very real delays or deficits in certain areas of functioning. Their developmental age may be quite different than their chronological age (Becker-Weidman, 2009). The significance of this is that the child's chronological age may only partially predict functioning across various domains. Consequently, a residential treatment facility that treats adolescents may assume that a particular teenage youth, with at least normal intelligence, is able to function consistently like other more typical adolescents. Yet if this youth has delays or deficits in some areas of functioning, it may not be readily apparent in the way that academic delays and deficits are fairly easily assessed.

This can create several important pitfalls for the therapist and facility. First, this youth may not have the maturity, judgment, and interpersonal problem-solving skills to handle the levels of autonomy or self-determination expected of a more typical peer, and may instead truly need greater structure and guidance. In such cases, the assistance and guidance of a parent or caregiver may actually be helpful instead of overprotective or controlling. Second, this youth may benefit from supports and activities that promote learning experiences associated with younger children. Third, typical content areas discussed with adolescents (e.g., sexual activity and personal responsibility) may not be normatively appropriate for a youth who is struggling with basic issues of trust and has very little sense of stable identity.

A therapist working from an attachment-focused approach in a residential treatment facility will need to ensure that the milieu is supportive of such an approach. Individuals with histories of early trauma, especially relational trauma, are likely to have a range of triggers that may not even be recognized, much less acknowledged, by the youth. Further, in general, children with attachment-related difficulties typically express their negative and distorted beliefs, derived from early traumatic experiences, in a range of behaviors.

When these children's difficult behaviors and reactions are responded to in ways that are perceived as confrontational or controlling, the behaviors may continue to escalate. If staff then responds with escalated efforts to confront and control the behavior, without concomitant efforts to help the child regain control, the child may quickly escalate to the point of requiring restraint. Subsequent efforts to process what happened and debrief in such a way that the child immediately takes responsibility for his actions may not be successful.

Many of these children have developed defenses such as splitting, projection, and denial. As with most defense mechanisms, these are mostly unconscious, automatic, and adaptive responses to perceived threat. These defenses can create significant conflict within and among staff, especially when the child's actions are viewed as purposeful manipulation. It is important that all staff members who work in the milieu have, at a minimum, training in trauma-informed care. This will help ensure that any trauma resolution work begun in sessions with the therapist is not undone by encounters in the unit that, instead, serve to reinforce the child's negative internal working model beliefs in the lack of trustworthiness of others and the relative danger in the world at large.

Study Guide

We hope that this study guide will assist the reader in processing the many concepts and principles contained within this book.

INTRODUCTION

Attachment therapy has been misrepresented within the media and literature for many years. It is not a specific model of treatment.

1. What are some models of treatment that are not synonymous with attachment therapy?
2. Name some components of attachment therapy as described in this book.
3. Why might touch and nurture be included in attachment-focused treatment?
4. Name some specific models of attachment-focused therapy that clinicians can use in their practice once they receive proper training.
5. What attachment-focused therapies would you like to learn more about?

We expect that the field of attachment-focused therapies will continue to progress as it is informed by research in neuroscience, attachment, and trauma, as well as the evolution of evidence-based practices for children and adolescents in order to more effectively address the unique needs and challenges of this population. In this evolving field, innovation and creativity support the ongoing refinement of effective strategies. We have tried to identify a framework that all therapies should embrace.

1. What are five of the core guidelines of treatment that are reviewed in more detail within the book? Do you use these in your treatment? If so, how?
2. Are you familiar with the guidelines listed above? If so, do you already include these in treatment?

For many disorders and treatment interventions, like disturbances in attachment and attachment-focused therapy, there is not yet sufficient data to establish evidence-based approaches.

1. Name the challenges to developing evidence-based approaches for this population of children.
2. Why have children with trauma and disorders of attachment historically been excluded from empirical studies?
3. Describe how studies and therapeutic methods related to the treatment of trauma could benefit attachment-focused therapy.
4. In what ways are trauma-focused cognitive-behavioral therapy and integrative treatment of complex trauma similar to attachment-focused therapy? In what ways are they different?

Chapter 1: TERMINOLOGY AND DIAGNOSIS

There is a lack of consensus and clarity about terms and diagnoses used in the mental health field regarding attachment. Reactive attachment disorder appears in the *DSM*, but terms such as *attachment disorder*, *attachment problems*, and *attachment therapy* have no clear, specific, or consensus definitions.

1. Describe one problem with the diagnostic approach of the *DSM-IV-TR*.
2. Why is a thorough, comprehensive assessment necessary for an accurate differential diagnosis?
3. Considering the seven domains of impairment associated with complex trauma, do you have clients for whom complex trauma would be a better diagnosis than reactive attachment disorder?
4. Describe two of the possible effects of prenatal exposure to alcohol. Are you treating any children to whom this may apply?

Chapter 2: OVERVIEW OF ATTACHMENT THEORY: SYNOPSIS OF KEY CONCEPTS

Several important components of attachment theory guide the application of attachment-focused psychotherapy. An understanding of these elements and the theory behind them is necessary for clinicians who treat children with disorders of attachment and complex trauma.

1. Which of the four primary patterns of attachment do the children you treat exhibit?
2. What patterns of attachment do your clients' caregivers exhibit? What is the relationship between parental patterns of attachment and the child's developing pattern of attachment with that caregiver?
3. What is the difference between patterns of attachment and disorders of attachment?
4. Attunement is an important dimension of treatment. How do you practice attunement with your clients? With their caregivers?
5. Interactive repair is another important dimension of treatment. How do you, or could you, use interactive repair in your practice?
6. Why is it important to understand a client's internal working model?
7. Do the treatment techniques you utilize address internal working models? How?
8. Intersubjectivity is an important dimension of treatment. Why might intersubjectivity be a more useful concept than attunement? What are the three elements of intersubjectivity? Give an example of intersubjectivity.
9. How might the level of reflective function that a caregiver exhibits affect treatment?
10. What treatment techniques do you use to foster a client's coherent narrative?
11. Within the context of treatment, how can caregivers and clinicians provide safety?

Chapter 3: OVERVIEW OF ATTACHMENT-FOCUSED THERAPY

Many different modalities of attachment-focused therapy exist today, each having its own set of techniques. However, all of the modalities contain the same core beliefs, values, and assumptions described in this chapter.

Attachment-focused therapy covers a range of different models and techniques. In an effort to provide guidance, we have outlined in this chapter core concepts and elements that should be part of any best practice.

1. What are the common goals of the various attachment-focused therapy modalities?
2. Elaborate the following basic assumptions of attachment-focused therapy:
   a. Attachment is fundamental to development.
   b. Disrupted or frightening attachment experiences place a child at risk for attachment disorder.
   c. Safety must be ensured in the therapy and healing process.
   d. Sensitivity and compassion in the caregivers and therapists are required.
   e. Relational trauma is the root of attachment trauma.
   f. Conditioned emotional reactions of maltreatment become generalized.
   g. Current relationships are the primary focus of therapy (child-parent, parent-therapist, and child-therapist).
   h. The historical attachment experiences of the parents play a key role in healing the child.
   i. Child resistance and regression in therapy is a function of attachment trauma.
   j. Parenting a child with an attachment disorder can have effects on family and marital dynamics.
   k. Children with relational trauma need multidimensional assessment.
   l. Attachment-focused therapy is driven by theory, principles, and empirical evidence.
   m. Nonverbal therapy modalities are an important aspect of attachment-focused therapy.
   n. The development of a secure base is essential to attachment-focused therapy. Therapists and caregivers need to understand the disparity between the child's functional and chronological ages.
   o. Intersubjectivity and interactive repair are important in attachment-focused therapy.
   p. Behavior is reframed through cocreation of meaning.

3. In what specific ways have your clients been placed at risk for developing disorders of attachment?
4. Why is it so important for your client to have a sense of safety when healing attachment trauma?
5. What has been your experience when sensitivity and safety are present in the process of healing? What has been your experience when safety and security have not been present?
6. Why is relational trauma at the root of attachment trauma?
7. Give examples of conditioned emotional trauma. How has the conditioned emotional trauma impacted your clients' caregivers?
8. How do you incorporate current relationships as the primary focus of therapy?
9. In what ways can caregivers' attachment experiences impact the healing of a child?
10. Give examples of resistance and regression you have observed with your clients. How have you worked with caregivers to better understand resistance and regression?
11. What effects can parenting a child with an attachment disorder have on family and marital dynamics?
12. How is a multidimensional assessment helpful when working with children with relational trauma?
13. Why is it helpful to rely on empirical research when working with children with relational trauma? If empirical research is not available regarding specific techniques or methodologies, what should you measure to determine whether or not the method should be used?
14. What nonverbal therapeutic modalities have you used to help access implicit memories of trauma?
15. How do you create a secure base in therapy?
16. Why is it important for therapists and caregivers to understand the disparity between the child's functional and chronological age? What experiences have you had where the caregiver does not understand the difference?
17. How can intersubjectivity and interactive repair be used in attachment-focused therapy?
18. In a therapeutic session, how would you reframe behavior through cocreation of meaning?

Coercion has no place in treatment. While there are valid uses for physical restraint when safety is an issue and other less intrusive interventions have failed, it is not treatment. Both caregivers and clinicians alike should understand and adhere to the safety principles outlined in this chapter.

1. Read Appendix A and discuss how safety and coercion affect your practice.
2. What is the overarching prerequisite of attachment-focused therapy?
3. In what way must the therapist and the caregivers collaborate to ensure the child's safety?
4. What strategies or techniques are specifically contraindicated?
5. How might you use touch appropriately in treatment?
6. Under what conditions may physical restraint be used?
7. How have you managed dysregulation in therapy?

We support a treatment framework grounded in several important core concepts. These core concepts provide a framework for the practice of attachment-focused therapy, regardless of the specific approach used by the clinician. All attachment-focused therapies rely on these core concepts (e.g. dyadic developmental psychotherapy, circle of security).

1. Define or describe the following core concepts:
    a. Relational model of change
    b. Focus on resolution of negative thoughts and beliefs
    c. Core self-regulation skills
    d. Secure base
    e. Emotional dysregulation
    f. Conditioned patterns of fight, flight, or freeze
    g. Behaviors based on developmental age versus chronological age of child
2. "When caregivers can ask the question 'why?' they will begin to be able to enter the child's world." What does this mean? How does this contribute to the therapeutic process?
3. What concern is raised if the therapist or caregivers only attune to the child's "false self"?
4. What is meant by the term *internal working model*?
5. Attachment-focused therapy relies on two interrelated concepts: theory of mind and reflective function or reflective capacity. Describe what is meant by these terms. How have you utilized them in therapy?
6. Another important objective of attachment-focused therapy is to assist the child in developing capacity for *metacognition*. What does this term refer to?
7. Describe the primary and secondary goals of attachment-focused psychotherapy.
8. Why is it important to challenge negative internal working models? What is a necessary client welfare issue that must be addressed before attempting this stage of treatment?

9. Explain why attachment-focused therapy is more concerned with identifying and resolving the child's underlying distorted beliefs that comprise the internal working model, rather than overt behavioral problems. What has been your experience when treatment has focused on overt behavioral problems?

10. The child's and caregiver's (and therapist's as well) shared experience of attention, emotion, and intention form the core of _____.

11. The client's ability to make sense of life experiences and integrate both positive and negative experiences into a more holistic understanding is referred to by what terms?

Chapter 4: CORE CONCEPTS OF TRAUMA & TRAUMA-FOCUSED THERAPY

Many children with complex trauma and disordered patterns of attachment have experienced simultaneous and/or sequential forms of maltreatment, as well as exposure to other trauma (e.g., domestic violence, parental mental illness or substance abuse, multiple placements, institutional care). Therefore, attachment-focused therapists must have a good understanding of trauma and the treatment modalities used to address relational trauma.

1. What behaviors are commonly exhibited by children who have experienced trauma within the caregiver relationship? How is this different than trauma experienced outside the caregiver relationship? What internal working models have your clients exhibited in each instance?

2. What are triggers or conditioned emotional responses and how might they affect behavior?

3. How do the storage and recall of traumatic memories differ from those of typical memories?

4. How might traumatic experiences affect emotional, cognitive, and behavioral functioning?

5. What are the typical biological responses to threat and how are they affected by trauma and by attachment-related trauma?

6. What role do the amygdala and the hippocampus play in the psychological, physiological, and neuromuscular traumatic stress responses?

7. What are the key similarities and differences between child trauma and adult trauma?

8. Define and give examples of implicit and explicit memories.

9. How does complex developmental trauma differ from PTSD?

10. What are the seven domains of impairment of complex developmental trauma?

11. Define relational trauma.
12. What are the possible outcomes of shifting parents' understanding to see child behavior as fear-driven rather than anger or oppositional behavior?

Provision of "Disparity"

To what does disparity refer and how is it relevant in treatment?

Focus of Treatment

1. Why is the focus of treatment primarily not the child's behavior?
2. What are the foci of treatment and why?

Exposure and Consolidation

1. Define *exposure* and *consolidation*.
2. How are exposure and consolidation effectively used in therapy?
3. What is the parents' role in therapy?

Therapeutic Window or Window of Tolerance

1. Define therapeutic window or window of tolerance.
2. What are some of the signs that a child may be under- or overaroused?
3. What strategies might a therapist employ to help a child remain within the window?
4. Discuss the importance of a therapeutic exploration that is balanced with positive historical events and experiences.
5. Discuss the roles of attunement, interactive repair, and the cocreation of meaning in therapy.
6. How might intersubjectivity be a more useful construct?

Arousal Modulation, Affect Tolerance, and Regulation

1. Discuss state versus trait physiological responses to acute and chronic traumatic experiences.
2. What changes in affect regulation and modulation occur as a result of trauma?
3. Discuss van der Kolk's concept of "befriending internal states" and its role in healing trauma.
4. What techniques are useful in managing arousal?

Resistance

1. Why are children resistant? What might be a more helpful interpretation of resistant behavior?
2. What interventions are helpful with resistance?
3. Why do traumatized children need to feel a sense of control?

Goal Sequence or Phase Approach

1. Why is it important to develop safety and coping strategies before exploring traumatic memories and experiences?
2. How does attachment-focused therapy differ from cognitive-behavioral approaches in trauma exploration?
3. How do exploration, consolidation, skill development, and safety interweave to create the therapeutic process?
4. Describe the relationships among the following phases:
   - Creating the alliance
   - Maintaining the alliance
   - Exploration
   - Integration
   - Healing

Development of a Coherent Trauma Narrative

Discuss the role of survival strategies in the creation of a coherent narrative.

Chapter 5: ASSESSING CHILDREN WITH ATTACHMENT ISSUES

A clinical assessment of a child who has a disorder of attachment is complex. Key historical or developmental data may be missing. Information from different sources will often conflict. There may be signs and symptoms that suggest a range of comorbid diagnoses. Given these many challenges, assessments should be multidimensional and cross-contextual and include a range of different methods.

The screening process should be focused on determining issues of client safety and appropriateness of provider's services.

1. Develop a flow chart for your practice, identifying referral sources, supervision, and peer support.
2. Identify your state's policy or law regarding:
   a. Consent to treatment by parents and by child, with respect to age
   b. Requirements for disclosure to child protective services
   c. Exchange and release of information (including HIPAA)
3. How have you seen presenting symptoms manifest in different contexts—family, school, teacher (one teacher more than another); with each, either, or both parents; with siblings; with close relatives (grandparents, uncles, and aunts)?

When considering a specific client you have or are currently treating:

1. Is there any pattern to the child's behavior when it is at its best or worst—context or triggers?

2. What are the parents' or caregivers' best guesses about the reasons for the child's symptoms?
3. How will you reframe or educate the caregivers about possible alternate explanations for the child's symptoms?
4. What do you think the challenges or limits are to the caregivers' understanding of the child's symptoms?

Assessments vary as to their ultimate uses (e.g., initial diagnostic assessment, termination of parental rights, custody hearings). Assessments that are carried out before beginning therapy are utilized to develop the initial treatment plan.

1. List the documents or releases that you currently use in, or will add to, the initial assessment phase.
2. If your assessment will be used for a legal purpose, now or possibly in the future, will participating in the legal process be part of your professional role? If not, how will you frame your working agreement to protect your client and yourself from an inadvertent use of your involvement in the case?
3. What are the rules about privacy and confidentiality in your state?
4. Have you received training or preparation to be an expert witness?

Attachment-related trauma has a wide-ranging impact on a child's functioning and development. Therefore, the assessment and record-keeping notations must address the various domains, symptoms, and issues being treated.

1. What is the importance of standardizing and annotating every contact you make in the process of collecting information about a child or a child's family?
2. Why must the assessment be comprehensive?

When considering a client you have or are currently treating who is presently in the family of origin:

1. What are the factors in the family that could have led to the child experiencing less than a secure base within this family? Are these factors situational or personal to either caregiver?
2. What contact has either parent had with the legal system? Are there issues of substance abuse or mental health? Has there been previous therapy or counseling?
3. What is the level of functioning of each caregiver in terms of psychological capacity and parenting capacity?
4. How do you imagine you would feel as a person living with this child's caregivers?
5. What is your understanding of the feelings of this child's caregivers regarding their level of competency in dealing with the child's issues?

It is important to recognize that the behavioral or surface symptoms of many disorders overlap. Taken alone, one symptom cannot indicate the true cause of a child's behavior.

1. When will you use a diagnostic classification system? What systems are you trained in? What are the strengths or limitations of the systems you use?
2. What is the purpose of your diagnosis? Will you be the only one using that diagnosis?
3. How will you test your diagnosis over time?

The focus of treatment in attachment-focused therapy is the caregiver-child relationship. Assessing the caregiver's ability to be a vehicle for change is an important part of any assessment when developing a treatment plan. When you consider a specific client you are currently treating:

1. How would an empathic strength-based intervention help the caregiver in an assessment situation?
2. Why do we assess the child's caregivers when it is the child who is being brought for treatment?
3. Why is it important to identify and address the caregivers' capacity to participate in treatment?
4. To what extent can caregivers empathize with children's experience of themselves or their issues?
5. To what extent is the caregiver taking the child's issues personally—too much or too little?
6. Describe how you might, formally or informally, assess the following important dimensions of caregiver capacity:

   Insightfulness
   Commitment
   Reflective function
   State of mind with respect to attachment (pattern of attachment)
   Sensitivity
   Ability to engage in positive intersubjective experiences with the child

In addition to the previous assessments, it is important to assess the current family as a whole to acquire a complete understanding of the child within the environment in which he or she lives. When considering a specific child you are currently treating:

1. How well has this family molded their functioning to meet the unique needs of the child?
2. Are there ways that the family functions that may impede optimal development of the child?

3. How would you work to help this family change their functioning?

When clinical interviews are supplemented with standardized instruments, the clinician can often begin to make sense of the complex set of symptoms presented in a more comprehensive and integrated manner.

1. Do you expect to use standardized instruments in your work? If so, which instruments and why?
2. If this isn't consistent with your training or expertise, do you have a relationship (referral or supervisory) with another professional who can add or support that component to your assessment process?
3. What types of information can standardized tests tell you that observation cannot?

Chapter 6: TREATMENT PLANNING

Consider the treatment planning process:

1. With whom (child, caregivers, other involved persons) should the treatment goals be established?
2. Which areas should the goals focus on?
3. What components should all attachment-focused treatment models include?
4. How can clinicians view a client's resistance or defiance? How would a clinician deal with resistance?
5. Why is it critical to celebrate the successes of the client? Why may the child struggle to accept success or positive responses? What can be done to help the child experience the positive responses?
6. What safety measures should be addressed by treatment planning?
7. Why is relapse prevention important to discuss during treatment planning?
8. Why does the healing of relational trauma require a healthy relationship?
9. The process of ongoing assessment is measured across which domains? How are the assessments qualified and quantified?
10. Why are coercive techniques contraindicated?
11. Why is it important to have a developmentally appropriate practice? What can happen if a child is treated according to chronological age instead of developmental age?
12. Children with histories of maltreatment with relational trauma may be biased toward which affective expressions?
13. Why is parental sensitivity critical to the progress of the child?

14. Why are out-of-home placements generally contraindicated in attachment-focused therapy? When out-of-home placements are required, what can caregivers do to help address the child's distorted working model beliefs?

Chapter 7: SPECIAL CONSIDERATIONS IN BEHAVIOR MANAGEMENT

While the focus of treatment in attachment-focused therapy is the development of the caregiver-child relationship, teaching the family how to manage their child's behavior will be a critical component of treatment. However, this is achieved not by focusing on the surface symptom or behavior. It is achieved by discovering what perceptions, meanings, and affects are driving the behavior. It is causes, not symptoms, that are treated.

1. Why would a child with a history of attachment-related trauma initially misperceive the intentions and actions of adults?
2. What beliefs may a child with a negative internal working model have about others?
3. What can the clinician or caregiver do when efforts to connect with the child are viewed by the child as threats or harm?
4. Suggest some ways in which the clinician and caregiver can respond effectively to child misbehavior.
5. Explain why behavioral techniques may not work with many children with histories of attachment-related trauma.
6. Why can behavioral techniques work with other, non-traumatized children?
7. What distorted beliefs can be reinforced through imposing consequences on a child with attachment-related trauma?
8. What is an effective way to address problem behaviors? Why can this work better?
9. Give examples of ways to provide safety physically, psychologically, and interpersonally.
10. What are some ways underlying shame can be expressed by a child with a history of attachment disturbances?
11. Why is it important to identify shame as the underlying emotion in the face of the behaviors you have listed above? What can caregivers do to avoid shaming a child?
12. What is the overriding goal of therapy? What must the adults demonstrate to the child?
13. How can one help a caregiver who perceives the child's behavior as purposeful rejection or defiance of the caregiver?

14. What outcomes have you experienced when you have helped the child "feel felt by" the adults?

15. In the examples section, how does reframing a situation in terms of the child's trauma history help the child? The caregiver?

16. When a caregiver is hurt, frustrated, and defensive in the face of a child's misbehavior, how can a clinician help the caregiver regain a position of empathy and self-control?

17. What are some approaches that may be effective in redirecting the child's behavior?

18. How can a session be structured if the child's behavior cannot be tolerated with patience and empathy?

19. Why is it important to discuss the rules and consequences?

20. Identify a way to reframe a child's behavior that could be viewed as misbehavior.

21. The text identified seven considerations that are needed in managing the behavior of children with histories of attachment-related trauma. Identify and explain each of the seven considerations and describe why each is important.

22. In Example 1, how can the traditional response cause the child to feel? How does the therapeutic approach differ from the traditional approach? What causes the therapeutic approach to have greater success with the client?

23. In Example 2, instead of "just being punished," what does the therapeutic approach do that the traditional parenting response does not?

24. What is included in educating others about the child's needs?

25. Suggest some ways the needs of the child can be communicated.

Restrictive Behavioral Management Techniques

1. What are restrictive behavioral management interventions? When should they be used?

2. Who should use a therapeutic hold? When should the hold be discontinued?

3. Why do we recommend those using therapeutic holds explain the rationale for the technique to the child?

4. Why is it appropriate to restrict certain freedoms and privileges for a child based on developmental needs?

Contraindicated Behavior Management Techniques

1. What behavior management techniques are not approved by ATTACh?

2. Identify why each specific technique is not recommended.

3. What interventions are not considered a restraint?

Chapter 8: TRAINING, CONSULTATION, & COMPETENCY

Specialized attachment-focused therapy typically encounters children with complex clinical presentations, severely disordered behaviors, and families in significant crisis. Therefore, clinicians need to be adequately educated for the level of need presented by these cases through specialized training before competency can be established.

1. Because the focus of treatment can shift from child to family to caregiver issues, clinicians should have training and ability to practice competently in what three areas of therapeutic work?
2. Why is it important for the clinician to seek supervision and consultation when working with clients who have experienced trauma and are struggling with achieving secure attachment?
3. What six criteria should the clinician consider when choosing a supervisor?
4. For clinicians who may have had their own experiences of insecure attachment as children, it is important that they have resolved these experiences and reach _____ _____ in their attachment style.
5. Supervision and consultation in attachment-focused therapy are critically important to monitor and manage what three specific areas of risk?

Chapter 9: ETHICAL CONSIDERATIONS

This book assumes an understanding on the part of the clinician that our role is to enhance the well-being of our clients while respecting their dignity and integrity. ATTACh recognizes a need for the highest standards of ethical practice in working with attachment-focused treatment, including the child and family or caregivers.

1. What are the professional codes and applicable laws and regulations of your professional organization and your state or regional licensing boards?
2. Do you periodically review the professional codes and applicable laws and regulations of your professional organization, as well as your state or regional licensing boards, to ensure compliance?

Competence

Clinicians are expected to provide services only within the boundaries of their competence.

1. What are the eight areas of training recommended by ATTACh for clinicians working in the complex area of providing attachment-focused treatment?
2. Rather than a one-model approach to treatment, what delivery approach do we recommend for attachment-focused treatment?
3. Why does an attachment and trauma clinician need perhaps a broader base of theory and practice than clinicians in some other fields?
4. What is the implication for the clinician in the fact that there are few attachment-focused resources to meet client needs?
5. Why is it critical for attachment-focused clinicians to continually engage in self-education, training, consultation, receiving supervision, and review of literature in the field?
6. What is the constant role of self-monitoring relative to providing attachment-focused therapy?

Informed Consent

The clinician has a duty to provide information to both the child and family in clear and understandable language.

1. What eight clear and understandable pieces of information should be included in informed consent when working with attachment-focused therapy?
2. Instead of a one-time event, how is informed consent offered in attachment-focused treatment?
3. What is particularly important regarding informed consent when working with both children and caregivers, and how is this handled in attachment-focused treatment?
4. Given that resistance is often a part of the client's presenting difficulties, how is the treatment of informed consent different than in many therapeutic relationships?
5. How would you adapt examples in this book to engage the family and child in developing a treatment contract and informed consent? Give at least three examples, based on your current client base.

Assessment and Professional Opinions

A practitioner is often asked to provide an opinion about a child or family to the court, child welfare, insurance companies, and other providers. The right to privacy belongs to both the child and his family and, therefore, they must be informed of both the right to confidentiality as well as the limits of such right.

1. What limits and uncertainties in the field of attachment-focused treatment make it difficult, at times, for practitioners to offer professional opinions and even assessment interpretations?
2. What are the legal responsibilities in your jurisdiction regarding the

client's rights to privacy and confidentiality, compared with your mandate to report?

3. Do you have a mechanism for reviewing with clients the mandates of insurance carriers with whom you work?

4. Clarify the division between your jurisdiction's laws and regulations relative to age of the client. Clarify the distinctions between individual, parental, and family rights to privacy and confidentiality when working with minor children and their families.

5. What special consents are required if you include audio or videotaping of client sessions? What are your jurisdiction's requirements around handling, storing, and destroying these tapes?

Conflicts of Interest and Dual or Multiple Relationships

Conflicts of interest occur when the clinician and client have dual relationships or in situations in which the client's needs may be at odds with those of the clinician.

1. Given that it is the clinician's duty to protect the client, what are the special considerations regarding the clinician's relationships with caregivers or other relationships that might create a potential conflict of interest?

2. Why is this particularly poignant in work within the attachment field?

Physical Contact With Clients

Attachment-focused interventions may involve the use of touch, for the purpose of resolving conditioned fear reactions to emotional or physical closeness.

1. What is the National Association of Social Workers (1999) Code of Ethics, Section 1.10, and why is it critical to understand and follow these guidelines in working in attachment-focused treatment?

2. What is "dosing" of physical contact and again, why is it critical to understand and practice in attachment-focused treatment?

3. What is the American Psychological Association's position on this subject?

4. What is the position of your professional association on this subject?

Documentation and Access to Records

All services provided should be documented and maintained in a confidential location.

1. What are your profession's mandated guidelines regarding timely and accurate documentation of services? Does your documentation storage meet professional and mandated requirements?

2. What special considerations should be taken regarding documentation of services in attachment-focused treatment?

Referrals

There are times when a clinician may not be able to help a child, and referral or termination of services would be in the child's best interest.

1. What are your criteria for making referrals for adjunctive treatment services and how do you determine that you are not being effective and should refer to another clinician?
2. Understanding that you should collaborate with the child and family to assess progress on a periodic basis, what is your method of determining readiness for termination?
3. If there is disagreement regarding readiness for termination, what is your documentation process and why is it critical that documentation be clear and comprehensive?
4. What must you provide when termination or transfer goes into effect?

Advertising, Endorsements, and Public Statements

Families who contact clinicians are often desperate and vulnerable to undue influence and promises, either implied or stated.

1. Why is a higher-than-usual degree of professional discretion required when working with caregivers and families involved in attachment-related traumas?
2. What are the professional recommendations concerning the use of endorsements by clients and the offer of guarantees of treatment effectiveness?
3. When engaging in education and advocacy concerning the needs of children with attachment-related trauma, what particular guidelines are needed?

Impaired Professionals

Treating children who have had attachment-related trauma can be hazardous for a clinician's own mental health.

1. Explain the reasons for constant self-monitoring regarding vicarious trauma, secondary traumatic stress, compassion fatigue, burnout, and countertransference. What steps should you take to avoid or address any of these common experiences as a clinician in this field?
2. What are we professionally bound to do if we suspect another's clinician's ability to effectively function in the field has been compromised?
3. What steps should you take, or have you taken, to avoid or address any of these common experiences as a clinician in this field?

Chapter 10: VICARIOUS TRAUMA & CLINICIAN SELF-CARE

This book assumes an understanding that is incumbent on the clinician to address traumatic, often uncomfortable, and even painful experiences with the client, which poses the risk of engendering secondary traumatic stress reactions in the clinician. Proactively managing this reaction allows the clinician to actively support his or her own well-being and to retain the best possible ability to help the client in treatment.

1. What are the various reactions that may occur in the clinician while attempting to stay attuned to both the traumatized child and the affected caregiver or family?
2. Since it is understood that in most attachment-focused therapy the caregiver is intricately involved in treatment, what should you do as a clinician if the caregiver gives signs of having significant emotional needs?

Occupational Hazards

1. Explain "vicarious trauma" and describe how it is different from "burnout."
2. Enumerate nine emotional reactions that may be experienced by a clinician who develops secondary traumatic stress.
3. How can a clinician most appropriately address these compassionate yet debilitating reactions?

Self-Assessment of Countertransference Reactions

1. Consider what might well happen if you experienced unresolved posttraumatic responses during the course of treatment with a traumatized child. Has this happened to you? What steps did you take to resolve your posttraumatic responses?
2. Regarding posttraumatic responses and countertransference reactions, explain four steps that we suggest using to monitor your own professional and personal functioning.
3. Using Phillips's (2004) list of consideration of one's personal responses to countertransference reactions, carefully review your own experience when working with a client during which you were aware of countertransference issues of your own. Can you identify the responses to which Phillips is referring?
4. What can be gained from a clinician completing his or her own attachment history with a trained attachment therapist?

Supervision and Consultation

Supervision and consultation are critically important in assisting the clinician in exploring countertransference responses and reactions. Maintaining a balance in one's life is critical for a clinician's emotional and physical health.

1. Now explore your responses and reactions in this (or another) client treatment process, considering how supervision and consultation may have been able to help you resolve these issues and keep the treatment process a safe holding environment for the child.
2. Using the same or another treatment situation, explore how consultation and supervision might also shed light on the client's unconscious reactions or traumatic memories that cannot yet be verbalized.

Other Supports for Maintaining Balance

1. Considering how stressful and draining trauma- and attachment-focused clinical work can be, explore your own lifestyle patterns, including sleep, rest, relaxation, diet, and so on.
2. Also, consider whether your lifestyle supports a balanced personal time and work ratio.
3. Understanding that children and their families can feel with the clinician, as well as the other way around, does your presence reflect health and self-care? Are you successful in balancing your caseload in terms of level of severity, types of presenting issues, and so on, or are there more ways that you can keep both your work and personal life balanced?
4. Are you careful to protect yourself from becoming overwhelmed by graphic traumatic material, both in your work and through media or personal life situations?
5. What are five areas of our own lives that are particularly susceptible to the effects of psychological trauma, according to Saakvitne and Pearlman (1995)? Consider why these areas are as critical to address as those of the clients.
6. What are five self-care strategies that clinicians in high-stress practices have found helpful?
7. Might it prove a helpful self-care strategy for you as a clinician in this difficult field to become active in advocacy or humanitarian efforts?

Appendix A: ETHICS GUIDELINES FOR CLINICIANS

This appendix provides guidance and standards for ethically and clinically appropriate treatment for children with attachment problems.

1. Describe what a coercive response to a child might look like and why it might be harmful.
2. Why is emotional safety so important to emotional repair?
3. How do we provide natural consequences and limits for the provision of safety with emotionally dysregulated children?
4. How are caregivers and clinicians advised to distinguish coercive interventions from acceptable authoritative practices? What makes this so difficult in practice?

When considering any type of treatment or behavioral technique, one must make a decision as to whether or not the method is coercive and, therefore, contra-indicated.

1. Describe the difference between coercion and therapeutic confrontation.
2. Identify a time when you used therapeutic confrontation in your practice. Was it effective?
3. Describe how ethical decision making can guide standards of appropriate behavior or intervention.
4. What are three important guidelines in making a determination of what is, and what is not, coercion?
5. What is the role of touch in therapy?
6. When is it appropriate to touch a child in therapy and how have you effectively used touch?
7. How would a sensory integration diagnosis affect your use of touch in a therapeutic setting?
8. Why do a therapist's or caregiver's intentions matter in the use of touch in therapy?

Decision making in complex treatment situations involves consideration of a number of important concepts and how the concepts apply to specific individuals and situations within the dyad.

1. Describe the characteristics of an emotionally regulated person.
2. Describe the characteristics of an emotionally dysregulated child. How does emotional dysregulation affect the therapeutic process?
3. Why does emotional dysregulation occur?
4. How have you helped a child regain regulation and manage distress?
5. When is it helpful to encourage a child to talk about a traumatic event that needs to be processed? When does this encouragement cross the

line and become coercive and hurtful to the child? How will the clinician know?

6. Why is gentle exposure considered more productive than forced exposure?
7. What factors does a therapist or caregiver need to consider when working with a chronically dysregulated child?
8. Describe the concept of a therapeutic window and its value of impacting change in treatment.

Psychotherapy with children involves special considerations.

1. Why is engaging in power struggles contraindicated in treatment or parenting?
2. How does a therapist and caregiver help a child make meaning of the therapeutic setting?
3. What is the role and prevalence of shame in this population of children?
4. How should adults handle their response to a child who feels shame in response to the communication?
5. Why might a child's developmental functions vary in different functional areas?
6. What is the role of regressive therapies in treatment?
7. Why might children need to re-create the feeling of security they may have missed at an earlier developmental stage?
8. Why is it important to consider the intention, effect, and process of any given behavior or activity?
9. Give an example of how a behavioral request can turn coercive in the clinical setting.
10. Why is it important to always implement an activity in a developmentally appropriate manner in the therapeutic setting?

In summary, we recognize that children with attachment-related trauma present with very challenging behaviors that are defensive reactions to profound fear and shame.

The use of coercive interventions is contraindicated and should never be used in treatment or parenting.

1. What are the primary principles of a corrective therapeutic experience?
2. Why do we look at internal beliefs and not behaviors?
3. How do we activate the therapeutic window without overwhelming the coping resources?
4. Why is it important for therapists to continue to study, receive additional training, and keep up with the most current literature and research in the field?

Appendix C: OUT-OF-HOME PLACEMENTS

This book was written primarily for therapists doing attachment-focused family interventions, which strengthen the attachment between the child and the primary caregiver. The therapist serves as a resource or guide to coach the caregiver and child toward greater security in their attachment relationship. Since the true form of this therapeutic approach is based on the development of this dyad, except when complicating factors arise (severe risks of imminent harm or chronic out-of-control behaviors), hospitalization and out-of-home placements are generally contraindicated in attachment-focused treatment.

When children must be placed outside of the home for either short or longer-term placements, the attachment-focused therapy described in this text must be modified.

In the case of acute psychiatric hospitalizations, one must consider the following:

1. What distorted internal beliefs might the child have as a result of the hospitalization? (For example, "Others don't care about me.") What distorted internal beliefs can you identify from your practice?
2. How important is it for this distorted internal working model to be addressed while in the hospital setting? Would it need to be approached in more than one way? How often?
3. Until the child's internal working model changes, when triggered, a child's behavior will be congruent with his or her core belief system. What would these behaviors look like? What might the triggers be?
4. How can you, the therapist, assist the hospital staff in understanding the child's behavior and caregiver's reactions, to facilitate responding to the caregivers in a positive way?
5. How involved should the parents be in treatment?
6. Do the caregivers need further respite care following hospitalization, to effectively parent the child?
7. How can normal protest from a child at the time of separation from the caregiver be reframed to assist the child in understanding that there is security in the relationship with the caregiver?

Residential treatment facilities are used for longer stays of months to years, which should occur only after a child has had several other levels of treatment.

1. What should the main considerations be when searching for a residential treatment facility?
2. What types of therapeutic models should the facility be using for treatment?
3. How can a therapist incorporate attachment-focused interventions into the treatment?
4. How can a clinician best assist the parent to communicate a clear, coherent statement about why the child is in care without inadvertently reinforcing the child's negative working model?

Adapting the Approach

The attachment-focused therapy approach can be adapted to residential settings by utilizing many of the concepts in this book.

1. Describe ways that therapists can help children achieve greater self-regulation skills.
2. How can the therapist help children understand the underlying reasons behind their problematic behavior?
3. Describe ways the therapist can foster the remediation of deficits in areas of social and emotional functioning within the context of an out-of-home placement?
4. How can the principles of attachment-focused therapy be adapted to individual and group settings?
5. How can a therapist assist staff to understand that the primary goal should be the building of relationships rather than the reduction of behavioral symptoms?

Challenges for Therapists

1. How can a therapist work effectively and respond to the needs of an attachment-disordered child in a facility that does not recognize the diagnosis nor subscribe to a relationship-based approach?
2. What tools will the therapist need to increase the likelihood of success in a behaviorally based program?

Special Considerations

Special considerations must be taken into account when monitoring the behavior of a child with significant attachment-related difficulties.

1. Why does improved behavior, by itself, create an illusion that a child is becoming healthier?
2. What signs are exhibited by children who are making progress in their ability to form and maintain relationships with caregivers?
4. How can developmental discrepancies be incorporated into treatment planning and programming?
5. How can a therapist working with an attachment-focused approach respond to difficult behaviors in ways that are not confrontational and controlling?
6. How can escalation be prevented?
7. What are ways of framing and understanding what may appear to be manipulative behavior?
8. What can be done to ensure staff consistency in responses, treatment, and daily care?

GLOSSARY

affect: Facial expression or body language that conveys what someone is feeling or experiencing.

antisocial: A continuum of behavioral responses, including mild to severe forms, indicating a pervasive pattern of disregard for others and rules. While there is some evidence of a possible genetic vulnerability, more commonly it can be a result of a basic failure in human attachment. This basic failure is then coped with through primitive defenses such as omnipotent control, denial, and projection.

attachment: A reciprocal process by which an emotional connection develops between a child and his or her primary caregiver. It influences the child's physical, neurological, cognitive, and psychological development. It becomes the basis for the development of basic trust or mistrust, and shapes how the child will relate to the world, learn, and form relationships throughout life.

attachment disorder: A treatable condition involving a significant dysfunction in an individual's ability to trust or engage in reciprocal loving, lasting relationships. An attachment disorder occurs due to traumatic disruption or other interferences with the caregiver-child bond during the first years of life. It can distort future stages of development and impact a person's cognitive, neurological, social, and emotional functioning. It may also increase the risk of other serious emotional and behavioral problems. Note: For a medical definition of Reactive Attachment Disorder of Infancy or Early Childhood 313.89, see the Diagnostic and Statistical Manual of Mental Disorders (IV-TR; American Psychiatric Association, 2000).

attachment style: The blueprint acquired from experiences in early relationships with caregivers that guides expectations about the self and how others will respond in significant relationships.

attunement: A strong empathic awareness of others' feelings or needs.

coercion: When immediate fear of consequences compels a person to act against his or her will. Coercion is contraindicated in attachment-focused therapy as it may create dysregulation in, or may retraumatize, the child. (Note: Mild and benign forms of coercion may be part of the normal process of socialization and protection of children when parents act against the wishes of the child, but these occurrences typically have only transient impact on the child's regulation and, while experienced as unpleasant and even distressing by the child, are not traumatic.)

coherent narrative: The ability to make sense of one's life experiences, integrating positive and negative experiences to form a new, more constructive understanding of oneself.

comorbidity: A medical term that refers to the presence of more than one disorder. Comorbidity is common in young children, especially those with problems of regulation, since the various behavioral symptoms can fit the criteria of multiple disorders.

complex trauma: "The dual problem of exposure to traumatic events and the impact of this exposure on immediate and long-term outcomes. Complex trauma exposure refers to children's experience of multiple traumatic events that occur within the care-giving system—the social environment that is supposed to be the source of safety and stability in a child's life. . . . [This] exposure to simultaneous or sequential maltreatment can result in emotional dysregulation, loss of a safe base, loss of direction, [and] inability to detect or respond to danger, and often leads to subsequent trauma exposure. Complex trauma can have effects across the following domains: attachment, biology, affect regulation, dissociation, behavioral regulation, cognitive function, and self concept" (Cook et al., 2003).

consolidation: A phase of trauma-focused therapy following exposure or other processing of traumatic memories that allows the individual to experience calm reflection on, and integration of, new perspectives and feelings. Consolidation is the process that promotes development of affect tolerance and regulation skills, as well as new perceptions and beliefs. Consolidation is supported as the individual experiences increased security, trust, and competency in the present.

developmental trauma: See complex trauma. These terms are often used interchangeably.

disorganized attachment: A pathologic style of insecure attachment that is marked by confusion, fear, and often contradictory behaviors of approach and avoidance toward the caregiver. This represents a disturbed response due to maltreatment or other trauma that is beyond the scope of normal development.

dissociation: A defensive process through which an individual attempts to distance from or ward off feelings, sensations, and thoughts that are too overwhelming to cope with. This disrupts the normal process of integration of these components into one's sense of self and personal history.

dysregulation: An intense state of arousal marked by loss of physiological, emotional, cognitive, and/or behavioral control and organization. This response to perceived threat or overstimulation may be evidenced in overt symptoms of distress and aggression, or more subtle symptoms of freezing and dissociation.

empathy: The ability to experience what someone else is feeling—"to put yourself in someone else's shoes and feel with them." This is different from sympathy, in which one might feel something for another, but remains less personally involved in the feeling.

explicit memory: A conscious memory, processed and stored with language that can intentionally be recalled for use in daily life.

exposure: (1) The experience of specific environmental factors, such as exposure to violence or exposure to alcohol during fetal development; (2) a treatment intervention used in trauma therapy to resolve defensive strategies of learned avoidance that increases arousal by confronting those aspects of experience, behavior, and sensation that are being avoided, while simultaneously preventing the use of maladaptive coping strategies.

holding: Holding refers to the coercive restraint of a child by an adult, as opposed to cradling, which is a cooperative, collaborative, and supportive experience. Although the term "holding therapy" has been used in the past, holding is not synonymous with attachment therapy. If non-coercive holding or cradling may involve a position in which the caregiver may have the younger child sit on her lap or may hold an older child's hand in order to help the child feel safe and comfortable while exploring painful or difficult memories or experiences.

implicit memory: An unconscious memory that involves sensory components (e.g., sights, sounds, smells, sensations), which are processed outside of conscious awareness and can become trigger reactions to stimuli in the present.

interactive repair: A repair that occurs when the caregiver recognizes a disconnection with the child due to misattunement and the child's negative feelings created by this disconnection. The caregiver then provides active assistance to help the child reconnect and reestablish the prior positive shared emotional state.

insecure attachment: Styles of attachment that are organized patterns within the normal range of development, but that lack the flexibility and comfort evident in secure attachment. The avoidant style of attachment (also known as dismissing in adults) is characterized by discomfort with strong emotions and reliance on others, coupled with more independent exploration. The ambivalent style of attachment (also known as preoccupied in adults) is characterized by anxiety about maintaining relationships, more intense signaling of emotions, and limited independent exploration.

internal working model: The core beliefs about oneself, others, and the world derived from early experiences with caregivers. These beliefs influence the individual's perceptions and related thoughts, which in turn exert significant influence on behavior. They persist relatively unchanged unless there is significant experience that challenges them.

intersubjectivity: A process of mutual interaction and engagement between the child and caregiver, in which each of these parties is able to understand the affect and the subjective experience of the other and to adapt to it. It has three components: shared affect, shared attention, and shared and complementary intentions.

kind attributions: Judging the cause of behaviors in a more positive context (e.g., recognizing a behavior as not intentional but based, instead, in fear).

misattunement: A break in an expected sensitive and empathic connection. Mild forms occur due to transient experiences of the attachment figure being distracted, preoccupied, or unavailable. When mild misattunements are handled well by interactive repair, the child learns frustration tolerance, ability to tolerate strong feelings, and trust in the help available from the caregiver. Severe, malignant forms result from serious and/or chronic experiences of maltreatment. In these situations, the child typically does not receive adequate interactive repair and is left alone to handle overwhelming feelings of distress and/or shame.

projective measures: A variety of personality tests in which the individual is presented with ambiguous stimuli (e.g., drawing, sentence fragment) and asked to provide meaning.

psychometric: Both instruments and processes of personality testing that are based on standards of validity (i.e., the test measures what it purports to measure) and reliability (i.e., the test yields measurements that are consistent over time).

rage reduction: A therapeutic goal, not a specific technique. In the early years of attachment work, the phrase referred to a confrontational and physically intrusive technique developed by Robert Zaslow and utilized to elicit rage in order to reduce resistance, thereby facilitating the healing of the child. In current practice, rage is not viewed as the primary basis for disordered attachments.

reflective function: The ability to recognize and understand one's own and another's thoughts, feelings, moods, and needs. Sometimes this is referred to as *reflective capacity*.

regulation: The developmentally acquired ability to flexibly organize one's feelings, thoughts, and behaviors in a constructive manner, effectively manage arousal and distress, and be able to return to a calm state of equilibrium.

relational trauma: A form of complex or developmental trauma that occurs within the caregiving relationship, involving the combined effects of maltreatment by a caregiver, resulting loss of the caregiver as a secure base, and the overwhelming dysregulation that children experience without access to safety or comfort.

restraint: The application of a physical, mechanical, or chemical force for the purpose of restricting the free movement of a person's body. Restraint is indicated and permitted as an emergency safety intervention for the protection of the person, others, and/or property. It is an intervention of last resort, not a therapeutic intervention (also sometimes referred to as a *therapeutic hold*).

> *chemical restraint*: The administration of medication for the purpose of restraint.
>
> *manual restraint*: A physical hands-on technique that restricts the movement or function of a person's body or portion of it. The following are not considered restraint: holding a person without undue force to calm or comfort; holding a person's hand to provide safe escort from one place to another; or prompting or guiding a person who does not resist to assist in the activities of daily living.
>
> *mechanical restraint*: The use of a physical device to restrict the movement of a person or the movement or normal function of a portion of his or her body.
>
> *seclusion*: Physically confining an individual alone in a room or limited space from which he or she is prohibited from leaving.

safety: Physical, emotional, and psychological freedom from harm or threat of harm.

secure attachment: A style of attachment that is marked by a balance between comfort with both emotional closeness and sharing of emotions as well as independent exploration.

secure base: The significant attachment figure who provides a balance of comfort and protection with support for exploration. Sometimes colloquially referred to as one's "safe harbor."

theory of mind (ToM): In general, an individual's ability to interpret accurately what another person may be thinking or feeling because the individual understands that the other has a mind that works similarly, yet may have different reactions to the same experience.

therapeutic window (Briere) or window of tolerance (Siegel): A range that exists between two boundaries of affect arousal. On one end is the boundary of too little arousal, in which the child's well-developed avoidance strategies continue unchanged. On the other end is the boundary marked by too much arousal, when the child is overwhelmed by intense affect that he is unable to tolerate or regulate. When a traumatized child is overwhelmed, there is greater chance that the child will feel forced to resort to the very defensive responses of withdrawal, avoidance, and/or dissociation, which the therapy is seeking to resolve and change. The window is that emotional and psychological space in which the child can experience feelings yet stay constructively engaged in the intervention.

trauma: An experience in which an individual perceives a significant threat to survival or of bodily harm that overwhelms the normal coping responses. Unless it is effectively resolved, such an experience will have lasting neurophysiological effects evidenced by automatic responses such as heightened arousal, avoidance of reminders of the trauma, and heightened physiological and emotional reactivity.

REFERENCES

Ainsworth, M. D. S. (1990). Some considerations regarding theory and assessment relevant to attachments beyond infancy. In M. T. Greenberg, D. Cicchetti, & E. M. Cummings (Eds.), *Attachment in the preschool years* (pp. 463–488). Chicago: University of Chicago Press.

Ainsworth, M. D. S., Blehar, M. C., Waters, E., & Wall, S. (1978). *Patterns of attachment: Psychological study of the strange situation.* Hillsdale, NJ: Erlbaum.

American Academy of Child and Adolescent Psychiatry. (2003). *Practice Parameter for the Assessment and Treatment of Children and Adolescents With Reactive Attachment Disorder of Infancy and Early Childhood.* Washington, DC: Author.

American Psychiatric Association. (1980). *Diagnostic and statistical manual of mental disorders* (3th ed.). Washington, DC: Author.

American Psychiatric Association. (2000). *Diagnostic and statistical manual of mental disorders* (4th ed., text rev.). Washington, DC: Author.

American Psychiatric Association. (2002). *Reactive attachment disorder: Position statement.* Washington, DC: Author.

American Psychological Association. (2005, July). *Report of the presidential task force on evidence-based practice.* Washington, DC: Author.

Anda, R. F., Felitti, V. J., Bremner, J. D., Walker, J. D., Whitfield, C., Perry, B. D., et al. (2006). The enduring effects of abuse and related adverse experiences in childhood: A convergence of evidence from neurobiology and epidemiology. *European Archives of Psychiatry and Clinical Neuroscience, 256*(3), 174–218.

Aponte, H., & Carlsen, J. (2009). An instrument for the person-of-the-therapist supervision. *Journal of Marital and Family Therapy, 35*(4), 395–405.

ATTACh. (2007). *White paper on coercion in treatment.* Lake Villa, IL: Author.

ATTACh. (2011). *Hope for Healing: A parent's guide to trauma and attachment.* Lake Villa, IL: Author.

Barnett, D., & Vondra, J. I. (1999). Atypical patterns of early attachment: Theory, research, and current directions. *Monographs of the Society for Research in Child Development, 64*, 1–24.

Barry, R. A., & Kochanska, G. (2010). A longitudinal investigation of the affective environment in families with young children: From infancy to early school age. *Emotion, 10*(2), 237–249.

Becker-Weidman, A. (2006a). Treatment of Children with Trauma-Attachment Disorders: Dyadic Developmental Psychotherapy. *Child and Adolescent Social Work Journal 23*(2), 147-171.

Becker-Weidman, A., (2006b). Dyadic Developmental Psychotherapy: A multi-year follow-up. In Sturt, S., (Ed.). New Developments in Child Abuse Research. NY: Nova Science Press, 43-60.

Becker-Weidman, A. (2007). *Assessing children with complex trauma and attachment disorders* [DVD]. Williamsville, NY: Center for Family Development.

Becker-Weidman, A. (2009). Effects of early maltreatment on development: Descriptive study using the Vineland Adaptive Behavior Scales–II. *Child Welfare, 88*(2), 137–161.

Becker-Weidman, A. (2010a). *Assessing caregiver reflective capacity, commitment, insightfulness, and sensitivity* [2-DVD set]. Williamsville, NY: Center for Family Development.

Becker-Weidman, A. (2010b). *Dyadic Developmental Psychotherapy: Essential methods and practices*. Lanham, MD: Jason Aronson.

Becker-Weidman, A. (Ed.). (2011). *The Dyadic Developmental Psychotherapy casebook*. Lanham, MD: Jason Aronson.

Becker-Weidman, A. (2012). *The Dyadic Developmental Psychotherapy Primer*. Williamsville, NY: Century.

Becker-Weidman, A., & Hughes, D. (2008). Dyadic developmental psychotherapy: An evidence-based treatment for children with complex trauma and disorders of attachment. *Child and Family Social Work, 13*(3), 329–337.

Becker-Weidman, A., & Shell, D. (Eds.). (2010). *Attachment parenting*. Lanham, MD: Jason Aronson.

Becker-Weidman, A., & Shell, D. (Eds.). (2011). *Creating Capacity for Attachment*. Oklahoma City, OK: Wood N Barnes.

Beebe, B., & Lachmann, E. M. (1988). The contribution of mother-infant mutual influence to the origins of self and object relations. *Psychoanalytic Psychology, 5*, 305–337.

Beebe, B., & Lachmann, E. M. (1994). Representations and internalizations in infancy of salience. *Psychoanalytic Psychology, 11*, 127–165.

Beery, K. (1997). *The Beery-Buktenica developmental test of visual-motor integration: Administration, scoring, and teaching manual* (4th ed.). Parsippany, NJ: Modern Curriculum Press.

Belsky, J. (1984). The determinants of parenting: A process model. *Child Development, 55*, 83–96.

Bennett, C. (2008). Attachment-informed supervision for social work field education. *Clinical Social Work Journal, 36*, 97–107.

Bernard, J., & Goodyear, R. (2009). *Fundamentals of clinical supervision* (4th ed.). Upper Saddle River, NJ: Pearson Education.

Bernier, A., & Meins, E. (2008). A threshold approach to understanding the origins of attachment disorganization. *Developmental Psychology, 44*(4), 969–982.

Beutler, L. E., & Clarkin, J. F. (1990). *Systematic treatment selection: Toward targeted therapeutic interventions*. New York: Brunner Mazel.

Blaustein, M., Cooke, A., Spinazzola, J., & van der Kolk, B. A. (Eds.). (2003). *Complex trauma in children and adolescents: White paper for the NCTSN*. Washington, DC: SAMSHA/NCTSN.

Bleiberg, E. (2001). *Treating personality disorders in children and adolescents: A relational approach*. New York: Guilford.

Borelli, J. L., Crowley, M. J., David, D. H., Sbarra, D. A., Anderson, G. M., & Mayes, L. C. (2010). Attachment and emotion in school-aged children. *Emotion, 10*(4), 475–485.

Boris, N. W., Hinshaw-Fuselier, S. S., Smyke, A. T., Scheeringa, M. S., Heller, S. S., & Zeanah, C. H. (2004). Comparing criteria for attachment disorders: Establishing reliability and validity in high-risk samples. *Journal of the American Academy of Child and Adolescent Psychiatry, 43*(5), 568–577.

Bouchard, M., Target, M., Lecours, S., Fonagy, P., Tremblay, L., Schachter, A., & Stein, H. (2008). Mentalization in adult attachment narratives: Reflective functioning, mental states, and affect elaboration compared. *Psychoanalytic Psychology, 25*(1), 47–66.

Bowlby, J. (1944). Forty-four thieves: Their characteristics and home lives. *International Journal of Psychoanalysis, 25*, 19–52.

Bowlby, J. (1951). *Maternal care and mental health*. WHO Monograph, 2. Geneva: World Health Organization.

Bowlby, J. (1969). *Attachment and loss: Vol. 1. Attachment.* New York: Basic Books.

Bowlby, J. (1973). *Attachment and loss: Vol. 2. Separation: Anxiety and anger.* New York: Basic Books.

Bowlby, J. (1979). *The making of affectional bonds*. London: Tavistock.

Bowlby, J. (1980). *Attachment and loss: Vol. 2. Separation: Anxiety and anger* (rev. ed.). New York: Basic Books.

Bowlby, J. (1982). *Attachment and loss: Vol. 1. Attachment* (rev. ed.). New York: Basic Books.

Bowlby, J. (1988). *A secure base: Parent-child attachment and healthy human development*. New York: Basic Books.

Bowlby, J., & Robertson, J. (1953). Discussion of a two-year-old goes to hospital. *Proceedings of the Royal Society of Medicine, 46*(6), 425–427.

Braungart-Rieker, J., Hill-Soderlund, A., & Karrass, J. (2010). Fear and anger reactivity trajectories from 4 to 16 months: The roles of temperament, regulation, and maternal sensitivity. *Developmental Psychology, 46*(4), 791–804.

Bretherton, I., & Munholland, K. A. (1999). Internal working models in attachment relationships. In J. Cassidy & P. R. Shaver (Eds.), *Handbook of attachment* (pp. 89–114). New York: Guilford.

Bretherton, I., Ridgeway, D., & Cassidy, J. (1990). In Greenbert, M., Cicchetti, D., & Cummings, E. (Eds.), *Attachment in the preschool years* (pp. 273–310). Chicago: University of Chicago Press.

Briere, J. (2002). The self trauma model. In J. E. B. Myers, L. Berliner, J. Briere, C. T. Hendrix, T. Reid, & C. Jenny (Eds.), *The APSAC handbook on child maltreatment* (2nd ed., pp. 175–202). Newbury Park, CA: Sage.

Briere, J., & Lanktree, C. (2008). *Integrative treatment of complex trauma for adolescents (ITCT-A)*. Washington, DC: NCTSN.

Briere, J., & Lanktree, C. (2011). *Treating complex trauma in adolescents and young adults*. Thousand Oaks, CA: Sage.

Briere, J., & Scott, C. (2006). *Principles of trauma therapy: A guide to symptom evaluation and treatment*. Thousand Oaks, CA: Sage.

Buck, C. (2010). *2010 ICD-10-CM, standard edition*. New York: Elsevier.

Bucks, J. (1995). *House-tree-person projective drawing technique: Manual and interpretive guide* (rev. by W. L. Warren). Los Angeles: Western Psychological Services.

Budzynski, T. H., Budzynski, H. K., Evans, J. R., & Abarbanel, A. (Eds.). (2008). *Introduction to quantitative EEG and neurofeedback: Advanced theory and applications* (2nd ed.). San Diego, CA: Academic Press.

Carlson, E. A. (1998). A prospective longitudinal study of disorganized/disoriented attachment. *Child Development, 6*, 1107–1128.

Carlson, G. A. (2007). Who are the children with severe mood dysregulation, a.k.a. "rages"? *American Journal of Psychiatry, 164*, 1140–1142.

Carlson, V., Cicchetti, D., Barnett, D., & Braunwald, K. (1989). Disorganized/disoriented attachment relationships in maltreated infants. *Developmental Psychology, 25*, 525–531.

Cassidy, J., & Shaver, P. (Eds.). (2008). *Handbook of attachment: Theory, research and clinical applications* (2nd ed.). New York: Guilford.

Cerney, M. (1995). Treating the heroic treaters. In C. R. Figley (Ed.), *Compassion fatigue: Coping with secondary traumatic stress disorder in those who treat the traumatized*. Bristol, PA: Brunner/Mazel.

Chaffin, M., Hanson, R., Saunders, B. E., Nichols, T., Barnett, D., Zeanah, C., et al. (2006). Report of the APSAC task force on attachment therapy, reactive attachment disorder, and attachment problems. *Child Maltreatment, 11*, 76–89.

Chasnoff, I. (2010). *The Mystery of Risk*. Chicago: NTI Upstream.

Chiriboga, C. A. (2003). Fetal alcohol and drug effects. *Neurologist, 6*, 267–279.

Cicchetti, D., & Rogosch, F. A. (1996). Equifinality and multifinality in developmental psychopathology. *Development and Psychopathology, 8*(4), 597–600.

Cicchetti, D., Rogosch, F. A., & Toth, S. L. (2006). Fostering secure attachment in infants in maltreating families through preventative interventions. *Developmental and Psychopathology, 18*, 623–649.

Clark, C., Buckwalter, K., Robinson, M., Blackwell, S., & McGuill, J. (2011). Dyadic Developmental Psychotherapy in impermanent settings (foster care, group homes, and residential treatment centers). In Becker-Weidman, A., & Shell, D., (Eds.), *Creating capacity for attachment*. Oklahoma City, OK: Wood N Barnes.

Clark, D. A., & Beck, A. T., with Alford, B. (1999). *Scientific foundations of cognitive theory and therapy of depression*. New York: Wiley.

Cobia, D., & Pipes, R. (2002). Mandated supervision: An intervention for disciplined professionals. *Journal of Counseling and Development, 80*, 140–144.

Cohen, J. A., Mannarino, A. P., & Deblinger, J. (2006). *Treating trauma and traumatic grief in children and adolescents*. New York: Guilford.

Colvert, E., Rutter, M., Beckett, C., Castle, J., Groothues, C., Hawkins, A., et al. (2008). Emotional difficulties in early adolescence following severe early deprivation: Findings from the English and Romanian adoptees study. *Development Psychopathology, 20*(2), 547–567.

Converse, B. A., Lin, S., Keysar, B., & Epley, N. (2008). In the mood to get over yourself: Mood affects theory-of-mind use. *Emotion, 8*(5), 725–730.

Cook, A., Blaustein, M., Spinazolla, J., & van der Kolk, B. (2003). *Complex trauma in children and adolescents*. White Paper from the National Child Traumatic Stress Network Complex Trauma Task Force. Los Angeles, CA: National Center for Child Traumatic Stress.

Cook, A., Spinazzola, J., Ford, J., Lanktree, C., Blaustein, M., Cloitre, M., et al. (2005). Complex trauma in children and adolescents. *Psychiatric Annals, 35*, 390–398.

Courtois, C. A., & Ford, J. D. (2009). *Treating complex trauma disorders: an evidence-based guide*. New York: Guilford.

Cozolino, L. (2010). *The neuroscience of psychotherapy* (2nd ed.). New York: Norton.

Craven, P., & Lee, R. (2006). Therapeutic interventions for foster children: A systematic research synthesis. *Research on Social Work Practice, 16*, 287–304.

Crittenden, P. (1985). Maltreated infants: Vulnerability and resistance. *Journal of Child Psychology and Psychiatry, 26*, 85–96.

Daniel, S. I. F. (2009). The developmental roots of narrative expression in therapy: Contributions from attachment theory and research. *Psychotherapy: Theory, Research, Practice, Training, 46*(3), 301–316.

Davies, J. K., & Bledsoe, J. M. (2005). Prenatal alcohol and drug exposures in adoption. *Pediatric Clinics of North America, 52*(5), 1369–1393.

Desmond, K., & Kindsvatter, A. (2010). Intentional practices in supervision of family counseling: The use of supervisory letters. *Family Journal: Counseling for Couples and Families, 18*(1), 31–35.

Dodge, K. A. (1985). Attributional bias in aggressive children. In P. Kendall (Ed.), *Advances in cognitive-behavioral research and therapy* (pp. 75–111). New York: Academic Press.

Dozier, M., & Lindhiem, O. (2006). This is my child: Differences among foster parents in commitment to their young children. *Child Maltreatment, 11*(4), 338–345.

Dozier, M., Stovall, K. C., Albus, K. E., & Bates, B. (2001). Attachment for infants in foster care: The role of caregiver state of mind. *Child Development, 70*, 1467–1477.

Dykas, M. J., & Cassidy, J. (2011). Attachment and the processing of social information across the life span: Theory and evidence. *Psychological Bulletin, 137*(1), 19–46.

Emde, R., Wolf, D., & Oppenheim, D. (Eds.). (2003). *Revealing the inner worlds of young children: The MacArthur story stem battery and parent-child narratives.* New York: Oxford University Press.

Ernst, M., Moolchan, E. T., & Robinson, M. L. (2001). Behavioral and neural consequences of prenatal exposure to nicotine. *Journal of the American Academy of Child and Adolescent Psychiatry, 40*(6), 630–641.

Field, T., Healy, B. T., & Goldstein, S. (1990). Behavior-state matching and synchrony in mother-infant interactions in non-depressed dyads. *Developmental Psychology*, 26, 7-14.

Figley, C. (Ed.). (1995). *Compassion fatigue: Coping with secondary traumatic stress disorders in those who treat the traumatized*. Bristol, PA: Brunner/Mazel.

Figley, C. (1999). Compassion fatigue. In B. Stamm (Ed.), *Secondary traumatic stress: Self care issues.* Lutherville, CA: Sidran.

Finkelhor, D., & Brown, A. (1984). The traumatic impact of child sexual abuse: A conceptualization. *American Journal of Orthopsychiatry, 55,* 530–541.

Fitch, J., Pistole, C., & Gunn, J. (2010). The bonds of development: An attachment-caregiving model of supervision. *Clinical Supervisor, 29*, 20–34.

Fonagy, P. (1996). The significance of the development of metacognitive control over mental representations in parenting and infant development. *Journal of Clinical Psychoanalysis, 5*(1), 67–86.

Fonagy, P., Gergely, G., Jurist, E. L., & Target, M. (2002). *Affect regulation, mentalization, and the development of the self*. New York: Other Press.

Fonagy, P., & Target, M. (1997). Attachment and reflective function: Their role in self-organization. *Development and Psychopathology, 9*, 679–700.

Ford, J. D. (2005). Treatment implications of altered neurobiology, affect regulation and information processing following child maltreatment. *Psychiatric Annals, 35*, 410–419.

Ford, M., & Collins, N. L. (2010). Self-esteem moderates neuroendocrine and psychological responses to interpersonal rejection. *Journal of Personality and Social Psychology, 98*(3), 405–419.

Fox, N. A., Hane, A. A., & Pine, D. S. (2007). Plasticity for affective neurocircuitry: How the environment affects gene expression. *Current Directions in Psychological Science, 16*, 1–5.

Geisinger, K. F., Spies, R. A., Carlson, J. F., & Plake, B. S. (Eds.). (2011). *The seventeenth mental measurements yearbook*. Lincoln, NE: Buros Institute of Mental Measurements.

Gillath, O., Sesko, A. K., Shaver, P. R., & Chun, D. S. (2010). Attachment, authenticity, and honesty: Dispositional and experimentally induced security can reduce self- and other-deception. *Journal of Personality and Social Psychology, 98*(5), 841–855.

Ginot, E. (2011). Self-narratives and dysregulated affective states: The neuropsychological links between self-narratives, attachment, affect, and cognition. *Psychoanalytic Psychology*, doi:10.1037/a0023154

Greenberg, M. T. (1999). Attachment and psychopathology in childhood. In J. Cassidy & P. Shaver (Eds.), *Handbook of attachment* (pp. 470–496). New York: Guilford.

Greenberg, M. T., Cicchetti, D., & Cummings, E. (Eds.). (1990). *Attachment in the preschool years*. Chicago: University of Chicago Press.

Gunnar, M. R., van Dulmen, M. H., & International Adoption Project Team. (2007). Behavior problems in postinstitutionalized internationally adopted children. *Developmental Psychopathology, 19*(1), 129–148.

Hanson, M. D., & Chen, E. (2010). Daily stress, cortisol, and sleep: The moderating role of childhood psychosocial environments. *Health Psychology, 29*(4), 394–402.

Herman, J. (1992). *Trauma and recovery*. New York: Basic Books.

Hesse, E. (1999). The adult attachment interview: Historical and current perspectives. In J. Cassidy & P. R. Shaver (Eds.), *Handbook of attachment: Theory, research, and clinical implications* (pp. 395–433). New York: Guilford.

Hofer, M.A. (1984). Relationships as regulators: A psychobiologic perspective on bereavement. *Psychosomatic Medicine, 46*(3), 183–197.

Hughes, D. A. (2006). *Building the bonds of attachment* (2nd ed.). New York: Aronson.

Hughes, D. A. (2007). *Attachment-focused family therapy*. New York: Norton.

Jernberg, A. M. & Booth, P. B. (1998). *Theraplay: Helping parents and children build relationships through attachment-based play*. New York: Aronson.

Johnson, S. C., Dweck, C. S., Chen, F. S., Stern, H. L., Ok, S., & Barth, M. (2010). At the intersection of social and cognitive development: Internal working models of attachment in infancy. *Cognitive Science: A Multidisciplinary Journal, 34*(5), 807–825.

Keck, G. C., & Kupecky, R. M. (1998). *Adopting the hurt child*. Colorado Springs, CO: NavPress.

Kobacks, R. R. (1999). The emotional dynamics of disruptions in attachment relationships. In J. Cassidy & P. Shaver (Eds.), *Handbook of attachment* (pp. 21–43). New York: Guilford.

Kobacks, R. R., & Sceery, A. (1988). Attachment in late adolescence: Working models, affect regulation, and representation of self and others. *Child Development, 59*, 135–146.

Kochanska, G. (2002). Mutually responsive orientation between mothers and their young children: A context for the early development of conscience. *Current Directions in Psychological Science, 11*, 191–195.

Kochanska, G., & Murray, K. T. (2000). Mother-child mutually responsive orientation and conscience development: From toddler to early school age. *Child Development, 71*, 417–431.

Koren-Karie, N., Oppenheim, D., & Getzler-Yosef, R. (2008). Shaping children's internal working models through mother-child dialogues: The importance of resolving past maternal trauma. *Attachment and Human Development, 10*(4), 465–483.

Kreppner, J. M., Rutter, M., Beckett, C., Castle, J., Colvert, E., Groothues, C., et al. (2007). Normality and impairment following profound early institutional deprivation: A longitudinal follow-up into early adolescence. *Developmental Psychology, 43*(4), 931–946.

Lacher, D., Nichols, T., & May, J. (2005). *Connecting with kids through stories*. Philadelphia: Jessica Kingsley.

Lambert, M. J. (Ed.). (2004). *Bergin and Garfield's handbook of psychotherapy and behavior change* (5th ed.). New York: Wiley.

Lanktree, C., & Briere, J. (2008). *Integrative treatment for complex trauma*. Washington, DC: NCTSN.

LeDoux, J. E. (1999). Fear and the brain: Where have we been and where are we going? *Biological Psychiatry, 44*, 1229–1238.

Levine, P. A. (1997). *Waking the tiger: The innate capacity to transform overwhelming experiences*. Berkeley, CA: North Atlantic Books.

Levine, P., & Klein, M. (2006). *Trauma through a child's eyes: Awakening the ordinary miracle of healing*. Berkeley, CA: North Atlantic Books.

Levy, T. M., & Orlans, M. A. (1998). *Attachment, trauma and healing*. Washington, DC: CWLA.

Lindsey, E. W., Caldera, Y. M., & Tankersley, L. (2009). Marital conflict and the quality of young children's peer play behavior: The mediating and moderating role of parent–child emotional reciprocity and attachment security. *Journal of Family Psychology, 23*(2), 130–145.

Liotti, G. (1992). Disorganized/disoriented attachment in the etiology of dissociative disorders. *Dissociation, 4*, 196–204.

Liotti, G. (2011). Attachment disorganization and the controlling strategies: An illustration of the contributions of attachment theory to developmental psychopathology and to psychotherapy integration. *Journal of Psychotherapy Integration, 21*(3), 232–252.

Luthar, S. S., & Zigler, E. (1991). Vulnerability and competence: A review of research on resilience in childhood. *American Journal of Orthopsychiatry, 61*, 6–22.

Lyons-Ruth, K., & Jacobvitz, D. (1999). Attachment disorganization: Unresolved loss, relational violence and lapses in behavioral and attentional strategies. In J. Cassidy & P. Shaver (Eds.), *Handbook of attachment* (pp. 520–554). New York: Guilford.

Main, M. (1991). Metacognitive knowledge, metacognitive monitoring, and models of attachment (pp. 127–159). In C. M. Parkes Jr., J. Stevenson-Hinde, & P. Marris (Eds.), *Attachment across the lifecycle*. London: Routledge.

Main, M., & Goldwyn, R. (1984). *Adult attachment scoring and classification system*. Unpublished manuscript, University of California at Berkeley.

Main, M., & Hesse, E. (1990). Lack of resolution in mourning in adulthood and its relationship to infant disorganization: Some speculations regarding the causal mechanisms. In M. T. Greenberg, D. Cicchetti, & E. M. Cummings (Eds.), *Attachment in the preschool years* (pp. 161–184). Chicago: University of Chicago Press.

Main, M., Kaplan, N., & Cassidy, J. (1985). Security in infancy, childhood, and adulthood: A move to the level of representation. In I. Bretherton & E. Waters (Eds.), *Growing points of attachment theory and research*. Monographs of the Society for Research in Child Development, 50 (102, Serial No. 209), 66–104.

Main, M., & Solomon, J. (1986). Discovery of the insecure-disorganized/disoriented attachment pattern: Procedures, findings, and implications for classification of behavior (pp. 95–124). In T. B. Brazelton & M. Yogman (Eds.), *Affective development in infancy*. Norwood, NJ: Ablex.

Main, M., & Solomon, J. (1990). Procedures for identifying infants as disorganized/disoriented during the Ainsworth strange situation. In M. T. Greenberg, D. Cicchetti, & E. Waters (Eds.), *Attachment in the preschool years: Theory, research, and intervention* (pp. 121–160). Chicago: University of Chicago Press.

Mallers, M. H., Charles, S. T., Neupert, S. D., & Almeida, D. M. (2010). Perceptions of childhood relationships with mother and father: Daily emotional and stressor experiences in adulthood. *Developmental Psychology, 46*(6), 1651–1661.

Marvin, R. S., Cooper, G., Hoffman, K., & Powell, B. (2002). The circle of security project: Attachment-based intervention with caregiver-pre-school child dyads. *Attachment and Human Development, 4*, 107–124.

Masten, A. S., & Coatsworth, J. D. (1998). The development of competence in favorable and unfavorable environments. *American Psychologist, 53*(2), 205–220.

Masterson, J. F. (2005). *The personality disorders through the lens of attachment theory and the neurobiologic development of the self*. Phoenix, AZ: Zeig, Tucker, and Theisen.

Mattson, A. (2010). The role of neuropsychological evaluation and intervention in the management and treatment of children with a history of early maltreatment. In A. Becker-Weidman & D. Shell (Eds.), *Attachment parenting* (pp. 107–124). Lanham, MD: Jason Aronson.

Maughan, A., & Cicchetti, D. (2002). Impact of child maltreatment and interadult violence on children's emotion regulation abilities and socioemotional adjustment. *Child Development, 73*, 1525–1542.

McCann, I., & Pearlman, L. (1990). Vicarious trauma: A framework for understanding the psychological effects of working with victims. *Journal of Traumatic Stress, 3*(1), 131–145.

McCarthy, G., & Maughan, B. (2010). Negative childhood experiences and adult love relationships: The role of internal working models of attachment. *Attachment and Human Development, 12*(5), 445–461.

McFarlane, A. C. (1987). Posttraumatic phenomena in a longitudinal study of children following a natural disaster. *Journal of the American Academy of Child and Adolescent Psychiatry, 26*, 764–769.

McFarlane, A. C., & Girolamo, G. (1996). The nature of traumatic stressors and the epidemiology of posttraumatic reactions. In B. A. van der Kolk, A. C. McFarlane, & L. Wersaeth (Eds.), *Traumatic stress: The effects of overwhelming experience on mind, body, and society* (pp. 129–142). New York: Guilford.

McNeill, B. W., & Worthen, V. (1989). The parallel process in psychotherapy supervision. *Professional Psychology, 20*, 329–333.

Mikulineer, M., & Shaver, P. R. (2005). Attachment security, compassion, and altruism. *Current Directions in Psychological Science, 14*, 34–38.

Milan, S., Snow, S., & Belay, S. (2009). Depressive symptoms in mothers and children: Preschool attachment as a moderator of risk. *Developmental Psychology, 45*(4), 1019–1033.

Minton, K., Ogden, P., Pain, C., & Siegel, D. J. (2006). *Trauma and the body: A sensorimotor approach to psychotherapy.* New York: Norton.

National Association of Social Workers. (1999). *Code of ethics.* Washington, DC: NASW Press.

Neale, S. (1992). Paul Grice and the philosophy of language. *Linguistics and Philosophy, 15*, 5.

Nelson, C. A., III, Zeanah, C. H., Fox, N. A., Marshall, P. J., Smyke, A. T., & Guthrie D. (2007). Cognitive recovery in socially deprived young children: The Bucharest early intervention project. *Science, 318*(5858), 1937–1940.

Neumeister, A., Henry, S., & Krystal, J. H. (2007). Neurocircuitry and neuroplasticity in PTSD. In C. A. Courtois & J. D. Ford (Eds.), *Treating complex trauma disorders: An evidence-based guide* (p. 32). New York: Guilford.

Newland, L. A., Coyl, D. D., & Freeman, H. (2008). Predicting preschoolers' attachment security from fathers' involvement, internal working models, and use of social support. *Early Child Development and Care, 178*(7–8), 785–801.

Niccols, A. (2007). Fetal alcohol syndrome and the developing socio-emotional brain. *Brain and Cognition, 65*(1), 135–142.

NICHD Early Child Care Research Network. (2004). Affect dysregulation in the mother-child relationship in the toddler years: Antecedents and consequences. *Development and Psychology, 16*, 43–68.

O'Connor, T. G., & Zeanah, C. H. (2003). Attachment disorders: Assessment strategies and treatment approaches. *Attachment and Human Development, 5*, 223–244.

Ogden, P., Minton, K., & Pain, C. (2006). *Trauma and the body: Sensorimotor approaches to psychotherapy.* New York: Norton.

Oppenheim, D., Goldsmith, D., & Koren-Karie, N. (2005). Maternal insightfulness and preschoolers' emotion and behavior problems: Reciprocal influences in a day-treatment program. *Infant Mental Health Journal, 25*, 352–361.

Oppenheim, D., & Koren-Karie, N. (2002). Mothers' insightfulness regarding their children's internal worlds: The capacity underlying secure child-mother relationships. *Infant Mental Health Journal, 23*(6), 593–605.

Oppenheim, D., Koren-Karie, N., & Sagi, A. (2001). Mothers' empathic understanding of their preschoolers' internal experience: Relations with early attachment. *International Journal of Behavioral Development, 25*, 16–26.

Ottenbacher, K. (1991). Sensory integration therapy: Affect or effect. *American Journal of Occupational Therapy, 1*, 571–578.

Pasco-Fearon, R. M., & Belsky, J. (2004). Attachment and attentional performance: Protection in relation to gender and cumulative social-contextual adversity. *Child Development, 75*(6), 1677–1693.

Pauli-Pott, U., Mertesacker, B., & Beckmann, D. (2004). Predicting the development of infant emotionality from maternal characteristics. *Development and Psychopathology, 16*, 19–42.

Paulussen-Hoogeboom, M., Stams, G. J. J. M., Hermanns, J. M. A., & Peetsma, T. T. D. (2007). Child negative emotionality and parenting from infancy to preschool: A meta-analytic review. *Developmental Psychology, 43*(2), 438–453.

Pearson, Q. (2000). Opportunities and challenges in the supervisory relationship: Implications for counselor supervision. *Journal of Mental Health Counseling, 22*, 283–294.

Perlman, L. A., & Saakvitne, K. W. (1995). Treating therapists with vicarious traumatization and secondary stress disorders. In C. R. Figley (Ed.), *Compassion fatigue: Coping with secondary traumatic stress disorder in those who treat the traumatized.* Bristol, PA: Brunner/Mazel.

Perrier, C. P. K., Boucher, R., Etchegary, H., Sadava, S. W., & Molnar, D. S. (2010). The overlapping contributions of attachment orientation and social support in predicting life-events distress. *Canadian Journal of Behavioural Science, 42*(2), 71–79.

Perry, B. D. (1993). Neurodevelopment and the psychophysiology of trauma II: Clinical work along the alarm-fear-terror continuum. *APSAC Advisor, 6*(2), 1–20.

Perry, B. D. (2001). Violence and children: How persisting fear can alter the developing child's brain. In D. Schetsky & E. Benedict (Eds.), *Textbook of child and adolescent forensic psychiatry.* Washington, DC: APA.

Perry, B. D., Pollard, R. A., Blakley, T. L., & Vigilante, D. (1995). Childhood trauma, the neurobiology of adaptation, and use-dependent development of the brain: How states become traits. *Infant Journal of Mental Health, 16*(4), 271–291.

Perry, B., & Szalavitz, M. (2006). *The boy who was raised as a dog.* New York: Basic Books.

Phillips, S. B. (2004). Countertransference: Effects on the clinician working with trauma (Module 7). In *Group interventions for treatment of psychological trauma.* New York: American Group Psychotherapy Association.

Richters, M. M., & Volkmar, F. R. (1994). Reactive attachment disorder of infancy and early childhood. *Journal of the American Academy of Child and Adolescent Psychiatry, 33*(3), 328–332.

Riggs, S. A., Cusimano, A. M., & Benson, K. M. (2011). Childhood emotional abuse and attachment processes in the dyadic adjustment of dating couples. *Journal of Counseling Psychology, 58*(1), 126–138.

Robertson, J. (1952). *A two-year-old goes to hospital* [Film]).

Rogosch, F. A., Cicchetti, D., & Aber, J. L. (1995). The role of child maltreatment in early deviations in cognitive and affective processing abilities and peer relationship problems. *Development and Psychopathology, 7*, 591–609.

Rothschild, B. (2000). *The body remembers: The psychophysiology of trauma and trauma treatment.* New York: Norton.

Rothschild, B. (2006). *Help for the helper: Self-care strategies for managing burnout and stress.* New York: Norton.

Rutter, M. (1981). *Maternal deprivation reassessed* (2nd ed.). Harmondsworth: Penguin.

Rutter, M., Colvert E., Kreppner J., Beckett C., Castle J., Groothues C., et al. (2007). Early adolescent outcomes for institutionally-deprived and non-deprived adoptees. I. Disinhibited attachment. *Journal of Child Psychology and Psychiatry, 48*(1), 17–30.

Saakvitne, K., & Pearlman, L. (1995). *Transforming the pain: A workbook on vicarious trauma.* New York: Norton.

Saunders, B., Berliner, L., & Hanson, R. (2004). *Child physical and sexual abuse: Guidelines for treatment.* Retrieved from http://academicdepartments.musc.edu/ncvc/resources_prof/OVC_guidelines04-26-04.pdf

Scheeringa, M. S., Zeanah, C. H., Myers, L., & Putnam, F. W. (2005). Predictive validity in a prospective follow-up of PTSD in preschool children. *Journal of the American Academy of Child and Adolescent Psychiatry, 44*(9), 899–906.

Schore, A. N. (1994). *Affect regulation and the origin of the self: The neurobiology of emotional development*. Hillsdale, NJ: Lawrence Erlbaum.

Schore, A. N. (1996). The experience-dependent maturation of a regulatory system in the orbital prefrontal cortex and the origin of developmental psychopathology. *Development and Psychopathology, 8*, 59–87.

Schore, A. N. (1997). Early organization of the nonlinear right brain and development of a predisposition to psychiatric disorders. *Development and Psychopathology, 9*, 595–631.

Schore, A. N. (2001). Effects of a secure attachment relationship on right brain development, affect regulation, and infant mental health. *Infant Mental Health Journal, 22*, 7–66.

Schore, A. N. (2003). *Affect regulation and the repair of the self*. New York: Norton.

Schuengel, C., Bakermans-Kranenburg, M. J., & van Ijzendoorn, M. H. (1999). Frightening maternal behavior linking unresolved loss and disorganized infant attachment. *Journal of Consulting and Clinical Psychology, 67*, 54–63.

Shirk, S. R. (2001). The road to effective child psychological services: Treatment processes and outcome research. In J. N. Hughes, A. M. Greca, & J. C. Conoley (Eds.), *Handbook of psychological services for children and adolescents*. New York: Oxford University Press.

Siegel, D. (1999). *The developing mind*. New York: Norton.

Simmons, K. J., Paternate, C. E., & Shore, C. (2001). Cognitions and self-esteem mediate attachment and aggression relationship. *Clinician's Research Digest, 19*(12).

Skowron, E. A., Kozlowski, J. M., & Pincus, A. L. (2010). Differentiation, self-other representations, and rupture-repair processes: Predicting child maltreatment risk. *Journal of Counseling Psychology, 57*(3), 304–316.

Slade, A. (1999). Attachment theory and research: Implications for the theory and practice of individual psychotherapy with adults. In J. Cassidy & P. R. Shaver (Eds.), *Handbook of attachment* (pp. 575–594). New York: Guilford.

Slotkin, T. A. (1998). Fetal nicotine or cocaine exposure: Which one is worse? *Journal of Pharmacology and Experimental Therapies, 285*(3), 931–945.

Smyke, A. T., Koga, S. F., Johnson, D. E., Fox, N. A., Marshall, P. J., Nelson, C. A., et al. (2007). The caregiving context in institution-reared and family-reared infants and toddlers in Romania. *Journal of Child Psychology and Psychiatry, 48*(2), 210–218.

Solomon, J., & George, C. (Eds.). (1999). *Attachment disorganization*. New York: Guilford.

Sonuga-Barke, E. J. S. (1998). Categorical models of childhood disorders: A conceptual and empirical analysis. *Journal of Child Psychology and Psychiatry, 39*(1), 115–133.

Sparrow, S. S., Balla, D. A., & Cicchetti, D. V. (1984). *Vineland adaptive behavior scales*. Circle Pines, MN: American Guidance Service.

Spitz, R. A. (1945). Hospitalism—An inquiry into the genesis of psychiatric conditions in early childhood. *Psychoanalytic Study of the Child, 1*, 53–74.

Sroufe, A. (1990). An organizational perspective of the self. In D. Cicchetti & M. Beeghly (Eds.), *The self in transition: Infancy to childhood* (pp. 281–307). Chicago: University of Chicago Press.

Sroufe, A., & Waters, E. (1977). Attachment as an organizational construct. *Child Development, 48*, 1184–1199.

Stamm, B. H. (Ed.). (1999). *Secondary traumatic stress: Self-care issues for clinicians, researchers, and educators.* Baltimore, MD: Sidran.

Steele, H., & Steele, M. (Eds.). (2008). *Clinical applications of the adult attachment interview.* New York: Guilford.

Stern, D. N. (1977). *The first relationships: Mother and infant.* Cambridge, MA: Harvard University Press.

Stoltenberg, C., McNeill, B., & Delworth, U. (1998). *IDM supervision: An integrated developmental model for supervising counselors and therapists.* San Francisco: Jossey-Bass.

Stroul, B. (2002). Systems of care: A framework for system reform in children's mental health. Washington, DC: SAMSHA and the National Technical Assistance Center for Children's Mental Health at Georgetown University.

Sundram, S. (2006). Cannabis and neurodevelopment: Implications for psychiatric disorders. *Human Psychopharmacology, 4,* 245–254.

Swingle, P. G. (2008). *Biofeedback for the brain: How neurotherapy effectively treats depression, ADHD, autism, and more.* Piscataway, NJ: Rutgers University Press.

Teicher, M.H. (2002). Scars that won't heal: The neurobiology of child abuse. *Scientific American, 286*(3), 68–75.

Terr, L. (1991). Childhood traumas. *American Journal of Psychiatry, 148,* 10–20.

Thompson, R. A. (2000). The legacy of early attachments. *Child Development, 71*(1), 145–152.

Tinker, R. H., & Wilson, S. A. (1999). *Through the eyes of the child: EMDR with children.* New York: Norton.

Trevarthen, C. (1993). The self born in intersubjectivity: The psychology of infant communicating. In U. Neisser (Ed.), *The perceived self: Ecological and interpersonal sources of self knowledge* (pp. 121–173). New York: Cambridge University Press.

Trevarthen, C. (2001). Intrinsic motives for companionship in understanding: Their origin, development, and significance for infant mental health. *Infant Mental Health Journal, 22,* 95–131.

Tronick, E. Z. (1989). Emotions and emotional communication in infants. *American Psychologist, 44,* 112–119.

Tronick, E. Z., & Beeghly, M. (1999). Prenatal cocaine exposure, child development, and the compromising effects of cumulative risk. *Clinical Perinatology, 26*(1), 151–171.

Tronick, E.Z. & Gianino, (1986). The transmission of maternal disturbance to the infant. In E.Z. Tronick, & T. Field (Eds.), *New Directions for Child Development,* No. 34. San Francisco: Jossey-Bass.

U.S. DHHS. (1994). *Treatment for abused and neglected children.* User Manual Series. Washington, DC: Author.

van Bakel, H. J. A., & Rikson-Walvaren, M. (2002). Parenting and development of one-year-olds: Links with parental, contextual, and child characteristics. *Child Development, 73*(1), 256–273.

van der Kolk, B. A. (2005). Developmental trauma disorder. *Psychiatric Annals, 35,* 401–408.

van der Kolk, B. A. (2007). Keynote address. Attachment in an Unattached World: Creating Caring Connections, 19th Annual International Conference on Attachment and Bonding, Providence, RI, October 10–13.

van der Kolk, B. A., McFarlane, A. C., & Weisaeth, L. (Eds.). (1996). *Traumatic stress: The effects of overwhelming experience on mind, body, and society.* New York: Guilford.

van der Kolk, B. A., Pelcovitz, D., Roth, S., & Mandel, F. S. (1996). The complexity of the adaptation to trauma. *American Journal of Psychiatry, 153*(Suppl.), 83–93.

Walker, R. F., & Murachver, T. (2011, September 19). Representation and theory of mind development. *Developmental Psychology.* Advance online publication. doi:10.1037/a0025663

Wallin, D. (2007). *Attachment in psychotherapy.* New York: Guilford.

Warren, S., Huston, L., Egeland, B., & Sroufe, L. A. (1997). Child and adolescent anxiety disorders and early attachment. *Journal of the American Academy of Child and Adolescent Psychiatry, 36,* 637–644.

Weathers, F., & Keene, T. (2007). The Criterion A problem revisited. *Journal of Traumatic Stress, 20,* 107–121.

Wigle, D. T., Arbuckle, T. E., Turner, M. C., Bérubé, A., Yang, Q., Liu, S., & Krewski, D. (2008). Epidemiologic evidence of relationships between reproductive and child health outcomes and environmental chemical contaminants. *Journal of Toxicology and Environmental Health, Part B, Critical Reviews, 11*(5–6), 373–517.

Wilson, J., & Lindy, J. (1994). *Countertransference in treatment of PTSD.* New York: Guilford.

World Health Organization. (1992). *The ICD-10 classification of mental and behavioural disorders.* Geneva: Author.

Yassen, J. (1995). Preventing secondary traumatic stress disorder. In C. R. Figley (Ed.), *Compassion fatigue: Coping with secondary traumatic stress disorder in those who treat the traumatized.* Bristol, PA: Brunner/Mazel.

Zaslow, R. (1975). *The psychology of the z-process: Attachment and activation.* San Jose, CA: San Jose State University Press.

Zeanah, C. (Ed.). (1993). *Handbook of infant mental health.* New York: Guilford.

Zero to Three. (2005). *Diagnostic classification: 0–3: Diagnostic classification of mental health and developmental disorders of infancy and early childhood* (rev. ed.). Washington, DC: Author.

Zhou, Q., Eisenberg, N., Losoya, S., Fabes, R., Reiser, M., Gutherie, I. K., et al. (2002). The relations of the parental warmth and positive expressiveness to children's empathy-related responding and social functioning: A longitudinal study. *Child Development, 3*(3), 893–915.

Ziegler, M., & McEvoy, M. (2000). Hazardous terrain: Countertransference reactions in trauma groups. In R. Klein & V. Schermer (Eds.), *Group psychology for psychological trauma.* New York: Guilford.

INDEX

Briere, J., 54
burnout, 147, 150
See also secondary traumatic stress

caregiver-child relationship
    abuse or neglect within, 92
    ambiguity in, 13
    attachment assumptions about, 48
    attachment behavioral system in, 28–29
    attachment styles in, 29–33, 44
    conditioned emotional responses affect-
        ing, 48–49, 50, 76–77
    cultural and racial differences within,
        102
    effects of early loss in, 17
    internal working models and, 39–42
    out-of-home placements and, 120–21,
        168–71
    parental sensitivity in, 120, 125
    as protective factor, 12
    proximity in, 29
    security development in, 56, 67, 116–17
    stress response system and, 76
    trust in, 8
    understanding behavior in, 5–6, 56
    See also intersubjectivity; synchrony and
        attunement
caregivers
    assessments of, 87, 94–97
    attachment styles in, 32–33
    challenges for, 49–50
    clinical interviews with, 97, 98
    definition of, 1
    functions of book for, 3
    internal working model navigation and,
        122–23
    primary roles for, 25
    reacting to child's experiences by, 76,
        111–12
    reflective capacity in, 5–6, 57–58
    resolution of complex trauma by, 92
    ToM and, 42–44
    treatment goals and objectives for, 60
    See also mothers
caregiver support
    for behavior management, 123, 125–26
    clinical interviews and, 97, 98
    importance of, 5, 14, 49–50, 109
    processing of coherent narratives in, 45
    security development in, 45–46, 54,
        57–58
    treatment success and, 8, 132
caseload balance, 153
CBCL. See Child Behavior Checklist (CBCL)

checklists, for RAD identification, 19
chemical restraints, 130
Child Apperception Test, 106
Child Behavior Checklist (CBCL), 104–5
child development
    attachment assumptions about, 47–48
    attachment changes through, 29
    beliefs and preverbal stages of, 41
    insecure attachment and risks to, 34–35
    limit-setting and, 129–30
    therapeutic window and, 68
    trauma's effects on, 21–22, 71–72, 75–76,
        127
children
    assessment of, 98–101
    attachment behavioral system and style
        in, 28–35
    balancing developmental versus chrono-
        logical needs in, 9, 51–53, 119, 162
    celebration of successes for, 113
    clinical interviews with, 101
    co-creation of coherent narrative in, 45
    compulsive self-reliance in, 17, 116
    discomfort clues in, 79
    effects of early loss and trauma in, 17
    histories of, 99–100, 101–2, 110
    honoring of trauma narrative in, 84
    informed consent of, 108, 139–43
    reenactment of fears in, 14
    treatment goals and objectives for,
        58–60
    vocabulary skills of, 110–11, 112
    See also behaviors; infants and toddlers
child welfare policy and practice, 33
choices, safety and security through, 83
claiming narratives, 84
clinical competence. See professional
    issues
clinical interviews, 97, 98, 101
clinical supervision, defined, 133
    See also supervision and consultation
clinicians. See professional issues
closeness. See proximity
cocaine exposure, prenatal, 26
coercion
    affect regulation and, 157–60
    decision-making process about, 156–57
    historical concept of, 20
    holding therapy as, 7, 8
    informed consent and, 160–61
    lack of reflective capacity and, 44
    meaning of behaviors and, 163–64
    safety promotion and, 53–54
cognition, complex trauma's effects on, 24

cognitive-behavioral therapy, 7
    See also trauma-focused cognitive-behavioral therapy (TF-CBT)
cognitive control strategies, 81
coherent narratives
    definition of, 6
    development of, 84–85
    overview of, 44–45
    reflective capacity and, 58
    of secure mothers, 32–33
    security in caregiver-child relationship and, 67
collaboration, 129
    See also family support network
communication, receptive versus expressive, 111
comorbidity, 21
compassion fatigue, 132, 133, 147, 150
complex trauma
    attachment and effects of, 23
    avoidance of intersubjectivity after, 13
    behavior escalations and, 127
    within caregiver-child relationship, 92
    chronological versus developmental age and, 162
    as consideration in diagnosis, 21, 22, 93
    contextual conditioning of, 74–75
    cyclical process in resolving, 83–84
    definition of, 11–12
    generalization of emotional responses after, 45
    overview of, 22–24, 71–72
    prenatal exposure to substances and, 26
    privacy limitations and, 144
compulsive self-reliance, 17, 116
concentration issues. *See* attention and concentration issues
conditioned emotional responses, 48–49, 50, 76–77, 80–81
    See also memories, traumatic
confidentiality. *See* privacy and confidentiality
conflicts of interest, 144–45
Conners Rating Scales–Revised, 105–6
consent for treatment. *See* authority to consent for treatment; informed consent
consequences. *See* protection and limit setting
consolidation, 78, 119
consultation. *See* supervision and consultation
control, 20, 83
    See also manipulation; resistance
control battles, 127

coping
    caregiver-child relationship and facilitation of, 12, 15
    dysregulation resolution during, 55–56
    exposure technique and, 78
    honoring of child's level of, 8
    source attribution error and, 45
    therapist's, 132, 133
    time-outs and, 119–20
corporal punishment, 130
cortisol levels, 39
countertransference, 132, 134–35, 147, 151–52
cradling, 8, 118
crisis management, 55
    See also safety planning
cultural differences, 102
cutting, 66, 73, 77

Davies, J., 26
DC:0-3R. See Diagnostic Classification of Mental Health and Developmental Disorders of Infancy and Early Childhood, Revised (DC:0-3R)
defense mechanisms. *See* behaviors
deprivation, effects of, 16
    See also institutional deprivation
despair, 29, 32
detachment, 32
    See also dissociation
The Developing Mind (Siegel), 160
development. *See* child development
developmentally appropriate practice, 9, 51–53, 119, 129–30, 162–63
developmental psychology, 16
developmental psychopathology. *See* psychopathology
developmental readiness. *See* child development
developmental trauma, 22–24
    See also complex trauma
diagnosis
    of bipolar disorder, 25–26
    clinical competence in, 20–21
    issues for differential, 20–22, 92–94
    problems with RAD, 18–19
    problems with symptom-driven approach to, 17, 19–20
Diagnostic and Statistical Manual of Mental Disorders. See specific *DSM* edition
Diagnostic Classification of Mental Health and Developmental Disorders of Infancy and Early Childhood, Revised (DC:0-3R), 19, 93

interactive repair, 37–39, 64–66, 80, 132

internal working models, 39–42, 63–64, 77, 82, 122–23

International Adoption Team, 25

intersubjectivity
    between caregiver and therapist, 49
    complex trauma and avoidance of, 13
    definition of, 6
    examples of process of, 62
    importance of development of, 49, 53
    overview of, 42
    secure base development through, 58

interviews. *See* clinical interviews

ITCT. *See* integrative treatment of complex trauma (ITCT)

kind attributions, 53, 61–62

Lachmann, E., 35, 38

learning brain, defined, 79

left hemisphere, 15

limbic system, 15, 79

limit setting. *See* protection and limit setting

Luthar, S., 12

Main, M., 31, 32, 44, 57

maltreatment. *See* complex trauma; neglect

manipulation, 19, 26–27, 44, 66

marijuana exposure, prenatal, 26

marital relationship, 50

Marschak Interaction Method, 106

Masterson, J., 36

media influence, 153

medication evaluation, 115

memories, explicit, 14–15, 45, 71, 72, 78
    See also coherent narratives

memories, implicit, 15, 78

memories, traumatic
    hyperarousal and, 73–74
    overview of, 48, 72–73
    strategies for accessing, 51
    therapeutic window and resolution of, 68, 69, 118

memories, unconscious, 41

memory storage, 72–73

mentalization. *See* reflective capacity

Mental Measurement Yearbook (Buros), 103

mindfulness, 81

misattunement, 37–38, 39

mothers, 32–33
    See also caregivers

multidisciplinary collaboration, 51

multiple relationships. *See* conflicts of interest

Myers, L., 22

narratives. *See* specific types

National Association of Social Workers, 27

National Association of Social Workers *Code of Ethics*, 145, 156

National Child Traumatic Stress Network (NCTSN), 11, 22, 23, 91

National Technical Assistance Center for Children's Mental Health, 11

neglect, 9, 25, 92
    See also complex trauma

neurobiology, 14–15, 23, 26–27, 51, 75–76
    See also stress response system

neuropsychological evaluation, 115

nicotine exposure, prenatal, 26

nurturing. *See* touch and nurturing

opposition, reframing of, 66

orbital frontal cortex, 15

orphanages. *See* institutional deprivation

outcomes, anticipated, 109–10

out-of-home placements, 120–21, 167–75

pacing. *See* goal sequence; therapeutic window

pain, as cause of attachment disorder, 91

parallel process, 152–53

parental loss, 22

parental sensitivity, 120, 125

parenting. *See* caregiver-child relationship

Parenting Stress Index (PSI), 103

pathogenic care, RAD and, 18

Pearlman, L., 154

Perry, B., 119

personality formation and integration, 76

phase approach. *See* goal sequence

phobias, 7

physical restraints, 55, 114, 129
    See also holding therapy

placements. *See* out-of-home placements

planning. *See* treatment planning

playfulness
    as arousal modulation technique, 82
    proximity and, 120
    safety and security through, 8, 38, 52, 54

post-traumatic stress disorder (PTSD), 13, 22, 71, 73, 150

poverty, cocaine abuse and, 26

prefrontal cortex, 15, 74

prenatal exposure to substances, 26–27

promotion of, 67, 81–82, 116–18
    protection and limit setting and, 124–26,
        129–30
    through playfulness, 8, 38, 52, 54
    See also felt security
safety planning, 113–14
    See also crisis management
Scheeringa, M., 22
schools, collaboration with, 129
Schore, A., 15, 25, 39, 120
screening, intake, and referrals, 88–89, 146,
    147, 165–66
secondary traumatic stress, 132, 133, 147,
    150
secure base, facilitation of, 51–52, 58
secure pattern of attachment, 30, 32–33,
    34, 43
security. *See* safety and security
self-care needs, of therapists, 132, 133, 136,
    147–54
self-concept, 24, 80, 84–85
    See also fears; shame
self-denigration, 124–25
self-injurious behaviors, 73, 124
    See also cutting
self-regulation, 21, 56
    See also affect regulation; behavioral con-
        trol
semistructured assessment tools, 106–7
sense of self. *See* self-concept
sensitive use of, 124–25
sensory experiences, traumatic memory
    and, 48, 72–73, 75
sensory integration, 21
    See also neurobiology
Sentence Completion Form, 140–41
separation distress, 28, 32
service providers. *See* family support net-
    work
sexual abuse, 42, 61–62
    See also complex trauma
sexual behaviors, 61–62, 73, 77
shame
    behavior issues and, 124
    ethical guidelines to deal with, 161–62
    honoring of trauma narrative and, 84
    trauma and, 8, 20
    as trauma reenactment trigger, 77
    witness guilt and, 150
Shell, D., 33
siblings, child's effects on, 50
Siegel, D., 35, 160
SIPA. *See* Stress Index for Parents of Ado-
    lescents (SIPA)
situational trauma exposure, 22

Solomon, J., 31
somatic sensations, attention to, 81
Sonuga-Barke, E., 21
source attribution errors, 45, 73
    See also fight, flight, freeze, or appease-
        ment responses
spanking, 49
Spitz, R., 25
Sroufe, A., 29
standardized instruments, 102–7
standards of practice. *See* ethical guidelines
stealing, as tension-reducing behavior, 77
Stern, D., 35, 120
Stovall, K., 33
Strange Situation Protocol, 106–7
stress hormones, 39, 72
Stress Index for Parents of Adolescents
    (SIPA), 103–4
stress response system, 76, 79
    See also triggers
substance abuse, 73
    See also prenatal exposure to substances
Substance Abuse Center and Mental Health
    Administration, 11
supervision and consultation, 133–35,
    152–53
survival brain, 79
survival mechanisms. *See* behaviors;
    fight, flight, freeze, or appeasement
    responses
symptoms. *See* diagnosis
synchrony and attunement, 35–37, 56–57,
    78, 80
"Systems of Care: A Framework for System
    Reform in Children's Mental Health",
    11

Target, M., 42, 43
tension-reducing behaviors, 77, 78
    See also sexual behaviors
TF-CBT. *See* trauma-focused cognitive-
    behavioral therapy (TF-CBT)
Theory of Mind (ToM), 42–44
therapeutic window
    coercion and, 54
    ethical guidelines for, 160
    exposure and consolidation and, 78
    overview of, 79–80
    process of, 67–69
    traumatic memory resolution and, 118
    See also consolidation; exposure
therapists, 49, 135
    See also caregiver support; professional
        issues
Thompson, R., 41

thought reframing, 39
See also reframing
threats
anxiety and, 29
attachment disruption and perception of, 31, 32, 82
attunement to real self as, 37
dissociation and, 44
fight, flight, freeze, or appeasement responses and, 73
hyperarousal as chronic response to, 73–74
neutral or positive interactions as, 108
time-ins, 126–27, 128
time-outs, 119–20
touch and nurturing, 8–9, 54–55, 118, 145–46
See also proximity
trauma
affect regulation and, 23, 120
areas susceptible to effects of, 154
as consideration in diagnosis, 21–22
definition of, 70–71
neurobiology of, 14–15, 23, 75–76
physiology of, 73–75
See also specific types
trauma-focused cognitive-behavioral therapy (TF-CBT), 12–13, 14–15
trauma-focused therapy, 76–85
trauma narratives, 13, 84–88
Trauma Symptom Checklist for Children (TSCC), 105
Trauma Symptom Checklist for Young Children (TSCYC), 105
trauma theory, 70–76
treatment
for attachment disorder behavior, 36–37
authority to consent for, 89–90
barriers to success in, 94–95
complexities of, 20, 71–72
diagnostic limitations and, 17
goals and objectives of, 56, 58–60, 109–10, 140
integrated approach rationale in, 116–20
predictors of success in, 8, 94
principles, roles, and responsibilities of, 110–12
progress monitoring and evaluation in, 112–13, 146

termination of, 146–47
terminology and issues in, 27
therapeutic experience and structure of, 80
See also developmentally appropriate practice; professional issues
treatment contracts, 140–41
See also informed consent
Treatment for Abused and Neglected Children (U.S. DHHS), 82
treatment planning, 108–21
triggers, 72, 73, 80
See also stress response system
Tronick, E., 35, 38, 120
trust
attachment and development of, 47
in caregiver-child relationship, 8
compulsive self-reliance and, 17, 116
conditioned emotional responses affecting, 49
problems with research and capacity for, 10
See also internal working models
TSCC. *See* Trauma Symptom Checklist for Children (TSCC)
TSCYC. *See* Trauma Symptom Checklist for Young Children (TSCYC)

unconscious reenactments, 74–75
U.S. Centers for Disease Control, 25

van der Kolk, B., 22, 119
van Dulmen, M., 25
vicarious trauma, defined, 150
See also secondary traumatic stress
Vineland Adaptive Behavior Scales–II, 104, 162
vocabulary skills, of children, 110–11, 112
Vondra, J., 40

Waters, E., 29
window of tolerance. *See* therapeutic window
witness guilt, 150

Zeanah, C., 22
Zero to Three, 19
Zigler, E., 12